get it
together

Surviving Your
Quarterlife Crisis

get it together

Surviving Your Quarterlife Crisis

damian barr

Hodder & Stoughton

Copyright © 2004 by Damian Barr

First published in Great Britain in 2004 by Hodder and Stoughton
A division of Hodder Headline

The right of Damian Barr to be identified as the Author
of the Work has been asserted by him in accordance with
the Copyright, Designs and Patents Act 1988.

10 9 8 7 6 5 4 3 2 1

A CIP catalogue record for this title is available from the British Library

ISBN 0 340 82902 8

Typeset in Sabon MT by Palimpsest Book Production Limited,
Polmont, Stirlingshire

Printed and bound by
Clays Ltd, St Ives plc

Hodder and Stoughton
A division of Hodder Headline
338 Euston Road
London NW1 3BH

For

John Anderson

You didn't make it through
yours but you got me through mine

Acknowledgements

I'd like to point the finger of blame at all those who made my quarterlife crisis possible. But I won't. I haven't got the time and my therapist says it's better to focus on the good things. So, thank you all.

The people you're going to meet in this book are in no way perfect – least of all me. But they were generous enough to talk to me about what's going on in their lives. I am very grateful to all of them – especially the ones who found it hardest. I owe many people many drinks.

My agent, Robert Kirby at PFD, was clearly a preacher/coach in a previous life – this book, like so many, would not have happened without him. If my editor, Katy Follain, turned her ink-stained hand to politics she'd fix our messy world in no time. But I am begging her to stay and help me work on my next book instead.

Thanks to all those at *The Times* who were generous with their knowledge and indulged me while I was writing. AS, PB – extra big love.

Friends are the new family. Mine is Catholic in size and Jewish in lovin': Mum & Dad, Tinie & Jamie, My Amazing Yorkshire Family, Laura, Big Sis, Jawan, Ruby Sue, Claire, Hil, Dee, Paul & Tony, Brian, Mischa, Julian & Ed, Nic & Jo, Liza, Lovely Rob,

Roni, Anna, Toby, Ben & Charlie, all the Kates and Katys, Chris G, Paul & Mick, Chaya, Michael & Kip, Sarah, Sally, Paul T, Paul O & Hannah. You all know who you are and you all know how important you are.

Extra Special Acknowledgement
Mike brought me cups of tea when I needed them. I deserved them as much I deserve him, which is to say barely. Unlimited true love tea on me.

get it
together Contents

Introduction 1

work

housing

money

relationships

Introduction

There are some things no twentysomething will admit to.
Nobody wants to say just how small their pay-packet is or
how big their debts are. Few will confess to feeling poorer than
their friends and wanting to say 'tap' when offered water in a
restaurant. And it's not just about money.

We're convinced everyone else is having more (and better)
sex, doing more (and better) drugs and generally having more
(and better) fun than we are. You know you're twenty-five – it
says so on your birth certificate – but you feel forty-five. What's
more, you're starting to look and feel older. Suddenly hangovers
affect you like never before and you're fantasising about furni-
ture. But aren't your twenties supposed to be the best time of
your life?

Well, yes, they are. But you aren't the only person your age
that hasn't bought a great house, snared a gorgeous partner,
paid off hideous debts and landed a dream job. In fact, very
few twentysomethings have what we've been led to believe we
should have. Most of us are actually just as freaked out as you
are that our twenties are bigger, scarier and harder than promised. It's just that nobody has ever really talked about it. Until
now.

Feeling you should be having, doing or being more is the essence of the quarterlife crisis. Suddenly, thirty is so close you can smell it and everyone is doing better than you. Real life is setting in and it's expensive, ugly and competitive. You feel stressed, inadequate and somehow not quite as good as your peers. You feel poorer, less successful and less together. You feel, even though you're only twentysomething, that your life is in crisis.

Over and over again men and women in their twenties, some graduates and some not, have told me – mostly in hushed tones, others loudly and proudly – that they're depressed. They haven't always said so directly, but you don't need to spend very long with someone to know they live their life in a dark unhappy place convinced everyone around them is sunnier and happier.

Twentysomethings are at greater risk from depression than any other age group. Although one in five people will be affected by depression at some point, the Depression Alliance estimate that as many as one in *three* twentysomethings are depressed. No wonder. No other generation has had so much choice or such great expectations thrust upon them. Another cheery little fact: suicide now accounts for a fifth of all deaths of young people. That's two twentysomethings a day. Who says your twenties are the best time of your life? Forget coke – pass the Prozac.

My grandmother, who lived through the war, doesn't believe in depression. A lot of people don't. Fair enough. But have a look at the official definition of depression and see if you recognise yourself or your friends. I hope you don't, but I bet you do.

The official definition of depression
- Two weeks of abnormal depressed mood
- Loss of interest and decreased energy
- Loss of confidence
- Excessive guilt
- Recurrent thoughts of death

- Poor concentration
- Agitation or retardation
- Sleep disturbance
- Change in appetite

Mild depression includes the first two symptoms and at least one other. Severe depression is the first two symptoms and at least five others.

(Source: World Health Organisation's International Classification of Disease)

Sound familiar?

Get It Together is the first book to capture the feelings and fears of a generation unprepared for life in an increasingly competitive and fragmented world. It's not about the colour of your parachute because nobody really cares about your degree. Nor is it about turning you into some high-performing Stepford twentysomething. This book is a source of support in the years between teenage angst and midlife meltdown when it's assumed we're having the time of our lives – a practical guide to recognising and overcoming the unique problems we now face in our twenties. (And it's cheaper than therapy.) It might read like *Dawson's Creek*, but all the twentysomethings in this book are British. To avoid being identified many have chosen another name (surprisingly, no one picked Pacey). But it's not all doom – there are highs as well as lows, dreams as well as 'mares.

There are no quarterlife 'experts' because no other generation has experienced the quarterlife crisis. No other generation has graduated into as much debt. No other generation has been thrown into a world of instant microcelebrity where you're no one if you haven't been on *Big Brother* or aren't the friend of a friend of someone who has. *We're* the experts on our own lives, even when we expertly fuck them up.

'It's really fucking hard when my mother tells me I've got it easy and even harder when my granny chimes in about how hard the war was,' says Ellie, 26, an advertising sales manager living with her family in London. 'My mother got paid to go to university and graduated into full employment. It took me a year to get a job after graduating. And I am living in a post 9/11 world that my granny, who has never even gone on a foreign holiday, hasn't got a clue about.'

'It's not that I feel stressed about any one thing,' says Gary, 24, who just landed his first job in the City. 'I just feel worried all the time and a little bit left behind. I know my job could go any day. And if the property market crashes I'll be stuck with negative equity.' Gary earns £5,000 above the average graduate salary and owns his own flat, but he feels poor. 'London sucks you dry – I'm sure other people my age earn more.'

Perhaps it's just that we're all spending more?

'I have £10,000 on two credit cards,' says Charlie, 28, a freelance photographer. 'I haven't started paying my student loans 'cos I don't earn enough, but I'm not going to stop going out. Everybody lives in debt now, don't they?'

I certainly do. And so do most of my friends. It's something our parents chide us about while busily drawing money against the equity in their houses to indulge their midlife crises.

Little research has been done on the quarterlife crisis. Until now. The psychologists and sociologists commenting on the midlife crisis do so because they're living it. By showing you how others are really tackling their twenties, *Get It Together* aims to help you turn trauma into triumph.

Is the pressure to get it together making you fall apart? If so, you're in good company. If not, fuck off. Nobody wants to hear about how fabulous your life is.

work

get it

together

1

To Postgrad or not to Postgrad?

The pleasures and pitfalls of being a permastudent

'I don't ever want to leave.'
Toni, 26, permastudent

Visiting friends who are still at university is guaranteed to make you feel envious and wistful. The grass seems greener on campus. You immediately suffer the reverse of the back-to-school effect: now you've graduated you want to go back and do it all again, but you can't. Or can you?

You certainly can't slip on campus unnoticed. For one thing, you're wearing clothes that have seen a washing machine and maybe also an iron. As a graduate you're an unwelcome prophet from the world of work bringing dark messages of days wasted in meetings and nights spent poring over presentations.

'I went back to uni every month for the first year after I graduated to hang out with my mates,' says Tom, 26. Why? 'It was hard going from seeing them every day to not seeing them at all. I missed everybody. Plus, beer is cheaper in the union.'

For the first few months Tom successfully recreated old times and all without the misery of essays and exams. 'It was great. I think I had more fun than when I was a student.' Although his starting salary was small – £15,000 – he bought round after round after round. But on Sundays, when his mates were tucking into bacon sandwiches and planning another big night out, Tom was packing to go back to London. And his office. 'I couldn't cut loose. It was all right for them – they could sleep in – but if I missed the train I'd be in shit at work. I don't think they understood that.'

Back on campus work is not the most important thing in the world. Nobody cares about promotions and demotions. Office gossip has no currency – work is boring. As Tom discovered.

'I started to feel left out. I lost track of who was shagging who. I wasn't part of the routine any more and we didn't have the same worries. They were stressing about exams and I was worrying about whether or not I could meet my targets at work.'

Campus eventually began to seem petty and small. Tom's student days jarred with the new life he was building at work. He found that he couldn't embrace the past and the future at the same time.

'I went back once after graduating to visit my best friend in the year below me,' says Anna, 24. 'It was great seeing her but it was hard because I knew I'd have to go back to work at the end of the weekend. I spent more time worrying than partying.' Sure enough, come Sunday evening, there were tears. 'I felt like I was leaving everything behind – not just my best friend, but all my chances to have fun and be young. I know it's stupid but it was a real wrench – almost worse than leaving home. I couldn't do it again so I didn't go back.'

Breaking up is hard to do. Some people just can't end their affair with academia. Anna's best friend graduated but rebounded back on campus after just one summer in the real world.

'I was totally shocked when she enrolled for an MA,' says Anna. 'Especially as she totally hated her dissertation and a Masters is just one massive essay.'

More and more graduates are postponing entry to the world of work by doing a postgraduate degree. And another. And sometimes even another. These are the permastudents.

For an increasing number of twentysomethings, one degree just isn't enough any more. According to the UK Graduate Careers Survey 2003, a quarter of final-year students were planning to go straight on to a postgraduate course – that's more than ever before. With 12,000 taught courses on offer there's plenty of choice. The permastudent trend is backed up by a report from the University of Warwick claiming that a quarter of all postgrads now come straight from their first degree. More graduates are going back to do more postgraduate degrees sooner. The number of postgraduate students is higher than ever – at around 400,000 they constitute 20 per cent of the UK student body.

I wasn't exactly thrilled about graduating five years ago. Yes, I had a first class degree, but I also had £6,000 in student loans, a £3,000 credit card bill, a £1,000 overdraft and not so much as a hint of a job. Which is why I went straight on to do a Masters in Contemporary Sociology. Would it get me a job? Probably not. Did I care? Certainly not. Like Anna's friend, I wanted to fend off adulthood and reality for just a little bit longer. And, even better, I managed to make someone else pay for it. Scholarships are beautiful things (mine came from the ESRC).

Tom thought briefly about becoming a permastudent. 'At uni we always laughed at people who came back to do a Masters or something because it was like they'd failed in the real world. But the first few months in my job were really hard and I did think about going back to uni – it was what I knew.'

So why didn't he go back? What stopped Tom becoming a permastudent?

'I couldn't afford to. Well, I could probably have got loans and stuff but I would have ended up with even more debts and no job to pay them off.'

But money wasn't all that stopped him. 'When I visited my mates I could see how stressed they were but they couldn't. It's almost like they were pretending to be chilled but really they were worrying about essays they hadn't even started and arguing about who'd finished the milk and stuff like that. Most of them were totally in denial about graduation – the closer it got the less they talked about it. It was like they never wanted to leave and if they didn't talk about leaving they wouldn't have to.'

Tom's face crumpled into his newly ironed work clothes when he realised he'd really romanticised his university days. 'I remember the exact moment because it was the first time I felt glad about going back to work. I'd forgotten all about not having any money and always feeling like I should be in the library instead of the union. I miss uni but not enough to go back again, not really.'

Realising and accepting university wasn't as completely amazing as he'd remembered it helped Tom face the challenges in his new working life. 'After a couple of months I started getting into my job, I even got a bit of a promotion. But I still miss wearing pyjamas all day.' This realisation, that his holidays in student-land were really about avoiding work-land and were stressful in themselves, ensured Tom would never be one of the permastudents he used to mock. 'I would have had to face reality eventually – I couldn't have studied for ever, even if I'd had the money.'

Permastudents share a common desire to stay in university for as long as they can. Their motivation for hiding out on campus varies. I did a Masters but stopped there – the thought of a Ph.D., one enormous deadline stretching endlessly ahead, was terrifying. For me, work was the lesser of two evils and I was sick of eating pasta. The classic permastudent is always studying and never learning. To them, grades are what you need to stay in one place, not what you want to get ahead.

But if you can afford it, is there really any harm in avoiding the real world? Could permastudentdom provide a valuable refuge?

Paul, 29, got a 2:2 in Computer Science. 'I wasn't exactly a high-flier.' After graduating he tried – and failed – to get a job as a programmer. 'I couldn't believe how competitive it was. I tried the government but they wouldn't take me 'cos I didn't have a 2:1.' This was at the height of the dotcom boom. 'I thought my degree would be in demand but it turned out the programming languages we learned at university weren't exactly in demand any more.' A common enough complaint.

'I moved back home after graduation but I really, really didn't want to. After three years living with my mates I felt like a prisoner. I felt like my parents were watching me all the time.' Paul's parents still didn't know he smoked but that didn't matter because soon he couldn't afford cigarettes. 'I had a degree but I was poorer than when I was a student. I felt like shit – a total loser.'

Everybody jokes about the graduate blues, but think of how you feel returning to work after a fortnight off and multiply that feeling by a hundred. Joking about postgraduate depression minimises its seriousness – but makes it harder to deal with, sadly, for many graduates whose feelings are serious and real. Graduation is a celebration loaded with pressures precipitating an existential crisis. Who are you? What now? You've got to make the best of it! The world is your oyster!

'I went from having a structure to nothing. For the first time in my life I didn't know what I was doing from day to day, never mind year to year,' says Paul. And it's not like he could easily get support from his friends. 'We couldn't just go down the pub because everyone was all over the country and I couldn't afford to visit them. It was hard to keep in touch.'

Had it not been for his judgemental parents and lack of funds, Paul would definitely have upped his cigarette intake. 'Everybody kept saying I should be having a fantastic time. I was going to scream if another fucking person told me the world was my oyster because I had a degree. What I really wanted was some good gear but I couldn't get any 'cos I didn't know any local dealers and I didn't have any fucking money.'

So back to university he went – they were only too happy to accept his 2:2 and his tuition fees of £2,100. 'I saw a thing about clearing in one of the papers. It took me a week to organise. I got a career development loan to pay my fees. My overdraft was already maxed out but it was still a student account so I didn't have to pay interest.' To cover living expenses he landed a job in the university computer centre. Once he was back on familiar territory with money (albeit not very much), a structure (albeit temporary) and a dealer, Paul thought everything would get better. And it did. But not straightaway. The feeling of being a loser that set in while he was stuck at home didn't lift as quickly as his fortunes.

'I still felt like shit. I wasn't sleeping. I was piling on weight and smoking way too much. I was missing more classes than I was attending.' Eventually a concerned tutor mentioned the university counselling service. 'No fucking way was I going to see some psychiatrist.' Paul developed insomnia. 'I started missing work as well. I swapped for a later shift but my mind wasn't on the job 'cos I was totally tired all the time.' Next term he was sacked. 'Then I went to see a counsellor but only to get help sleeping.'

Free therapy! It's not an advertised benefit of a university education but it should be. Like Paul, I refused to see a counsellor despite the fact that my friends thought it was a good idea and I rather liked the idea of having a therapist. I imagined casually mentioning 'my therapist' at dinner parties and instantly appearing interestingly troubled yet smart for tackling my issues. My problem was I thought I'd solved all my problems simply because everything that was wrong with my life was in the past which I'd already lived through, so that was that. Why dredge it all up?

'I was totally stressed when I got there,' says Paul. In fact, he missed his first two appointments – one because he slept in, the other because he bottled out. 'I remember sitting in the waiting room. A woman came in and called my name. I got up and left. She didn't know it was me because I'd made the appointment on the phone.' Denial: not just a river in Egypt. Paul's cover was blown when he finally turned up and got the therapist he should have seen in the first place.

'She acted like nothing had happened but I thought it was funny and started laughing. I couldn't believe it. She asked me why I was laughing. I told her and she laughed too. Then she looked serious and asked why I'd left the first time. I started crying.'

Paul saw his therapist once a week during term time and less often in the holidays. 'I am not going to say I enjoyed it because I didn't,' he says. 'And I don't think my therapist enjoyed it 'cos a lot of the time I just sat there and said nothing.' Fun or not, it did the trick. 'I felt really bad after some sessions – I couldn't go to class or work or anything because I was thinking about stuff that had come up. I even stopped going for a while. But after about fifteen sessions I started sleeping better so I knew it was working.' Perhaps it was just exhausting.

'All in all I went about thirty times. That would have cost me thousands of pounds if I wasn't a student.' Better value than a free McDonald's or 10 per cent off at HMV.

Suddenly, it was the final term. A life without structure loomed once again. All around Paul saw the familiar signs of panic – big queues at the careers office, CVs flying off the printer at the computer centre and preparations for the impending milk round. This dominated his therapy sessions. 'I hadn't really enjoyed my Masters but, at the same time, I couldn't think of anything else I wanted to do. I was back to square one again.'

Graduation came and went again, but this time it was different. 'I was scared but not as scared as last time 'cos I knew what to expect.' Rather than moving back home Paul got a flat in London with someone from his course. They worked in a bar for six months to raise the cash for plane tickets and are now travelling the world. 'I never thought I'd do that but I am doing it,' says Paul, emailing me from New Zealand. 'I don't know what I am going to do when I get back but I am not that worried about it. I know I won't be going back to university again.'

Paul's postgrad became, completely unexpectedly, about therapy. His M.Sc. won't exactly hinder him in the job market, but his new-found, if directionless, confidence will certainly stand him in good stead. 'I am more in debt and travelling is going to make that worse, but I am starting to view debt as an investment in myself. Know what I mean?'

A postgrad can buy you space and time to ponder what it is you do or don't want to do with your life. You can spend a year on campus recuperating from the rigours of work planning your next move. Or of course, if you already know where you want to be, a postgrad can be an effective route there, which is why vocational qualifications, like teaching, are now so popular. And you can do one at any point, even after getting a taste of the real world.

Kate, 29, is about to finish a PGCE. Her undergraduate degree was in Fine Art. 'I am going to be an art teacher,' she says proudly. Her new career couldn't be more different from the one she relentlessly pursued after graduating. 'I was a PR girl for five years. I totally loved it. It was my life.' Kate worked twelve hours most days and often longer. When she finally did go home it was to Peter, a guy from her office.

'I never stopped talking or thinking about work. It was the most important thing in my life. Looking back it seems ridiculous that I got really excited about getting a mention for some crappy company in a shitty trade mag, but that really was my life then.'

Her dedication was rewarded with a salary that dwarfed her fellow Fine Art graduates. 'I started on £18K then went to £20K then £22K then £26K.' As an account manager for a big City technology PR firm she earned £36K. 'The money was amazing. I paid all my students debts off – every single one. And I had fantastic clothes and great holidays.' She had it made. 'And then I got made redundant.'

When the dotcom bubble burst Kate was left on her arse. 'The firms we worked for just didn't have the budgets for big parties or lavish campaigns any more.' Like many others, Kate hadn't seen it coming. Peter also lost his job. 'I had no savings or anything 'cos I'd been clearing my debts and basically having a really good time.' Fortunately they both got six months' redundancy. 'The first thing I did was get really fucking drunk.'

Kate's hangover was unpleasant. 'I'd been working so hard for so long and doing so well that I hadn't questioned anything. I mean, I'd had the job I wanted, a gorgeous boyfriend and a great flat. So many of my friends were still struggling years after graduation. I'd felt lucky most of the time.'

But not all of the time, she soon realised. Her peers may have been cash poor but they were time rich. 'It's true, I hadn't had much spare time. I'd spent most evenings dining with clients.' Dating a co-worker was the only way for Kate to have a relationship. 'That's what everyone did because at least that way you'd be guaranteed to spend some time together, even if it was work.'

When they stopped working together they stopped sleeping together. Soon they stopped living together. 'I think it was partly the stress of wondering what we were going to do next. We suddenly had all this free time and our big common interest – work – wasn't there any more. We were arguing a lot and not having sex. Basically, we realised that work was pretty much all that had kept us together.' Fast train to Splitsville.

Kate began contacting the people she'd been at university with. 'It felt good hooking up with people I hadn't seen for ages. I was a bit nervous because I thought they'd see me as some PR bitch, but they didn't, not all of them anyway.'

More than half the people she'd hung out with on her Fine Art course had gone on to do teaching, a career she'd never considered. 'Some were in little private schools and others were in big state schools. They all seemed to love it – especially the long holidays.' Which got Kate thinking. 'I talked about it. Different people said different things. Everyone who was doing it already said I should go for it, but the people from my old PR job thought I was nuts.' A week's work experience made her mind up.

For Kate, going back to university was a means to an end.

'The government paid my fees and gave me £6,000. I got a flatmate in to help me with my mortgage and I stopped drinking champagne.' Kate's redundancy meant she didn't have to work during the holidays. 'I didn't have any money left at the end of the course but I didn't have any debts either.'

Wasn't it strange, being back on campus after spending so much time swishing around an office? 'Yes and no. I treated the whole thing like a job. I wore my work wardrobe to lectures and when I was working in school. It wasn't about being a student again. Frankly, I hate the idea of not washing my hair and wearing those big ugly green coats.' Spoken like a true PR princess. 'As far as I was concerned I was there to get a professional qualification.'

Kate's motivation was completely different from Paul's, yet both ended up doing a postgrad. Having got what they wanted from going back to university, neither Kate nor Paul plan to set foot on campus again. Toni, 26, is unlikely ever to leave.

'I'm just finishing my Masters. I've focused on the representation of feminine insanity in nineteenth-century literature. It's fascinating.' It certainly is but it's not going to get you a golden handshake at Deloitte. 'I don't care about all that shit. Why should I go and work in some fucking company?' Why indeed.

Toni is making the transformation from permastudent to lecturer, or at least she hopes to.

'I love learning and I love university. It's hard to explain, it's not that I love being a student. It's not easy being poor all the time and I don't drink so that whole scene isn't me. But this campus is my world.'

Toni is doing her Masters at Sussex where she did her BA and where she will also do her Ph.D. Doesn't she want to move to another university at the very least? 'I considered moving, but when I really thought about it I realised it would be change for the sake of change. I love being by the sea and I know my way around here.'

For Toni, the campus is a comforter and the students and staff her little sleepover friends. She doesn't want the slumber party to end. 'After I graduated I went straight on to my Masters. I am taking a break of six months to go travelling before my Ph.D. though.' But only to go to Harvard and their library. 'That is a holiday for me.'

Because she spends little time in the bar, Toni's grades are ridiculously high. 'I got a first and I am on course for a distinction.' Which means she got scholarships which means her debts are ridiculously low. 'I don't own a credit card and I have invested my student loans.' Scary.

What is it about university that keeps Toni there? 'A lot of people on my course are there 'cos they have nothing better to do. I think that's a waste of their time and a waste of resources. I am at university because I want to spend my time learning. I don't want to give my life to a company, which seems to be what everyone is expected to do as soon as they get a degree.'

The fact that most universities are now run as companies and that education is now a product does not deter Toni. 'University has its faults and I am sure there are things I will hate about being a lecturer – the pay is rubbish. But the holidays are good.' Her dream job would keep her in her beloved Sussex, but she'll go anywhere so long as she's in academia. 'I'll do whatever it takes to become a professor and I'll go wherever the work takes me.'

Clearly, being a permastudent is not synonymous with a lack of ambition.

Would you go back if you could? If someone offered you all the time and money needed to spend a year back on campus, would you go?

Andy did. 'My company runs a sabbatical scheme. After three years you can take six months off to go and work on an approved project or undertake an approved project so long as you guarantee you'll return to the company and work for a further three years.'

Such Faustian pacts are increasingly common. Many companies now sponsor their employees to go and find knowledge and experience so long as they promise to bring it back and share it with their colleagues. For some, this is an ideal way of going back to university (just for a while). Andy did an MBA with a minor in Creative Writing.

'I deliberately didn't go back to the same university where I did my undergrad,' says Andy, 26, who got a 2:1 in Linguistics from Lancaster before going on to become a management accountant. 'Lancaster does an amazing MBA, but it would have been too tempting to go and see old mates and revisit all my old haunts. Don't get me wrong, I was tempted, but I wanted to go somewhere new and have a different experience.'

With a salary to feed, clothe and entertain him, no fees to pay and a guaranteed job at the end of it, Andy was set. 'There wasn't a single day I didn't enjoy. It was very different from when I was a student the first time around because I didn't have any money worries and I knew what I was doing at the end of it all. Obviously I drank a lot and took full advantage of late nights and late mornings, but I could do it all because I knew that, so long as I pulled it out of the hat at exam time, I'd be okay.' After three years of getting up for the office, every single second of every single lie-in was bliss. 'I made the most of everything.'

Andy minored in Creative Writing because he'd never done anything, well, *creative* before. 'My A levels were science and my degree was science. I wanted to do something artsy but I couldn't do English or anything 'cos I didn't have the knowledge. Creative Writing appealed because everyone thinks they can churn out a novel or something, don't they?' Indeed they do. Thankfully, most don't try.

'I did some poems which were awful and everyone in my group hated them. It was embarrassing really. My girlfriend thought it was hilarious.' Slowly his writing improved. 'By the end of the year people weren't laughing unless they were supposed to.' Back at work, reports and presentations, previously a chore, were a breeze. 'I became more critical of other people's writing and more able to express my thoughts more clearly.' In secret he pinned a poem on the office notice board. 'It was called "Back to school". I didn't put my name to it.'

If you decide to go back, think about why you're going. Really think about it. Are you being driven by a passion to fully understand Russian history, or do you just want to escape the rule of a cruel and corrupt office Tsar?

If you're going back to university to escape the world of work – a perfectly natural impulse – remember you're only putting reality on pause. As Paul found, you're no sooner back on campus than it's time to leave again. I remember all too well the inexorable approach of another graduation, another existential crisis. Kate got the extra letters after her name needed to become a teacher, and Andy took the chance to discover and indulge his creativity. Toni will never leave campus because she doesn't want to and there's no reason why she should. For Paul, permastudentdom provided a much-needed pause; he's still not sure what he wants to do but he feels more confident and together than ever.

Could you be a permastudent? According to a Labour Force Survey, a postgraduate degree earns you, on average, an extra

£1,778 per year, but fees can cost up to £20,000 – and then there's all the coffee and cigarettes needed to see you through your thesis. Would you swap appraisals for exams, wages for an overdraft and early mornings for late nights? Only you can decide.

Next time you visit a friend who is still studying, try imagining yourself staying beyond Sunday and into the week where missed lectures, dirty dishes and other guilty pleasures await. Is a postgrad an expensive delaying tactic or a worthwhile polishing process? Discuss.

The small print

There is no doubt, more graduates are going back for more education. But what are they studying, how much does it cost and what do they get from it?

Average cost of a taught postgraduate degree
Fees range from £250 to almost £20,000. The average fee for a part-time course is £1,550 rising to £3,780 for full-time. (*Source: National Postgraduate Committee survey*)

Most common postgrad degree
The most common Masters degree programmes are the Master of Arts (MA) and Master of Science (M.Sc.). (*Source: ECCTIS*)

Most studied subject
Business and finance are the most attractive postgraduate subject areas amongst finalists. An incredible 49 per cent of respondents were interested in a business/MBA programme. (*Source: survey by www.topgraduate.com*)

Average age of permastudent at start of postgrad degree
There doesn't seem to be a definitive figure. Full-time students

tend to be younger than part-time students. And age varies a lot with subject studied – vocational degrees (like law) generally attract younger students than academic ones (like English literature). I was twenty-five when I graduated with my MA in Sociology. Go figure.

Will you earn more?

Yes. Postgrads expect to make at least £22,000 in their first year (*source: National Postgraduate Committee.*) Most will. The average earnings for graduates aged 25–34 in 2001 were £25,334 for first-degree holders and £27,112 for those with a postgrad.

People who can help you find useful information, university places or money:

- National Postgraduate Committee: *www.npc.org.uk*
- *www.topgraduate.com*
- The Course Source: *www.thecoursesource.co.uk*
- Prospects Postgrad: *www.prospects.csu.ac.uk*
- EducationGuardian (a great site):
  www.education.guardian.co.uk/courses
  www.education.guardian.co.uk/universityguide
- See *The Independent* for places in Clearing around July. And get *The Times Higher Education Supplement* for the most in-depth and authoritative analysis of what's going on in Education
- UCAS: *www.ucas.co.uk*
- Find a Ph.D. at *www.FindAPhD.com*
- Jobs for non-science Ph.D.s: *www.phdjobs.com*
- Jobs and studentships in the academic community: *www.jobs.ac.uk*
- Details of undergrad and postgrad scholarships and studentships: *www.scholarship-search.org.uk/post_info.html*

2

I Want to Go Travelling

The next flight to Anywhere-but-here is leaving from Terminal Twentysomething

'Would you tell me, please, which way I ought to go from
   here?'
'That depends a good deal on where you want to get to,'
   said the Cat.
'I don't much care where–' said Alice.
'Then it doesn't much matter which way you go,' said the Cat.
'–so long as I get somewhere,' Alice added as an explanation.
'Oh, you're sure to do that,' said the Cat, 'if only you walk
   long enough.'
From Alice's Adventures in Wonderland, Lewis Carroll

'Same shit, different country.'
Harriet, 27, teacher-turned-traveller

Wouldn't it be nice to get away for a few months? Just fuck off somewhere hot with someone hot and not worry about work or money? Kick back on a Californian beach and cultivate a tan or sample the dubious delights of Thailand . . .

The right to stop commuting and start travelling is now completely ingrained in twentysomething culture. For many twentysomethings, work is just the thing you do to pay for your next trip. The office has become a departure lounge. No longer content with mere holidays we demand odysseys – journeys that continue affecting us long after the tan has faded. Mum and Dad might settle for a fortnight in Fuerteventura, but we want six months in Malaysia.

It starts simply enough with a post-GCSE break. Parents who used to pay a tenner for every A grade are now packing their high-achieving offspring and ten of their best friends off for some hard-earned rest in a Spanish villa. More drinking than resting is done, resulting in at least one trip to the local hospital. *Duration:* four weeks. *Cost:* parents pick up the tab.

Good girls then spend the summer after the first year of A Levels or Highers working as au pairs. Bad girls join the boys serving drinks and sex in beach bars in Ibiza. *Duration:* summer. *Cost:* parents pick up big costs like flights, but you must live on your meagre salary.

And then comes the gap year, so named because of the chasm it leaves in your bank balance and on your CV. Initially the reserve of the middle classes, this sojourn between school and university is now a rite of passage. 'Where did you do your gap year?' has overtaken 'What school did you go to?' as the standard Fresher ice-breaker.

Last year 25,310 students of the 401,854 who accepted places in higher education deferred entry to take a gap year, according to UCAS. That's a record 14 per cent increase, but the final numbers are likely to be much higher because some people choose to apply for courses during their year out. Nor do these figures include those who intercalate (take a year out while studying) or take a gap year immediately after graduating. And then there are those lucky bastards who take a year out at both ends.

Between post-GCSE holidays, summers working abroad and gap years, most of us have done some kind of travelling before we get to university. Those experiences – cleaning the chalets, tending the children, learning Spanish for 'stomach pump' – are great practice for the travels we take while we're at university.

'For me, vacations were about getting out of the country, not getting on with my essays,' says Jane, 24. 'During Easter break in my first year I went interrailing around Europe with mates from uni.' She loved France so much she spent the summer working in bars in St Tropez. 'I didn't make any money but I had a great time. My French is very, erm, colloquial now.'

Coursework increased in her second year, but still she went away for the summer – this time to the US with BUNAC. 'I worked at a kid's camp in California for two months then spent a month travelling around America by bus.'

Finals and the prospect of finding a job meant Jane travelled no further than the library in her third year. Until summer, when she took a trip with a vocational slant. 'I did TEFL for two months. I went to Nigeria so I could use my French. I made fairly good money teaching Business English and came back in time for graduation with money in my pocket and something to put on my CV.' *Très* sensible.

Although she has more air miles than she knows what to do with, Jane is not unusually well-travelled by today's standards. Most students now take at least one non-essential trip a year (not counting acid ones). Some take more, some take less. Student travel agencies are booming.

But not everyone can afford to jet off between terms – students increasingly spend their holidays clocking up work experience or keeping the bank manager off their back. NUS figures show that over 40 per cent of students are forced to work during term time, and around 90 per cent work during vacation.

In my first year at Lancaster University I couldn't afford to travel further afield than Morecambe. Most of my friends spent their holidays paragliding across Australia or breastfeeding endangered otters. I could only look with envy at their exotically stamped passports. My parents couldn't afford to indulge my wanderlust and I would never earn my round-the-world ticket waiting tables. I looked set to remain bound to Blighty until I discovered the miracle of the Student Exchange Program. But even that cost a pretty penny.

Thanks to a year spent at the University of Texas at Austin, I now know everything there is to know about barbecues, cowboys and cacti. Studying abroad, for a term or a year, is, in many ways, better than just travelling. It's about immersion – you aren't just passing through. For however short a time, you have to build a life – find a place to live, open a bank account and discover that tea isn't always served hot (or even served at all). And you learn a lot about yourself.

Despite sleeping in for the interview, I won a year-long scholarship to study English Literature and Sociology, which meant I didn't have to pay tuition fees – a big bonus as they were $10,000. I had barely finished celebrating when it dawned on me that I had to find living costs. For a year. This meant cutting back to one meal a week or laying my hands on some cash.

A mass email appeal to all my friends and plenty of people I barely knew yielded nothing but good wishes. Months passed and I raised just £500. The sun was setting on my Texan dreams and I hadn't even raised the air fare. I was about to surrender when the phone rang. It was a former teacher of mine in Scotland telling me to catch the train up there for an interview the very next day. I was to meet the lawyer of an anonymous businessman who'd heard about my plight and wanted to help but wished to remain anonymous.

In the spirit of *Great Expectations*, I changed my name to Pip and boarded the train for the meeting which changed my life. Mr Dick, the unfortunately named lawyer of my mysterious benefactor, agreed to give me at least £5,000, and a well-paying job at his law practice. By the end of the summer I had more than enough money to fund my year abroad. The only condition was that I write a letter each term describing my progress. I never enjoyed writing any letter more, though I was careful to leave out the bit where I was nearly arrested in full *Ab Fab* drag during a rather rowdy Halloween party on Austin's infamous Sixth Street.

When I arrived in Texas, the immigration people wanted to know why I'd come all the way to America to study Shakespeare. Good question. At the time I couldn't answer it. On my way back I told them I'd heard a girl from a poor suburb of Houston recite Hamlet in perfect iambic pentameter. That's why I went to Texas. That and the sunshine.

Travelling while studying gave me a focus and structure. I knew what I was doing and when – the weeks were mapped out for me but I still had time to do my own thing. I didn't want to go travelling in my mid-twenties, when I guessed (rightly) that I would need to be focused on building my career and saving my pennies.

As a student I automatically got lots of support. When things went wrong – I got ill and didn't understand health insurance, I set my room alight, a poisonous spider lunched on my leg – there were professionals on hand to help me.

For those who cannot afford the time or money for a gap year or study abroad, twentysomething seems the best age to see the world. In fact, the urge to go travelling appears to get stronger the closer to thirty we get.

'I feel burnt-out,' says Kate, 25, who has just ditched the office to go travelling. 'I've gone from school to college to university to work without a break.' To keep the pressure up she completed a postgraduate diploma while working full time as a charity fund-raiser. 'It's too much. I need time to think about where my life is going. My friends travelled after university but I started work because I couldn't afford to get into more debt. Now it's my turn.'

Bye-bye commuting, hello backpacking. Kate quit her job. 'My boss was not thrilled but she did say I could interview for my old job when I got back. She assumes I'll want it; I don't think I will.'

In February Kate and a friend jetted to Bangkok to begin their year-long adventure. She has budgeted £1,000 per month and plans not to work. 'I've let my flat to two friends and I am going to supplement that with my savings. I can just about afford it.'

Kate's two-bedroom flat in Kennington will yield £800 a month, covering her £400 mortgage payments and leaving enough to buy a Vuitton backpack. Managing agents will take 15 per cent. She's happy to pay for peace of mind: 'I don't want to trek the rainforest worrying about my boiler. I am also leaving my dad some keys, just in case.'

But why go 'travelling'? Why not take a luxurious holiday?

'A holiday is about a specific activity or location like scuba-diving or the Red Sea. Thinking is what I want to do, and I suppose I could think here in England but I need to get away from everything that's familiar and challenge myself to think about what I really want. Who do I really want to be? What do I really want to do? Obviously I want to get a good tan, too, and maybe meet a guy who has a different perspective on the world.'

Almost none of the people I spoke to said they wouldn't spend at least a few months exploring some far-flung corner of the world given the chance. The same fantasy was described over and over again with slight variations. 'Escape' was the mantra. Some craved a challenge, others a chance to reflect. Travelling is seen as a last hurrah before the three Ms: marriage, mortgage and monogamy. *I have to go now while I can still enjoy it.* One girl I know (who is afraid of flying) plans to hitch a ride on one of those container ships that constantly circle the globe and find a lover in every port.

Harriet, 27, is an accidental traveller. She recently returned from a year in Asia which started out as a fortnight's holiday in India. 'I was having the definitive quarterlife crisis,' she says.

And she was. She had quit teaching – only to go back into teaching six months later; moved from Brighton to London – only to move back a year later; and got into – and out of – an utterly disastrous relationship.

'Not one aspect of my life was sorted – even my friends hated me because I'd treated them so badly when I was still with my horrible boyfriend. Everywhere I looked I saw evidence of my mistakes. I wanted to get away and think about what had gone so wrong and why. My therapist suggested a holiday, so I went to Goa.'

Her two weeks flew by and Harriet had focused more on her beach books than the problems that drove her out there. 'It was time to go but I couldn't leave. It was too soon. The thought of seeing everyone again made me sick. I called my parents in tears. Then I called my best friend and she said, "Why don't you just stay out there?" So I did.'

With the rental income on her house in Brighton, Harriet scraped together the cash to turn her holiday into an odyssey. To ease herself into travelling she booked another package tour in India. 'I went to an elephant sanctuary, saw the Taj Mahal and did all the touristy stuff.' After that she was on her own – for a while.

'At first I was terrified. I didn't know anyone or speak the language and I had all these limbless beggars screaming at me.' What scared her most was the realisation that, for the first time in a long time, her destiny was her own. 'I could do what I wanted when I wanted with who I wanted. I had an open return ticket but it felt like one-way because I didn't know if or when I was coming back.'

She ploughed through the multipack of condoms packed as a hopeful precaution. 'I would meet people at a hostel and hang out with them for a while. If they were going somewhere interesting I'd tag along and if they weren't I'd go my own way. It was very liberating.'

A few months into her travels, Harriet felt homesick. 'I don't know what happened. I think it was an email I got from a friend about the weather in England. She said it was rainy and I was sitting in full sunshine in a bikini and it all seemed a bit unreal. I started thinking about all the things I was missing.' Cue another tearful phone call to Mum and Dad.

'They were wonderful. They flew out two days later and I spent a week with them in a luxury hotel. I caught up on all their news, told them a few stories and ran up a huge bar bill.' But a little England goes a long way. 'By the end of the week I was ready to be on my own again – I had just needed pepping up.'

Harriet kept a diary of what she calls her 'emotional journey'.

'I often flick through the pages to remind me of where I went and who I was. I look at some of the things I've done and think "Wow – I went white-water rafting in New Zealand! That was cool!" But I also read about when I felt homesick and the time I ran out of tampons.'

This is her final entry: 'Tomorrow I catch the flight back to reality. I fly from Sydney to London with a stop in Bangkok. I am not looking forward to the flight but I feel I really started to come back a couple of months ago. It's time to put the new me to the test. It's the start of another journey.'

Harriet is now very clear that she doesn't want to go back to teaching or get into another relationship (not for a while anyway). She is back in her house in Brighton and is getting by on the rental income. 'I am lucky I don't have to find work straightaway, but I can't live like this for ever. Right now I am working out what I enjoyed about travelling. Maybe I'll live abroad or something. I don't know. Right now I am making a list of options. I'll keep you posted.'

Craig, 28, was by no means an accidental traveller – he worked hard to earn his time away. Despite being determined to see the world, he very nearly never left Manchester.

'Travelling was always on my mind. Some days I just wanted to stay on the train till it got to the airport and then catch the first flight I could get. I wondered how long it would take for anyone to notice I'd gone. I wondered what people would say.'

While his friends were at university, Craig was working his way up in a local estate agency. He was still there long after they graduated.

'I didn't feel destined to be an estate agent, but I didn't want to go to uni either. I'd done it since leaving school but wasn't sure I'd do it for ever. I saw everyone I knew go off to these amazing places and come back with amazing stories and I was doing the 18–30 thing and coming back with a hangover. I felt jealous. I couldn't imagine getting all that time off.'

But it wasn't just time: 'I was a bit scared, I admit it. I didn't think I could cope with getting lost in a rainforest or missing a plane or something. I like my home comforts and my football.'

With every email from a friend in New Zealand or Nepal Craig grew more envious. And with every birthday that went by he felt more trapped.

'My girlfriend was talking about marriage and kids and I knew that I would never get away if that happened. I was really into my job and they wanted to promote me to branch manager, and that would have been another commitment that was too hard for me to break.'

It was now or never.

'I'd bought a house. Instead of living in it I renovated it and sold it on for a big profit and used the money to buy tickets. I couldn't have gone otherwise. Selling my security gave me the money I needed to get away.' Craig then had to find work abroad to fund his travels.

'I got a job in a temp agency in Sydney. It was all right and the money was good. Everywhere I went I bumped into these people who seemed to know one another already. Eventually I realised it was 'cos they were all students. There were people like me who were working, but most of them were graduates too. I felt out of it but I didn't let that get me down 'cos I was there to do my own thing.'

Working in a temp agency helped Craig realise he actually enjoyed being an estate agent. 'I saw the sorts of jobs we'd send people out on and I was glad it wasn't me.'

What you do while you're away can determine what you do upon your return – in predictable and unpredictable ways. You could, like Jane, pick up a language that makes you more marketable or, like Craig, happily return to your old job having tried, but not liked, other things. Of course, you might never return.

'I never thought I'd come back. I couldn't imagine what I'd do in England,' says Tim, 26, who spent four years abroad as a serial TEFL teacher. 'A couple of months before the end of every contract I started feeling like I should be doing my CV and applying for jobs in England, but I never actually did it. It was a lot easier to just take another teaching job in another country than come back and start all over again.'

And so he spent four years tensely ignoring his own future and conjugating verbs. 'I started in Italy, then went to Russia, China and Venezuela.' Each post lasted a year. His salary was around £7,000. 'I had more than enough to live on – I actually felt quite wealthy.' But each time his contract ran out he'd never saved enough to travel for more than a few weeks. 'I always ended back at home with my parents. A month of that and I was ready to leave.'

'My degree was in English. I got into TEFL because I wanted to go travelling. A TEFL company ran a seminar in my department which I went along to. Because I had a first they offered me a slightly higher starting rate and my pick of the posts – they even paid for my training.'

Like Jane, Tim taught Business English: 'Because I really hate children.' And the money was better. 'I also thought the experience of dealing with business people in four different countries and several different languages would make me attractive to employers.' It didn't. Well, not to the employers Tim wanted to wow.

'I'd been working for four years and still not earned £10,000. I was sick of leaving a place just as I was beginning to feel like I really knew it. For four years I never saw the same season in the same city more than once.'

Letters and emails from friends revealed a different life back home. 'They were making a lot more money than me and building up careers and getting married and stuff. I was getting sex but I couldn't have a relationship because I knew I would be leaving eventually.'

Had he chosen to, Tim could have taken an MA in TEFL and gone on to run a language school or write the textbooks he taught from. 'It was in danger of turning into a career.'

Back in the UK, Tim discovered he didn't know anything about adding value, leveraging assets or singing from the same hymn sheet. He was bamboozled by corporate language. The irony of this was not lost on him.

'HR people would talk to me and I swear I didn't get half of what they were saying.' Admittedly he was applying for consultancy roles – notorious for their impenetrable jobspeak. 'At one interview they repeated the same question three times. I still don't know what "strategical exiting" means.' Probably best.

Tim now works in a travel agency helping others make strategical exits. 'I stopped trying to understand corporate bullshit and decided to use my experience of other countries. I find it very satisfying but it's not just vicarious travel – I get great discounts. Maybe I'll make this into a career.'

Working abroad in a role or industry you don't wish to make a career of isn't necessarily a waste of time. Transferable skills is one of those hateful careers teacher terms, but if you can drive a truck in Borneo you can drive one in Birmingham, and people need correct change and perfect Martinis wherever they are.

There is little point worrying about the supposedly stellar careers of your peers. Part of the reason you have gone away is to forget about what's going on back home, so forget about it until you need to. Don't be eaten up with envy by the real or imagined success of others. Instead, luxuriate in the fact that they undoubtedly envy you. Is their grass greener? Who knows, but your sky is certainly bluer.

Tom, 27, very nearly returned from his travels in a coffin.

'It wasn't cold at 27,000 feet but windy and cloudy. The descent down the couloirs from the summit of Lhotse wasn't difficult but demanded concentration. All of a sudden I slipped and before I could react was tumbling down the upper slopes of the fourth highest peak in the world. My life span in a whirl of disorientation accelerating out of control. Somehow 500 metres later I stopped myself. At 8,000 metres there is no help at hand, no helicopters, just silence and that sickening feeling you are going to die.'

Sure beats the 'We missed our flight' and the 'I broke my ankle during a mad binge' stories told by most twentysomething travellers.

'I had been living my dream but it was quickly turning into a nightmare.'

Tom was rescued – his friendship with the man who saved him is one of the most enduring aspects of his travels. 'I lost three toes and 15 kilos of fat.' There are easier ways of making friends.

Craig, who'd got the job in the temp agency in Sydney, never got the chance to thank his saviour.

'I decided to stop off in Africa on my way back to the UK. It was all going really well. We were at a beach party in quite a remote bit of Mozambique. There were about five of us and we were really drunk.'

Craig was so drunk he stepped over a windbreak without realising there was a twenty-five-foot drop on the other side. 'I nearly broke my back.' Fortunately, he didn't. Luckier still, one of his fellow travellers was a medical student from Germany on a gap year. 'I was panicking but I didn't pass out. He gave me anti-inflammatory drugs and painkillers that he had on him. Then he used the bars from his backpack as a kind of splint for my back. I couldn't move for three days. I was in agony. There was no hospital and no way of getting in touch with anyone. I would have died if I'd been on my own.'

Bruised but not broken, Craig flew home as soon as he could move. 'At least it happened towards the end of my trip.'

Emails from friends on the move rarely tell you about what's gone wrong. After all, they want you to think they're having the time of their lives. The nearly fatal experiences of Tom and Craig are extreme, but most travellers return with at least one really good tale of woe that becomes more horrifically hilarious with every telling. Like when Harriet had to visit casualty after having an allergic reaction to the phlegm sprayed on her by a sneezing elephant, or when Tim had his tires slashed after making an ill-advised Mafia joke with a Mafioso in Moscow.

Travel is about moving around, but it does not necessarily follow that your life is moving forwards. Tim felt just as unsure about what he wanted to do in Russia as he did in Italy, China and Venezuela. Only after he returned to the UK and began applying for jobs and delving deeper into the success stories spun by his friends did he get anywhere. 'Their jobs weren't as amazing as they'd made out. After a while I realised that almost all had some kind of problem, usually with work.' Same shit, different country.

'It was as much about working out what I didn't like, you know? It's a process of elimination that's still going on.'

Harriet's circumstances are pretty much the same as they were before she went travelling by accident. She's still jobless and single. 'My attitude is different and that's what's important. I can look at my life and see where I went wrong. Distance – in time and space – gives you perspective. If you decide to look back it might be painful, but it can help you look forward and avoid making the same mistakes again.' And her friends have forgiven her.

From my vantage point in Texas I looked back across the Atlantic to my past in the UK. It was like getting an aerial view of a giant puzzle. Suddenly I could see patterns I was too close to notice before – ways of behaving and feeling that I had never recognised, let alone understood. And that was the start of another journey.

Whether you like it or not, you will probably have to stop travelling eventually. But there's nothing to stop you going away again. And again.

Tim is packing his bags once more but he's leaving the books behind this time. 'This time I won't be working – I'll just be enjoying myself. I have a job to come back to and a boyfriend too. I won't need to worry about a gap on my CV because, to other travel agents, travelling is research.'

Kate, who quit her job because she felt burnt-out, is still travelling. She's thinking of extending her stay as she's met a rather delicious man in Sydney. 'I don't know if it will work out or not – I hope it does. But if it doesn't, I am having an amazing time and the relationship thing just makes it a bit more special. I do think about coming home, but never for very long.'

Your twenties are a journey. You can take them anywhere, but your life isn't going to change just because you're living it in a different country. Here are some travellers' tips to help you make the most of your odyssey.

Bon voyage.

The small print

Questions to ask yourself:

When foreign shores beckon
- Why do I want to get away?
- Will going away really change my situation?
- Do I need to go travelling or do I just need to take a holiday?

When you've decided to go
- How long will I go for?
- Where will I go? Is it safe for me to go there?
- Who will I go with?
- When will I go?
- Will I come back? If so, when?
- Do I need structure, like TEFL, or some time where I can do my own thing?
- What do I want to get out of going away?

Practical stuff
- Can I get out of my lease?
- How will I manage my mortgage/student loans/credit card payments while I'm away?
- How easily can I quit my job?
- Do I want a job/flat/relationship to come back to?
- How much will travelling cost? (Make a budget.)
- Will my employer or university sponsor me?
- What about visas?
- What equipment do I need and how much of it can I safely buy secondhand?
- How can I access money while I'm away?
- Do I need to keep up national insurance and tax payments?
- Will I/can I work while I travel? Am I insured for that?
- How do I make travelling attractive to potential employers?
- What vaccinations do I need?
- How can I keep in touch while I am away?

How do universities feel about a year out?

According to a recent survey, over 90 per cent of university vice-chancellors believe that a structured year out *during a course* can benefit students. By 'structured' they mean a year spent either working or travelling (or a combo) that will allow you to develop valuable skills. (*Source: keyCLIPS 2001*)

How do employers feel about a year out?

Most employers feel the same way as universities. HBOS (formerly Halifax Plc) say: 'From our point of view a year out shows independence, strength of character and the ability to plan ahead.'

Providing you want to go back to your old job, there is no reason why you can't ask your boss if you can take time out. Point out that it will be cheaper to hire you back than it will be to hire a completely new employee and train them up. Find out if your salary, role or job title will change. Ask other people at your company who've gone travelling how they went about it.

If you're self-employed, keep in touch with key clients while you're away – an email every couple of months should do. But keep it professional, not personal (unless you have that kind of relationship).

If you're thinking about TEFL:

www.Tefl.com
www.eslcafe.com
www.teaching-abroad.co.uk
www.ihworld.com
www.britishcouncil.org
www.ef.com

Year-out organisations:

www.gap-year.com A great resource.
www.gap.org.uk What it says.

www.yearoutgroup.org Ditto.

www.adventure.co.uk Voluntary work in Africa and Asia.

www.conservationafrica.net Conservation experience in Africa.

www.afs.org Dedicated to building a peaceful world through international student exchange.

www.arthistoryabroad.com Art history fest.

www.artts.co.uk Yorks-based entertainment courses for aspiring theatrical types.

www.auscharity.org Charity-based placements in Oz.

www.bunac.org Summer camps and more in the USA, SA, Canada and Oz.

www.cat.org.uk UK-based projects with the Centre for Alternative Technology.

www.cesalanguages.com A year of languages.

www.challengeuk.com Academic and work placements in the USA and France.

www.ciee.org Study and work with the International Educational Exchange Council.

www.coralcay.org Worldwide conservation projects specialising in reef and rainforest.

www.britarch.ac.uk/archabroad Archaeological digs abroad.

www.britishinstitute.it Learn about pasta . . . in Italy.

www.bses.org.uk Serious expeditions to the very remotest places.

www.councilexchanges.org Work, study, teach or volunteer abroad.

www.csv.org.uk UK-based volunteering for 16–35-year-olds.

www.donquijote.org Learn Spanish in Spain or Mexico.

www.eiluk.org Cultural immersion with a host family abroad.

www.euroacademy.co.uk Learn a language in Europe.

www.frontierprojects.ac.uk 4- to 20-week conservation projects in remote locations.

www.icye.co.uk Promotes intercultural awareness and empowerment.

www.i-to-i.com Everything from internships to teaching.

www.mbg.org Business and community projects in the UK and Gambia.

www.pgl.co.uk Activity holidays in the UK and Europe.

www.questoverseas.com Projects and expeditions in Africa and South America.

www.raleigh.org.uk One of the biggest and best – a real mix of people and projects.

www.spw.org Health and environment projects in Africa and Asia.

www.sunseed.org.uk Volunteer research placements in arid regions.

www.trekforce.org.uk Science, conservation and community projects in Central America and South-east Asia.

www.windsandstars.co.uk Projects and travel in deserts for 16–23-year-olds.

www.world-challenge.co.uk Three- to six-month placements worldwide.

www.worldwidevolunteering.org.uk Search engine for volunteering.

www.yearoutdrama.com Does exactly what it says on the box: based in Stratford-upon-Avon.

3

Internship or Internment?

Make working for nothing pay

'It worked for Monica Lewinsky.'
Alison, 26, intern turned employee

'What do you mean you can't source an artificial wedding cake? You'll never work in television! I am just glad we're not paying you!'

Those words, screamed at me by a producer, summarise my brutal internship at Planet 24. While everyone was enjoying their Easter break I was hauling my ass into the offices of the hugely successful television production company. Nothing could have prepared me for having to find five tiers of fake cake for a re-enactment of the nuptials between Frank and Peggy from *EastEnders* on the set of the *Big Breakfast*. Nothing.

Other tasks included one day of hard nipple labour cleaning a collection of fake breasts and two days watching Richard and Judy to ensure our shows stayed 'fresh and hot'. Finding a venue for a party to be thrown in honour of *Watercolour Challenge* presenter Hannah Gordon was almost impossible. 'Ms Gordon,' I was told, 'will not go north of the river.'

Amazingly, Planet 24 offered me a job at the end of my internship. My four fellow interns – one of whom was still trying to break into television in her forties – gawped with envy as I was invited to be a runner. On £250 a week. A quick calculation confirmed such a wage wouldn't keep me in shoelaces let alone put a roof over my head in London. Runners are road kill on the motorway of TV production; studios are littered with their dead and forgotten bodies. I determined to do something better and let the other interns fight it out to take my place.

Work is no longer a linear trajectory beginning with a golden handshake and ending with a golden carriage clock. Not that it ever was, not really. But the image of the job-for-life persists even though it's a reality for precious few people. We are now likely to switch jobs – and careers – many, many times (to the chagrin of our parents). This is partly because we're far more likely to be made redundant or downsized, but also because we're far more independent, fluid and, in some ways, risk-taking. We know it could all be over tomorrow. And if it is, we're going to be happy on that day. We're discovering what we really want to do and doing whatever that is. Postgrads are one route, internships another.

Doing a Monica can lead to bigger and better things. Ms Lewinsky now has her own range of handbags, a permanent chair on the talkshow circuit and a television show about relationships. Interning probably won't get *you* that far. But it might.

'I turned my internship into a job,' says Alison, 26, a Glasgow-based radio reporter, 'but it took nearly ten years.'

That's ten, count them, ten years. Aged fifteen, Alison began making herself useful at her local radio station. She was there long enough to see CDs replace vinyl. 'It's a cliché, but I started off making tea. I was always getting drinks mixed up so I made a reference chart for milk, sugar and mugs, which they laminated. It hung on the wall by the kettle for years.'

Alison progressed to cataloguing albums with the same efficiency. 'It was mainly men at the radio station – they definitely needed a woman's touch.' A year later she began handling calls from the public. Soon after, she was given her own identity badge. 'It made me feel like a real part of the team. I still have that badge.'

But still no money, not even bus fare. 'It was hard because my friends had Saturday jobs and I couldn't work because I was at the radio station.' Still, Alison sensed the knowledge and skills she was garnering were more valuable than money. 'I got on to my journalism degree course straightaway because I had more work experience than any other applicant.'

She spent university holidays juggling her internship and a bar job. 'I was skint – I became a vegetarian because I couldn't afford meat.' At last, the station coughed up expenses. 'If they hadn't I would have had to give up.'

In the second year of her degree Alison did her first short report on air. 'I did a live broadcast from a student protest. It came so naturally, I felt like I'd been doing it for years. It was amazing.' Her bosses thought so too and paid her freelance rates, thus ending her career as a barmaid.

Alison was formally hired on graduation day.

'I'd been at the station for nearly ten years, but becoming a staffer wasn't an anticlimax. I finally felt on the same level as everyone else. I mean, I'd worked with them for years doing almost every aspect of the job, but, in the end, I always felt like a "work experience girl".' Not any more. Alison now has her own show and her own intern. 'I told him what I took in my tea the first day he started.'

Some kind of internship is a prerequisite for even the lowest rung on the media ladder. By the time I landed my first job, editing an online student magazine for *The Times*, I'd worked on ten newspapers, four magazines and countless web sites generally whoring myself about as much as possible. Sometimes I got paid.

For many companies, interns are an artesian well of fresh, keen and free labour. Don't be surprised if no one knows your name because, to them, it's not worth memorising – you'll be gone in two weeks. Expect to be sucked up, used and spat out. That way, anything good that happens is a bonus.

It's worth bearing in mind that you can very easily give too much of yourself for nothing. You must have a cut-off point or you're in danger of slaving from here to internity. Ask yourself what you want to get out of it. How long are you willing – and able – to work for free? How far will you go to get the job you think you really, really want?

James, 27, now works in PR, but his ambition was to be a VJ on a popular music video television station. 'At school I was the first to get cable and everybody came to my house to watch music videos. Being a VJ seemed like the best job – it was just so fucking cool.'

Scoring an internship at the station's swanky HQ in London was a dream for James. 'When I went for the interview there were all these gorgeous people walking about looking important. There was a sense of urgency. I was desperate to be a part of it. I wanted to know everyone and get all the insider info.'

When he got the call James couldn't believe it. 'I'd just finished uni and was waiting to graduate. The woman who interviewed me rang to say I'd got the internship. She asked me if I wanted it. I thought she was mad, but if I'd known then what I know now I would have said no.' He promptly signed his summer away.

'I bought new clothes and stuff because I didn't want to look like I'd just graduated.' James turned up for his first day looking like he'd worked there for years. 'When I walked into reception I really felt like I'd made it. I'd arrived.' Then he was taken behind the scenes. 'I was shown into this manky little room. It was nothing like the rest of the building. There were overflowing ashtrays and dirty cups everywhere.' And lots of other interns.

'That shocked me most of all. It's not like I thought I'd be the only one, but there were loads – at least ten. I was introduced to everyone. Some smiled but most sort of nodded. I was given a little radio to keep me in constant contact and a rota so I knew when to turn up. From that moment they treated me like a member of staff.'

Except he was unsalaried and expected to work longer and harder than paid employees.

'Every day I got in at 7.30 a.m. and did a coffee run to Starbucks. I then spent the morning doing whatever had to be done. The only fun job was preparing dressing rooms for stars – I had to find special kinds of flowers and all sorts of luxuries. Thank God I never got Mariah: imagine trying to buy kittens!'

James never took a break. Then again, he was never offered one. 'We had to keep our radios on in the toilet! We ate lunch on the run – at least they bought it.' The station also paid for pizzas at dinner time. 'I thought they were generous, then I realised they just wanted us to work into the evening. I don't think I ever finished before 9 p.m.' That's a fourteen-hour day. 'And I worked six days a week. I slept right through most Sundays.'

Three weeks into his stint, James had to visit his family in Leeds. 'When I asked for Saturday off you'd think I'd asked for a million pounds. They demanded to know why I wanted that particular day off and scoffed when I told them it was my sister's wedding. I told this to another intern and she looked at me like I was mad – she worked every day including Sunday and this was her fourth summer there!'

James asked around and found that almost all the interns had already served at least one sentence there. 'I couldn't believe it. Some of them were in their late twenties, early thirties. They believed they'd get a job if they went that bit further than the next person or did yet another internship. It was megacompetitive.' He took his Saturday off and came back to a cold shoulder. 'It was like I'd never existed. My supervisor pretended to forget my name. I don't know, maybe she really did – there were so many of us all working for free.'

Summer ended and so did James's career in music television. 'I wasn't offered a job, nobody was. Come to think of it, I didn't meet a single person there that had started as an intern. They didn't promise jobs but sort of dangled them. It was delayed gratification but no one was ever gratified.'

He wasn't even offered another internship. 'I was told I "lacked commitment". I think they confused commitment with addiction. Once was enough – I wouldn't have gone back even if they'd paid me. But I know plenty of others did, for free.'

James went on to join the PR firm where he is now an account director. 'We have interns but they get expenses and the same rights and respect as staff. We work hard but we have boundaries. If people need to take time off they can.' He has never worked another Saturday.

In the end, Alison's internship got her where she wanted to be. But she knew it would. 'Two of the people I worked with had started out as interns and they were really encouraging.' James's internment took him in a very different direction. 'My dream became a nightmare. It was a massive disappointment. But I'm sort of glad it happened. I feel sorry for those people who keep hoping that one day they'll be the person handing out the radios and hunting down the interns.'

A taste of what you think you want can whet your appetite or kill it completely. But having a go and deciding something just isn't for you – as James did – is definitely not a waste of time. Far better to find out sooner rather than later that you'd rather lag pipes than design bras. Think of interning like dating: a process of elimination that will hopefully bring you to the Right One.

I had always dreamed of being a doctor. From an early age I was obsessed by obscure skin disease, ferocious fevers and medical paraphernalia. I spent hours memorising Latin terms and perfecting illegible handwriting. My parents were excited, rather than worried, and fuelled my unhealthy interest with books. Grey's *Anatomy* booted Enid Blyton off the shelf. Only when I had to deal with actual sick, dying and dead people did the boil of interest burst.

In my final year at school – just months away from med school – I worked at a geriatric hospital for two weeks. Despite being improbably young, nurses addressed me as Dr Barr because I wore a white coat and was improbably tall for my age. I rather liked this and only bothered to relieve them of their misapprehension when asked specific medical questions.

On my first day a patient ('they're not inmates') set my arm alight. Next day the same patient tried to torch another in a row over cigarettes. I became intimate with the workings of adult nappies and their contents. But it wasn't just the grossness of bodies that deterred me, it was the emotional consequences of death, which I had imagined as the closing sequence of *Beaches*, that barred my medical ambitions. As the fortnight drew on I watched a lovely old lady die. Daisy shrunk before my eyes, getting smaller every day. My last day was also hers. She disappeared from her room but the flowers brought for her remained, shrouding the scent of death.

I discovered I loved reading about death and disease but hated dealing with it. It took an internship for me to realise that – far better then than on my first ward round. At university, friends studying medicine told horror stories from tours of duty and I shuddered, thinking how close I'd come to having blood swill around my ankles in an ambulance. (I am stuck with the doctorly handwriting as those with a signed copy can see.)

Working for free is an essential component of vocational degrees like Law and Medicine. Geoffrey, an ex-housemate of mine, had a glamorous way of paying for the unpaid work he had to do as part of his studies. Far taller than my six-foot-three and with cheekbones you could use to cut glass, he combined medicine with modelling.

'The two occupations were completely incongruous,' admits the model/medic. 'I remember cramming for a biochemistry exam on a private jet back from Milan after a Calvin Klein shoot. I was looking out over the Alps thinking that in four hours I'd be sitting an exam. It was like *Absolutely Fabulous* meets *Casualty*.'

But he managed it.

'I started modelling in my first year after being approached by an agent on campus. At first it was just catalogue stuff – you know, standing in a silly pose wearing a pair of pants and trying to look serious.' Pretty soon, someone in London noticed his work and he was put on the books of a big agency where he started doing magazine shoots.

I remember being very jealous. Each weekend I skulked around our dirty student flat in Edinburgh thinking up interesting things to do with pasta, while Geoffrey swanked around Paris, New York and Rome. At least he brought me good presents.

'I made less than £10,000 in my first year,' he says. Still, far more lucrative than flipping burgers. His earnings soared when he began working abroad. 'The last year I almost made six figures.' Although he was rich – far richer than he'll ever be as a GP – Geoffrey wasn't tempted to become a full-time model. Well, not that tempted.

'It was glamorous – I'm not going to lie and say it was really hard work because it wasn't. I stayed in beautiful hotels and had hundreds of people running after me all the time. Compared with being a doctor it was easy. There was a lot of standing around and I didn't like everyone, but that's hardly the end of the world.'

So why didn't he swap the operating theatre for the catwalk?

'Fashion was fun but that's all. It was very shallow and frivolous. It made me realise that I really wanted to do something serious and important with my life. I couldn't have modelled for ever – the jobs would have stopped when my looks went. I'm happy being a handsome doctor.' And so are his patients.

While studying law, Tashi, 24, spent her summers working as a legal secretary. 'It was a great way of getting a grass roots understanding of how a practice works.' And of earning £10 per hour. 'I saved so I could afford not to work while I was interning during my course. Most of my friends didn't need to work at all – their parents funded them. If I hadn't saved I would've had to work and intern during the course at the same time, though I don't know how.' Although her faculty frowned on it, many of Tashi's fellow students did exactly that. 'They'd finish at the office and go straight to their other job. Not one of them did as well as they should've because they were shattered.'

Geoffrey and Tashi both had to intern as part of their studies – no internship, no degree, no career. Understandably. Who'd want a doctor that had read about, but never seen, a broken limb or a lawyer that had never actually won a compensation claim? These internships often attract some financial assistance from universities or a stipend from employers, but there is rarely enough money to go around.

Any pretence of pay disappears when you volunteer your services as Alison, James and I discovered. Not only are most internships unpaid, but they actually cost. Interning requires investment – new clothes, a place to stay, transport to work, lunch and drinks and, if you're a media whore, drugs with colleagues. And it's up to you to find a way of making up the lost income. (You're more likely to temp than model.)

Those without relevant work experience are at the end of the career queue whether they're seeking their first job or starting a new career. But interning, like travelling, is a luxury not everyone can afford. That's why university is the best time to do it. Budget time and money and you can make good use of holidays. Nobody expects students to look great and your standard of living is appalling anyway, so you might as well go for it.

So how do you get those supposedly golden opportunities?

I got my Planet 24 internship by replying to a newspaper ad then blagging my way through the interview. It's worth reading job papers, even if you're not actively seeking a job, to see the sorts of roles – and salaries – you might get. If you have a specific company in mind, keep checking their web site. And, providing you spellcheck, there is no harm in sending a prospective email or letter. Such prosaic routes are often the only way into straight-edged jobs. Indeed, the BBC and other big institutional employers have limited numbers of internships which you have to apply for. Don't expect to get in just because you're offering to work for free, because there are plenty of other equally desperate applicants.

Your chances of scoring an internship are linked to the industry you're aiming for. Wannabe spies should not expect to spend the summer at MI6, but time spent picking up skills in a corollary profession – like translation – would be a good investment. Consider security and background checks. If you recently trashed a bank at an anti-war demo you may find awkward questions being asked at your job interview with the police. Because of fears about paedophiles, prospective teachers and all those who plan to work with children must undergo security checks, as Kate, who we met in Chapter 1 discovered.

'I had to get classroom experience before I could apply for my PGCE to become an art teacher,' says the former PR girl, 'but I had to wait before I could do that while the police ran checks to make sure I wasn't a danger to children. I didn't mind them doing it because I knew they wouldn't find anything, but it felt strange to be suspected.'

Although her criminal record was whiter than white, Kate was concerned about unteacherly activities that might show up on other tests. 'I did a lot of coke when I was working in PR – I mean, *a lot*. If they'd done a drugs test I would have been screwed, which would have been unfair because it's not like drugs I did a year ago would stop me teaching a class now.' Depends how good they were.

Although legally you don't have to comply, many companies now make job offers conditional on passing drugs tests. This same courtesy has been extended to internships, as Simon, 24, found out.

'I was after a consultancy role at Accenture or somewhere like that,' he says. Having graduated with first class honours in management studies from one of the country's best business schools, this seemed likely. Sure enough, he was invited to apply for a paid summer internship at a big consultancy. 'I had a short interview on campus, then they discussed my grades with a tutor and that was that.' Except for the drugs test.

'They told me I didn't have to take it. I knew it would show up weed, E, speed, acid, mushrooms and coke. I didn't ask what would happen if I didn't take it, but I got the impression that my place would have gone to someone else.' Which it did: rather than take – and fail – the test, Simon pretended to have a better offer. 'I found out how long I have to wait before the drugs won't show up. I'll reapply then.'

Those dreaming of being 'creative' face the toughest fight to get noticed – everybody wants to be a television presenter, nobody wants to be a camera person. The more creative the industry, the more creative you have to be to get an internship and break in.

'I only ever wanted to make beautiful hats,' says Kai, 26, a graduate of fashion from St Martin's. 'I did lots of work experience all through my degree and it was all very practical.' As practical as fashion can be. Kai was offered a trainee job with a big department store after graduating but turned it down. 'Sure, I would have been working as a designer and I know that is a great privilege, but I didn't want to make hats for white trash weddings, you know?'

So, posing as a customer, he presented himself at the London shop of one of Britain's most celebrated milliners. 'We got talking about his work and before I knew it I'd been standing there for three hours.' The chat became lunch. 'This guy was my idol – I'd only ever seen him from a distance at shows or in magazines or on television.' Lunch was delicious and the pair got on famously. I can't say Kai is now working for him or even that he did. 'I told him I'd just graduated and that I wanted to make hats, not buy them. He was great and put me in touch with a friend who looked at my designs and loved them. She was my first private client – I made her the most fabulous hat you can imagine!' A direct approach can work, but only for those brimming with confidence.

Travelling and interning can be a fruitful combination, but it's doubly hard to organise. Unless you get a lucky break.

While sipping iced tea in a café in Austin, Texas, I overheard a local journalist interviewing people about what they were doing in the Lone Star state. I sat listening to the quotes he was getting – they were dull. Leaping from my seat I presented myself as a case study for his story. I was, I said, a journalist. At the end of our interview I was given a business card and invited for lunch. I couldn't believe my luck. A week later we lunched. The internship program was full at the moment, he said, but did I fancy doing some freelance work instead? Did I? Did I!

Did I also fancy being deported? My student visa cleared me for studying and interning, not working. But was freelancing working? Yes, in that I did work, but no, in that I was not a worker. It was all very bureaucratic. I took advice from everyone I could think of – some said do it, others said don't. I did it, as I knew I would the instant it was offered. And I didn't even get shipped back to the UK.

The reporter who gave me my first big break was Michael Barnes, arts critic for the *Austin American-Statesman*. He also gave my ego its first big thump. 'This piece you've written,' he said, of my first story, 'it's not publishable.' The story was indeed bad. It rambled, bumbled and sucked. But Michael helped me fix it. And the next one.

The US government is particularly evil about visas, although the line between interning and working can be blurred to your benefit. Thankfully there are organisations that can help (see end of chapter for details). Providing you speak the language, it's far easier to intern in Europe.

Sally, 29, was part of the European Parliament for a summer. 'I sort of attached myself to our local MEP,' she says. 'The toughest bit was finding out who he was.' Once she'd done that there was no stopping her. 'I started out in his UK offices between terms assisting his assistant. Then, the summer after I graduated, they flew me to Brussels.'

A graduate of French and Law, this was exactly what Sally wanted. Or so she thought. 'I loved the job. My language skills were very good but after a month they were great. I started dreaming in French, which I'd never done before. People say government is slow to respond, but when you're inside, everything happens very fast. I researched proposed legislation and proofread draft amendments. It was very high level.'

All she had to do to stay legal was register with the local police station and commit no crime. 'Because it's the EU there was no need for visas, but I did have to pass quite a few security checks for work.' For money, she lived off a parental allowance. 'I know, I was very lucky.'

Despite enjoying her role and making a great success of it, Sally was not completely happy. 'I loved everything about my internship and I made some great friends, but everything was work-focused. On the weekends we'd end up talking about what we'd done the week before at work and what we planned to do next week. I wanted more fun. And I missed my family.'

At the end of the summer, Sally returned to England with a glittering CV. 'I realised I really wanted to work in European Law but didn't want to work in Europe.' She now works at a London-based think tank with strong European links.

Sally's skills were directly transferable across international borders (as were mine, once I'd developed them), but it's worth checking beforehand that experience gained abroad will be recognised by UK employers.

Once you're in you have a limited amount of time to discover whether or not this really is the place for you. You can decide quickly, like James, or consider your options, like Geoffrey. Whatever you decide, it's going to look good on your CV, providing someone gives you some kind of reference. Many places issue fairly naff certificates, but these will do, as will standard letters stating where and when you worked.

If you like what you find, the next challenge is turning your internship into a job offer. I'm not sure how I did this at Planet 24, given that I couldn't find a fake wedding cake or shine boobs very well. Alison got hers by hanging around for ten years and making herself useful.

'There was a clear procedure at the end of our internship,' says Sally. 'We were evaluated, and, if we did well, invited to apply for certain positions. These might not be with the team you interned with, but they would be at the same level.'

The summer after his hateful internment at the music television station, James was surprised to receive a phone call from their HR dept. 'This woman wanted to know if I'd be interested in another internship. I said no and told her why. She said she was sure there would be plenty of other interested parties and hung up.' And she was right. 'They did say they would file my details, but I can't believe they actually did.'

Geoffrey, now working as a GP near Dundee, still gets the odd call on his mobile from agencies interested in booking him. 'It's flattering, but I always say no. If there was a really amazing gig or a cause I was interested in, like PETA, I'd think about it.'

Ideally, you should approach an internship like a job – dress, act and sound like a professional. Of course, employers should treat you like an employee – pay you, remember your name and care. They probably won't. But if they are equally vile to paid employees you just have to deal with it.

If you're already in a job and looking to switch careers, an internship is the perfect way to hedge your bets. Discover if the grass really is greener without giving up the security of your current job.

'I hated banking,' says Jo, 29. 'It was a drudge. I despised the people, the job, the office – everything. I ended up on anti-depressants because I couldn't face work.' What she really enjoyed was clubbing. 'That was the only time I was really happy.' During a therapy session, Jo discovered exactly what it was about clubbing that she loved so much. And it wasn't being loved up.

'It was the music. I loved dancing with my mates, but when the club closed it was the music I really missed. When I thought about my life I realised I had music everywhere – in my house, in my car and even in my shower.'

And so the banker became a DJ. 'Everybody thought I was mad. I didn't tell anyone at work. I told my friends and my therapist. I couldn't quit – I couldn't afford to – but I had to do something.' Inspired by the cellist-turned-DJ on TV's *Faking It*, she enrolled on a DJing course. 'I took two weeks' holiday. We did classes during the day and practised in bars at night. On the first night I got the biggest buzz. Making music was very different from listening to it. I loved knowing what beat was coming next – it was like sex.'

At the end of the course Jo passed, but not with flying colours. 'I didn't think they'd tell me I was amazing because I wasn't, but I wasn't rubbish. It just felt good to do something fun for myself and develop new skills.' Jo now does a free monthly set at the bar she cut her decks in. 'I still hate working at the bank,' says Jo, 'but I can stick it now I've got something else to look forward to. DJing has given my life some balance.'

If you are going to intern as a way of trying out a new career, make sure your current boss doesn't find out. Don't tell colleagues what you're doing (a fake postcard from the Bahamas should throw them off the trail). Using your holidays means your internship will effectively be paid so you don't lose income, but you do lose valuable chilling time. And if the grass really isn't greener on the other side you may end up feeling even more bitter.

Working for nothing *can* pay, but only if you make it. Should an amazing job not be forthcoming, plunder paper clips, contacts, experience and knowledge. You can profit from your internship whether it's here or abroad, voluntary or compulsory, paid or unpaid, before, during or after university. And if nothing else, you can, as James and Geoffrey did, find out what you really *don't* want to do.

The small print

Whether you're starting out or switching careers, you'll face less competition in autumn and spring than you will in summer. Students will find it more difficult to intern during term. Also, think small. You don't need to be at a big company to gain experience. In fact, smaller companies often offer more tailored hands-on programmes. And you'll face less competition.

People who can help you find an internship:

www.bunac.org Summer camps and work placements in the USA, SA, Canada and Oz
www.ciee.org International Educational Exchange Council
www.councilexchanges.org Work, study, teach or volunteer abroad
www.icye.co.uk International exchanges and voluntary work
www.i-to-i.com Everything from internships to teaching
www.klc.co.uk Interior and garden design courses in the UK
www.travellersworldwide.com Do whatever you like, wherever you like
www.world-challenge.co.uk Three- to six-month placements worldwide

Ten rules for indispensable interns:

1. *Talk, but don't talk people to death*

You may not get paid, but you are an employee (albeit temporary). So act like one and talk to your colleagues (but don't take
up too much of their time).

2. *Ask for work*

Sick as this sounds . . . Suggest tasks you want to do, but don't
start work without being asked to. Don't do more or better
work than your supervisor as they're unlikely to hire someone
that's going to show them up.

3. *Suck up information*

Eavesdrop, read what you shouldn't and go where you're not
supposed to. Find out everything you can – information is rarely
useless. Try convincing HR to let you see CVs of successful
applicants.

4. *Get in the loop*

Try and get on internal email – that way you can maintain a
presence inside the organisation and be privy to internal commu-
nications.

5. *Don't be overfamiliar*

You can be friendly, but don't start following people home or
stalking them at lunch time.

6. *Go to meetings and events*

Little of note actually happens at meetings, but you can pick
up on interdepartmental dynamics and learn some useful buzzwords. Turning up and helping out shows willing.

7. *Never burn a bridge*

Even if you hate the place and everyone in it you may well need
somebody at some point, so it's worth smiling at people you
wouldn't normally spit on.

8. Know your rights

Remember: you're not being paid and you're not fully trained. If you're asked to do anything difficult or dangerous or put in a situation that makes you uncomfortable, you can walk away.

9. Know your limits

If you're on your third internship in the same organisation and it looks like you're not going to get a job, you're probably never going to. Stop wasting your time – take your knowledge and skills to a competitor willing to pay for them.

10. Keep tabs on yourself

Write a diary of your internship – use this as the basis for updating your CV. Include buzzwords (but only if they're current). Be honest – is this really the job for you?

How to turn your internship into a job:

1. Be realistic

If the industry is full of freelancers, don't expect a staff job.

2. Accept the odds are against you

Don't be disappointed if you don't make it this time.

3. Stay hot

Regularly update contact details for key people and send a monthly email keeping them in your loop.

4. Whenever you can, get face time

You'll find more out that way, and it's harder to say 'no' to a face.

5. Stay ahead of the game

Watch the company's web site and read the industry press – you can spot openings and sound smart at interview.

6. Go the extra mile (if you can)

Offer to extend your internship or do another at an agreed date – make it easy for them to keep you.

7. Talk yourself up
Nobody else will. But don't talk yourself up too much.

8. Debrief
Find an employee who started out as an intern and pump them for info.

9. Sleep with the boss's PA
Befriend admin staff – they often know what's really going on and are best at reaching key people.

And if they do manage to get rid of you . . .
Schedule an Exit Interview and get someone to acknowledge your contribution in writing or tell you where you went wrong. Before you go make sure you get numbers/email addresses of cute potential colleagues.

4

Too Old to Be Young, Too Young to Be Old?

Coping with your inbetween years

*'There's always someone younger and better coming down
the stairs after you.'*
From Showgirls

O nce upon a time your eyebrows sat quietly and unobtru-
sively on your face. Like your waist, they required no maintenance. Now, suddenly and without warning, your eyebrows
are turning to topiary and your waist is, well, where is your
waist?

Your bum, squashed into an office chair since leaving university, is looking decidedly dumpy. You're still getting spots only
now they take weeks, not days, to clear and hangovers become
a two-day affair. Sex? Tiring and too messy.

What's going on?

You're getting old. Boisterous body hair, an expanding waist
and slowing sex drive are three sure signs that you're aging. Yes,
you. Okay, you're not forty. Far from it. Perhaps you're not even
thirty. But you will be. Are you closer to twenty than thirty? Or
delicately poised exactly in between? At twenty-five I started
my countdown to thirty. I have three years to go. Early, mid or

late, our twenties are the decade when time stops being about development and starts being about decay. Hair growing in the wrong places. Fat staying where it's not wanted. Energy being spent faster than money. All of a sudden pop stars are younger than you and Madonna is having babies and you haven't written a bestseller, got to Number One or released your own celebrity skin care range.

Aging is not a symptom of the quarterlife crisis, but feeling like you're suddenly too old – to change, take risks or have fun – is.

So what to do?

First of all, accept your share of responsibility for the agist society we live in. Youth is currently the only currency higher than sterling. And don't we know it. It is – or was – the unwritten qualification on all our CVs – YOUTH.

INTERVIEWER: So why should we give you this job?
INTERVIEWEE: Because I am precociously young and much younger than you.
INTERVIEWER: Congratulations, welcome to the company.

Admitting that you once traded on the fact that you were closer to the cradle than the grave may make it easier to accept that the balance is now slowly shifting out of your favour. You might not understand it now, but one day you'll be the one lusting after youth in the boardroom and the bedroom. (Or so I'm told.)

'I started off as a graduate trainee,' says Gayle, 28, a business development director at a software company. When she joined the firm everything was, well, firm. 'I'm sure my age and youthful good looks were part of the reason I was hired, not that I'm a model or anything. This is a male-dominated industry and it makes some sense to have a young, pretty woman in a front-line sales position.'

It certainly does. Gayle was promoted twice in her first year and her salary rose from £18,500 to £22,000. 'I was doing better than the other graduates hired at the same time. It was all performance-related, so I was able to make a direct correlation between how well I was doing and how well I was paid. I was a bit of a star.'

In newish industries, like tech, youth is an even greater asset. Gayle leveraged this. 'It was dotcom boom time. I don't think I knew anyone over thirty. I'm not kidding – and I thought thirty was old! To do my job you needed energy.' Lots of it. 'I did hundreds of client presentations and pitches for new business. Very often I'd fly to Europe or America and sometimes to India to deal with our contractors. It was always go, go, go.'

In her first year Gayle did eight trips abroad, each lasting around a week. 'And I was always visiting clients up and down the UK.' As well as travelling there was wining and dining to be done. 'I always had good food and wine when the company was paying, whether or not I was entertaining clients.'

Then the miles and the meals began to take their toll.

'At the start everything was exciting. I remember the first time I flew business class, I took all the little cosmetics off the plane as trophies. I was one of those people who couldn't wait to graduate and get into the real world. I loved the hotels and taxis and everything.'

But after two years it started to get a bit boring.

'I began to dread being picked to go to sales conferences. I didn't want to travel so much. I bought a flat but it seemed like I hardly spent any time there at all. And I wasn't seeing my friends very much – my best mate had a baby and I wasn't there for the birth and that really upset me.'

But Gayle still enjoyed sales. 'That's the thing – I loved my job. I loved the buzz of going into an office and coming back out having sold hundreds of thousands of pounds' worth of products and services. Especially as I was on a bonus.' To continue selling Gayle had to continue travelling. 'I didn't want to quit but I couldn't do one without the other.'

So she kept on going. And going. 'I was at an airport in Europe somewhere, I honestly don't remember where. And I was looking at the board with all the flights on. There were all these destinations and I couldn't remember which one I was going to next. I couldn't visualise where I'd be when I got off the plane.' Gayle looked at her ticket. 'I was supposed to be going home.'

And that was that. Her performance hadn't changed – she was still meeting her targets – but her situation had. She wanted to keep going but she couldn't. 'On one trip a guy, not from our company, offered me some speed. He said it'd perk me up. I actually thought about taking it.'

Something had to give.

'I went to my boss, the business development manager, and told him I was feeling quite tired. He asked if I needed a holiday and I said yes.' Gayle took two weeks off. But she didn't go anywhere. 'I stayed at home and finished decorating my flat. I went through loads of papers and did a bit of a life laundry. I caught up with my mates and saw my family. By the end I felt ready to go back to work.'

After two days in the office she was told she'd need to do a site visit with a potential client. In Australia. 'I couldn't believe it. I'd never been to Oz – I wanted to go but I didn't want it to be about work. I'd only see the inside of a hotel and they're the same everywhere. I wanted to go travelling and see it for myself. But I couldn't not go.'

Gayle approached her boss with her concerns. 'He sat me down and talked to me like he hadn't done before. Basically what he said was, "You're too old". I was shocked. I was twenty-six. How could I be too old?'

Like it or not, she was. The pace of work was no longer sustainable – not when she wanted to do things like spend time at home and see her friends. 'I couldn't have a life and do the job I was doing. It wasn't even a question of balancing any more. I was just too tired to work all the time. I hadn't noticed age creeping up on me, but it had. I just didn't have the same energy levels any more.'

Luckily for her, it wasn't a question of quitting or going elsewhere. 'I wanted to stay and they wanted to keep me. I actually got promoted to business development manager.' This meant more time on strategy (desk) and less time on tactics (planes). 'It worked. I still get to go out on big presentations, but I'm not travelling all over the place. I still get tired, who doesn't, but I'm not permanently exhausted any more. I actually do things in the evenings and on weekends now.'

Gayle realised that her youthful energy had been at least partly what got her the job. When it expired, so did her time on the sales front line. 'I could have felt used, but I didn't. I got as much out of them as they got out of me. And now I'm in a higher, easier position.'

Gayle was able to stay at the same company, but not everyone has that choice. There are businesses where aging is simply not an option. 'The only place I could have got decent work after forty was in a Marks & Spencer catalogue,' says Geoffrey, our model/medic from the last chapter. How many fortysomething footballers (with the beponytailed exception of David Seaman) are there in the Premier League? And how much Botox will Kylie have to inject before she becomes more statue than icon?

The moment when we realise we no longer count as 'youth' can be painful.

'I remember it very distinctly,' says Leon, 28, a senior marketer for a big brand consultancy. 'I was hired after doing a summer internship in my last year at university. There was a group of us and we were all hotshots.' On a starting salary of £30,000, Leon could afford to rid himself of burdensome student debts and dress the part for his sexy job. 'We were the rebellious teenagers in the company family.'

Leon and his friends were almost encouraged to go in late. 'We never got pulled up. So long as we'd been out at the latest club or done something cool it was okay. I think we'd have got into trouble if we'd rocked up late because we'd been watching morning television or catching up on our laundry.' Widely agreed to be handsome, Leon had a good degree from a good university. His colleagues were pretty much all the same. 'We were the beautiful people.'

Whenever his company was pitching for a youth account, like Levis, Leon was consulted. 'I remember sitting in a meeting with my boss's boss and he listened to my every word and didn't interrupt me once. I was just talking shit about how spending was the new saving or something like that, but you would have thought I was a prophet preaching a new gospel.'

Any new product or service targeted at the jaded-but-essential 18–25 demographic was bought and trialled by Leon and his colleagues. 'It was called "competitive analysis". We decided what was hot and what was not. It was purely opinion.' But, as a twenty-two-year-old, Leon's opinion was automatically valid.

Freebies included: 1 micro scooter, 1 bike, 1 scooter, several holidays to cool destinations, wardrobes of clothes and trolley loads of drinks, booze and food as well as myriad other trinkets. 'I got something free every day.'

The office was a place to check in and out of. 'Apart from team meetings, I came and went as I pleased. I could go anywhere so long as it could be passed off as research – clubs, bars, shops, wherever. I had a company mobile, always the latest model, so they could get me any time they wanted.'

A charmed life for one of the beautiful people. Then it turned ugly.

'I was in a meeting. We were preparing a pitch for Diesel. I knew the product well, though I didn't particularly like it, but I had very clear thoughts on it. For once I'd even done some research so I could back myself up, as my boss had started challenging me. Anyway, the meeting started and I got up to give my presentation. This new girl stood up at the same time. I didn't even know she had a job, I thought she was an intern. Anyway, I looked at her as if to say "sit down" but she stayed standing. I turned round to my boss who nodded his head at me to sit down. I was stunned. I barely heard her presentation and I didn't say a single word in that meeting. As I left the room my boss came over to me and patted me on the shoulder. Do you know what he said? He said, "Don't worry, Leon, happens to us all".'

And that was that. Only it wasn't. 'I didn't have a clue what he was talking about.'

Back at his desk Leon pondered his boss's pronouncement alone. 'I wanted to tell one of my colleagues, but held back – it's like a failure shared is a mistake multiplied, you know? But I kept it to myself. I thought I'd put a foot wrong or offended someone or something. Advertising has a lot of egos so I just assumed it was that.'

And then he was passed over again at another meeting. 'After that I told the guys who were recruited at the same time as me. Turns out we were all experiencing the same thing. One girl was even told to shut up when she didn't get the hint. I couldn't believe it.'

Not sharing concerns about failure, or perceived failure, is a key component of the quarterlife crisis. We assume errors lie with us rather than the organisations that shape our lives. We're desperate to been seen by our peers as outrageously successful. After all, nobody wants a loser for a mate. Unbeknownst to one another, Leon and his mates were in the same boat. Would sharing have changed the situation? Almost certainly not, but it would have changed how they felt about it – and did. 'It felt good to know I wasn't the only one.' Had Leon, or one of his colleagues, 'fessed up faster they would have felt a whole lot better a whole lot sooner. Instead they all spent two weeks wondering what they'd done wrong and why they'd been singled out.

Leon and his mates were all the same age – twenty-five – and had been with the company for the same time – three years. 'And it was the same person who'd told us all the same thing – we were too old to speak for youth any more. The same thing must have happened to every employee when they hit twenty-five – some sort of sick birthday present. It wasn't just coincidence.'

With the loss of his gilded status came the end of his privileged workstyle. Leon had to be at his desk by 10 a.m. 'And that's where I spent most of my day. I also had to go to more meetings and generally do more work. It was a real change and it basically happened overnight.'

Although his job title and salary didn't change, his status did and it happened because he got older. 'I couldn't believe that, at age twenty-five, I was "too old". It's like I lost the right to speak on my twenty-fifth birthday.'

Leon and his group weren't thrilled with the new regime, especially when they were ousted from their shared desk by a new clutch of creative cuckoos. 'That was the last straw. I thought about confronting the boss – we all did. But what could I say? "I am older but I still feel young and my girlfriend is only twenty-three." I looked around and noticed that almost everyone in the agency dressed and acted younger than they were, especially the women. I'd never noticed they were emulating me, or at least my age group.'

Although only twenty-five, Leon opted for voluntary redundancy. 'The company needed to shed jobs and I wanted to go, so I took the money and ran. I couldn't stay – I knew I'd never have it so good again.' His peers took the same deal and the group went into business together. 'I am still in branding but I have a different focus. I'm sick of youth culture, so we're capitalising on the fact that a lot of people are living longer and giving a bit of oomph to companies selling to older people.'

Like Gayle, Leon became too old to do the job he was hired to do in the eyes of those who hired him. Unlike Gayle, Leon felt he could continue in the same role despite his advancing years, which is why he left and set up his own business. Both had to accept that other people's perception of their age overruled their own. If your boss thinks you're too old, you're too old. Deal with it.

It's not only bosses who force you to accept your age.

Amanda, a PA, now 27, slid comfortably into her first experience of office culture. 'I was only twenty-one but I felt very grown-up. There were loads of people my age and we had a great social life. We went out most nights and compared hangovers the next day. Everybody got on, even though there was all the usual bitchiness. I mainly stuck with two girls who'd gone to college with me. I had my own little gang. It was a bit like being back at school.'

Christmases, birthdays and break-ups were marked by trips to the local bar, whip-rounds and cheekily cheap gifts. 'My boyfriend worked in our sales department so I managed to see a lot of him even though he went away for business.' Like many people in their first job after seemingly endless years of education, Amanda recreated a school-like structure. Only progression in the workplace isn't always welcome.

Then: 'The two girls I worked with had degrees, but I only had an HND.' One by one her friends were promoted. 'We were still in the same building but not the same room. We talked on the phone and emailed, but we didn't see each other at coffee break or lunch as much.' Eventually, they stopped seeing one another at all. There was no row or rift, just slow and inevitable separation.

Bereft of her buddies, Amanda tried to make friends with the new girls. 'They were cold right from the start. I thought it was because they were new to the company. I thought they were intimidated by me because I knew how everything worked. I went with them on fag breaks but they ignored me. I thought I was being paranoid, but they didn't ask me to go for lunch or drinks after work.'

Her suspicions were confirmed one Friday afternoon. 'I got sick of feeling left out so I asked if I could join them for a drink. I wasn't desperate or anything and I played it nice. They said, "Sorry, it's an under-twenty-five night" and started laughing. I went to the toilets and burst into tears.

'Those girls were the same age I was when I joined the company. Obviously I knew I was getting older, but I didn't think I was getting *old*.' Amanda worked out that she was now closer in age to the office stalwarts than the new girls. Realising this, she tried to deal with suddenly feeling ancient by hanging with an older crowd.

'I'd never socialised with older women before. They were nice enough and quite happy to have me with them, but I wasn't into bingo and line dancing. It was like going out with my mum.'

Amanda struggled with a classic quarterlife quandary: she was too old to go clubbing but not old enough to start knitting.

'I realised the girls I tried to be with actually weren't right for me any more. They were talking about boyfriends and silly stuff when I wanted to talk about getting married and maybe having kids. They were sharing a flat with one another and I was trying to get a mortgage. But the older women already had kids and a house and a husband so they weren't as excited about it all as I was.'

Set adrift from her peers, Amanda felt isolated. She spoke to her (older) boss about it. 'He didn't want to lose me but accepted something had to be done. I was miserable. It sounds sad, but I really missed my mates – they were one of the best things about my job.'

A transfer to a different department with a more suitable demographic provided the answer. 'I'm much happier. I don't feel so old now there are other girls my age. I don't dislike older or younger girls, it's just that I don't have much in common with them.'

Age dynamics become even more complicated when, as a whippersnapper, you have to *manage* older colleagues.

Jay, 27, joined the force after a degree in economics. 'It comes in handy for fancy-dress parties – I just wear my work clothes. I got on the fast-track scheme.' Now a detective, Jay was a special constable at university. 'I got plenty of stick for that. My flatmates stubbed out joints when I walked into the room and pretended I was going to arrest them and stuff. They still call me Bobby. But getting into the force was my life's ambition.'

His experience as a special and his fast-track status meant he wasn't on the beat for long. 'I had sort of done the job already but there was still a lot to learn. It's mainly about attitude and that's the one thing you can't learn that I have always had.'

Within a year, Jay had risen above many of the colleagues he'd been supervised by shortly after signing up. 'Everyone was pleased for me, but there was something else, a sort of jealousy. People that had sat with me in the staffroom didn't automatically pull a chair out for me any more and a couple of people started calling me Sarge, even though I was barely above them rankwise.'

The jokes went on. Jay didn't pay too much notice until he opened his locker and got a shock. 'A shitty nappy fell out.' There was nobody else around to see. 'I didn't know what to do. It was stinking. I finally got the message.'

In an attempt to avoid formal action, Jay confronted the chief suspect – a much older man who was now technically Jay's junior. 'He didn't deny it. I was amazed. It was a big joke for him but I wasn't laughing. I have to say, it was only really the men who took issue with my age – the women were pretty much all right.'

A formal warning later, Jay's colleague wasn't laughing, and the jokes and pranks stopped. 'I thought I'd earned their respect, but actually they saw me as a sort of grass, which was ironic. As part of my training I got moved quite a lot so I didn't have to see them again. But that was the first and last time I got serious grief for being so young.'

In actual fact, age wasn't the issue – it was seniority. Jay's older colleagues were really objecting to the conferment of power on someone younger. As far as they were concerned, it was unfair and possibly unwise. 'They were always laughing about how young policemen looked these days.' Like many other graduates, especially those on a fast-track scheme, Jay had to learn to manage upwards. 'Getting people older than you to take you seriously is an invaluable skill but it's not easily learnt,' he says.

Like Leon and Amanda, most of us seek others our own age, but there are some who do the opposite.

'That's why I went into social services,' says Tina, 27, a social worker specialising in care of the elderly. 'There's something callous about our culture. Experience isn't valued here, not like in Japan. Our older people aren't listened to. I hate the whole "bang them in a home" culture. It's disgusting.'

Tina is unusual – most of us are only too happy to take granny's money for a house deposit, but we can't bear to hear another story about the war. 'Most of the older people I deal with are surprised to have such a young person working on their case. One or two have asked for older colleagues, but that's okay.'

So far, so PC.

'I have plenty of friends from university who are my own age, but I don't feel the need to surround myself with clones of myself. Everywhere I look I see people my age. It's nice to go to work and interact with people who have different concerns. People have always said I was "wise" for my age, which made me feel a bit awkward – old, somehow. But I can use that side of myself at work.'

Tina admits that part of her likes being the only person under thirty in her office: 'Most of my colleagues are in their forties. I benefit from their experience and feel quite safe in their hands, but they don't patronise me or anything. Actually, they make quite a fuss of me.'

Sarah, 29, works in a crèche. 'Why would anyone want to work with adults? I mean, I have adult colleagues and I deal with the children's parents, but my life is basically about children.'

So why this (slightly unusual) dedication? 'It's not like it sounds. Children are more innocent than us. When I'm with children I feel less jaded and more optimistic. You start to see the world through their eyes.' And it's not always pretty. 'There's all this stuff about paedophiles and whatever – a lot of children are scared to trust adults. I want to help children understand that not all adults are dangerous. And I want to help make the world a better place for children.'

Sarah and Tina have gone to extremes to escape our all-pervasive youth culture. Neither totally rejects it, but both choose to spend 9–5 in a different demographic. 'At the end of the day I go home to my boyfriend,' says Sarah. 'He tells me stories about his office and I am glad I don't have to deal with that kind of crap.'

'I believe you should treat others as you want to be treated yourself,' says Tina. 'I am not a wounded helper, but I feel like I'm storing up karma – I don't want to end up rotting in a home. I'd like to think things will be different by the time I'm seventy.'

Sarah and Tina have to acknowledge their peer group every time they open a magazine or turn on the TV. The cult of youth is inescapable and with it the notion that younger is better. That's all right when you're young: Gayle had her vitality and Leon his privileged point of view; then we're all too happy to buy in. But, as we age, the rewards we got just for being young are taken away. We're expected to 'act our age'. There are new recruits eager to make their mark. So let them. 'My job gets easier the older I get,' says Jay. 'People respect me more.'

Our inbetween years are only awkward and difficult if we try to cling to our twenties. No man should wear bootleg jeans beyond twenty-five and miniskirts are a crime much beyond thirty. (That's not to say you can order your clothes from the back of the Sunday papers and be in bed by 10 p.m.) Getting older has its rewards – salary, for one – but you won't see what they are until you accept your age. Gardening becomes the new clubbing, Echinacea the new E.

Perhaps, as Gayle hopes, our society will stop favouring the young. But it's unlikely.

We may be able to stop the signs of aging, but we cannot stop the clock or make getting older trendy. All we can do is age gracefully and gratefully. And I don't mean nightly application of cold cream and daily application of sunscreen. We must be less harsh on ourselves. So you're not running the company by the time you're thirty – who is? You don't have to do everything now. You can do it later, or not at all.

'I won't live till fifty, I know I won't,' says Elizabeth, 27. 'I have hypertrophic cardiomyopathy. I don't know exactly how long I'll live, but I know I won't have to worry too much about wrinkles. It makes me sad to see my friends wasting time worrying about getting old. It's a luxury I don't have.' Terminal illness hasn't stopped her from living abroad, getting a degree and snaring a boyfriend. 'I don't waste time, I can't afford to. I'm 27 – proportionately, according to my life expectancy, I am really in my forties. I suppose my quarterlife crisis is actually my midlife crisis.'

All of which makes me think that having eyebrows like caterpillars isn't such a bad thing after all.

The small print

Five ways to manage your inbetween years:

1. Grow older and wiser (hopefully)
You're getting older, which means you're getting more experience. If you've launched a product or dealt with a tough situation, you can do so again. A new graduate can't. Use this to your advantage.

2. Be honest
Lying about your age is illegal. Make sure your boss knows that, although you still look young, you're actually an experienced colleague – which means you need more pay and perks! If your boss thinks you're twenty-one and you're actually twenty-six, you'll get a twenty-one-year-old's wage (and you won't like it).

3. Act your age
Don't try to keep up with the kids – you'll look ridiculous and lose the respect of your peers and elders. Don't go overboard and dress like a biddy, either.

4. Know your rights
It's illegal to ask someone's age in a job interview – so don't answer. If asked, challenge them as to why your age is more important than your experience or skills.

5. Avoid age rage
Don't get frustrated with yourself – you'll get where you want to be eventually. There's no point giving yourself an ulcer in the meantime. You'll be old before you know it.

5

I Work Therefore I Am

How our jobs become our lives

'Is it all just work, consume, die?'
Hugh, 29, bank manager

'Every time a friend succeeds, I die a little.'
Gore Vidal

You have the worst job in the world. No, you really do. The pay is shit, your boss is evil and your office was designed by a sadistic architect on a tight budget. Your friends have it easy compared with you. If you could open the windows you'd jump. But you can't, so you send envious emails to friends employed elsewhere and fantasise about stapling the receptionist to death.

This job envy is an essential ingredient in the glue that holds our civilisation together: we bond in our shared hatred of micro-managers, bitchy colleagues and energy-sapping offices. The success of *The Office* proves that work feels the same whatever you do. Estate agent or editor, police officer or pastry chef, we all love to hate our own David Brent.

Not content with having a bad job, we compete with our friends to have the worst job. My boss is meaner than your boss. My team is lazier than yours. Even in our misery we overachieve.

It's partly about garnering sympathy but there is covert kudos in having the worst of anything, so we exaggerate.

Not everybody hates work. Take a deep breath – I know it sounds like sacrilege, but for every person that feels like walking out at 5 p.m. and never coming back, there's another person who can't wait for 9 a.m. to roll around again. Some people actually enjoy working. They probably enjoyed getting their report card at school and viewed exams as an opportunity to shine. What's more, they like the people they work with and the space they work in. For many people, colleagues are the new family. But even they complain about their jobs.

Why do we pretend to hate our jobs and actively covet those of our friends? Well, job satisfaction just isn't cool. It wasn't cool to love school, it's not cool to love work. Which makes it tough for those who do. Nobody wants to admit they really like selling advertising space or enjoy dressing bed sores. But that's not quite it. Job envy is an integral part of our culture of consumption – it could not function without envy. We are constantly encouraged to believe the grass is greener somewhere else. You'll get paid more, have more power, get more respect if you just . . .

Today's grotesque overemphasis on work has blurred the line between who we are and what we do. When we're little we're not asked what we want to *do* when we grow up, but who we want to *be*. So when we get there it's 'I'm a bank manager', not 'I manage money', and 'I'm a plumber', not 'I fix sinks'.

'I don't tell people what I do,' says Hugh, 29, a bank manager. 'They imagine me as some sort of miser or control freak. It's such a cliché, but people really switch off and start treating me differently when I tell them I work in a bank.' Having his job acknowledged can be worse than having it ignored. 'I've been to so many dinner parties where the person next to me won't stop talking about money or asking my advice about interest rates because they think I am fiscally obsessed. I hate it. Now I just say I work in an office.'

Hugh enjoys moving around piles of pounds and pennies. 'I wouldn't work in a bank otherwise,' he says. 'But I don't dream about money. At the end of the day I want to switch off and talk about something else. I think it's a real problem that we define ourselves so much by what we do for a living. Surely we're more than just a job?'

If you don't know 'who' you want to 'be', you're more likely to be dissatisfied with your job. And if you hate what you do, you will inevitably envy what other people do.

Alec, 26, has had a bad case of this – he has had five different jobs, each lasting a year, since graduation. 'I've been an ad salesman, a barman, a temp, a trainee teacher and a *sous-chef*.' Not what you'd expect from someone with a 2:1 in history.

'What *would* you expect? I mean, everybody thought I'd go into teaching. I listened to all the advice and that's exactly what I did.' And he hated it. 'I am *sooo* not a teacher it's not even true. I don't know what I was thinking. It's not that I don't like kids – I have a two-year-old son. I just hate school.' Alec later told me he was bullied from the age of twelve to fourteen. 'As a trainee teacher I was put into classrooms with kids that age. It sounds sad but I felt edgy every time I went in. I knew it couldn't happen again, but it brought a lot of memories back.'

For Alec the only good thing about being a teacher was the grant he got to train. Even though he had a miserable year, Alec remembers his friends being envious. 'They were jealous that I had a structure – if I stuck with teaching I'd know what I was doing and how much I'd be getting paid ten years from now.' They stayed envious even when Alec told them he was having a tough time and considering quitting. 'One girl told me to stick with it because, however bad teaching was, it was better than what she was doing. She wanted me to do it more than I wanted to myself.'

Alec chucked his duster in. 'I had no idea what to do next.' He drifted into working behind a local bar. Before he knew it he'd been pulling pints for a year. 'I'd spent enough time on the other side of a bar so it was a nice change!' Then he developed his own case of job envy. 'This is going to sound really stupid,' he says. Go on. We've all done stupid. 'It was a bar-restaurant, right, quite a nice one. I got miffed when I realised people came for the food, not the drinks I was making.'

No longer proud of his trademark pomegranate Martini, Alec announced his intention to defect from bar to kitchen at the Christmas party. ('I was a bit insulted that the bar replaced me so easily.') He settled down to a life of scrubbing, peeling and boiling. 'I am not an idiot – I'd been in the kitchen, I sort of knew what it was like. But it was harder than I thought. Behind the bar I could stand and chat to customers. In the kitchen I only had colleagues to talk to, but I was usually too busy to chat. It just wasn't as much fun as it looked from behind the bar.'

Another Christmas party, another job change. This time Alec didn't know what to do next. Luckily he didn't have to wait too long for job #3. 'I was having leaving drinks at the bar and some of the regulars were there. One of them told me he thought I'd be a good salesman because I'd always managed to make him run up a big tab.'

A couple of interviews later and Alec was selling advertising space in a monthly trade magazine for TV and film production people. 'My mates were all dead jealous – they thought I was working with celebs. Truth is, I never once spoke to, saw or even sniffed a star. It was all boring business-to-business work.'

Alec stuck it out for six months. 'I told my boss I wanted to quit. He offered me more money to stay. So I stayed for another six months.' But dolly grips, gaffers and sparkies just aren't glam. 'And I have to say, good guys were in the minority in sales. What a bunch of wankers.' Again, to the shock of friends who thought Alec was one step away from the red carpet, it was all-change. 'Apart from hating sales I got to see a bit of the film and TV world and I liked that, but I knew I couldn't get into it in a million years.'

Right now Alec could be photocopying reports or minding phones in your office. 'I'm temping because I can't make my mind up about what to do next. This gives me a taste of lots of different jobs and keeps my girlfriend off my back.' Of course, his friends envy his flexible workstyle. 'I'd like more stability but I'm not going to rush into anything.'

Five jobs in five years is a lot, but does that make Alec a job-slut? 'I don't think so. I think it's wrong to keep doing something if it makes you unhappy, even if other people think you should stick at it.'

Stability wasn't enough to keep Alec in teaching, the bar lost out to the kitchen because food seemed more important than drink, and secondhand celebrity couldn't make up for the dullness of sales. It seemed the action shifted each time Alec moved to where he thought it was. The grass never got greener. Alec is suffering from 'negative' job envy because it's not taking him anywhere.

'I'll keep temping till I find an office or job I really like, then I'll go for it. I'm not bothered about what my friends think – it's me that's got to do the job, not them.' Sure. 'But it would be nice if they thought it was cool.'

There is the added complication today that, in a world where contract working is the norm and companies are as stable as the average *Big Brother* contestant, we can no longer rely on a job for life even if we wanted one. I learned this aged 12 when I was made redundant from my paper round. My first job after university went bye-bye when the magazine I was hired to edit folded. I was made redundant three times in three years. Nothing personal, you understand. We can no longer rely on work to provide our identity for us, which makes us feel less secure generally. We have to think beyond our jobs to discover who we are. Is a paperboy without a round still a paperboy?

Job envy is inevitable because what we do has become who we are. Your job is a lifestyle. We overidentify with our jobs and work steals far too much of our time. And if we're not happy at work, we're not happy in life.

'I really thought special things would happen to me after I graduated,' says Elizabeth, 23, a law graduate. Didn't we all. The first person from her family to go to university, she made it to Cambridge. 'There was a real sense of entitlement, which the university magnified. I wasn't alone in thinking I had the world at my feet just because I had a degree from the world's best university. We all assumed life would be there for us when we left.'

Only after graduation did she discover that a degree does not guarantee a vocation or a route to financial, intellectual and emotional gratification. By then it was too late. Elizabeth was unemployed for nearly a year – unusual for a Cambridge graduate and especially odd for a law graduate, as, according to *Legal Business*, law firms take up to 58 per cent of their trainees from Oxbridge.

'There was a glut of law graduates that year, but it wasn't just that. I started to question what I was doing. I saw friends from other courses do jobs that seemed so much more exciting and interesting. I still thought that law equalled lawyer. I didn't imagine I could do or be anything else.'

During her year-o-dole she grew increasingly envious of her seemingly happy friends. 'They complained about their jobs, everybody does, but I could tell they were happy really.' Their happiness made her miserable. 'I felt such a failure. I wasn't going out much because I wasn't working, and I was sick of hearing work-talk all the time. Whatever I started a conversation about, politics or the news or anything, it always came back to work.'

Eventually Elizabeth gave up on law. She hadn't applied for many jobs; she hadn't, as promised, been courted by big law firms with big budgets. 'I know I'm good – I got a first – but I started to think maybe it's not meant to be. I'm not a fatalist but it seemed like somebody was trying to tell me something.' Directionless and consumed with job envy and job over-identification,

Elizabeth paid for advice from a career counsellor. 'She was a total waste of money. Basically she told me I have a great degree and that it's up to me to find out what I really want to do and go for it. I knew that already; I wanted answers.'

Almost two years after graduation Elizabeth is still *sans* job. 'I'm not going to take a job unless I'm sure it's what I want to do. I'm lucky, I don't need to worry about money because my boyfriend supports me. I'm not going to take a job just for the sake of it, but I'm no closer to knowing what it is I want to do. I just know I'm not meant to do law – especially when I hear stories from friends who are now practising. It's not me, but I don't know what *is* me.'

Elizabeth's fear of not liking her job (i.e. her life) has stopped her getting a job or a life. Of course, Elizabeth's parents don't understand. 'My mother works in a building society and my father drives a taxi. They've done the same jobs for twenty years. They think I should just get on with it. I don't want to be like them. I don't want my job to be my life, because if I hate my job it means I hate my life.' She needs to work out what she actually does want.

Our parents, like Elizabeth's, seem satisfied with their 9 to 5 lot. Job envy and job over-identification are the curse of *our* generation. More than ever we define ourselves by what we do. Yet work is less secure than ever, there is more choice than ever so there is more job envy than ever. You look at your fellow commuters and imagine them going to a swanky corner office with cappuccino on tap. We're all imagining the same thing. We're scared that everyone has a better job, bigger pay-packet and more job satisfaction. In Claire's case, this meant she did not give her friend the best advice.

'I know it was wrong,' says Claire, 25. It certainly was. 'Looking back I can't believe she did that to me,' says Jess, 25, Claire's ex-best friend. As far as I can see this is what happened.

Claire and Jess went for the same job – PA to the director of a big energy firm based in London. Jess got the job. Claire didn't. End of story. You'd think.

'If I couldn't have it she shouldn't have it either,' says Claire. 'I honestly think I deserved the job.'

'It started out great,' says Jess. 'I thought I was lucky to have such a nice boss – we were more like mates, even though he was older and in charge. It felt too good to be true.' And it was.

One month into the job Jess received flowers. 'They were from my boss, but it wasn't my birthday or anything. He said it was to celebrate our "one month anniversary" and told me my probation period was over.' Now she really had the job.

Claire was totally jealous. 'I got another job, which paid more, but I wanted that job – it was nearer to my house and the offices were nicer. Anyway, I had to sit and listen to all these stories about how great her boss was. Nobody gave *me* flowers.'

Jess was chuffed to bits. Every Friday they'd meet after work and Claire would sit silently as Jess extolled the virtues of her new job and her new boss.

When Jess began to express doubts about some of the things her boss was saying ('I love you') and doing (touching her – *lots*) Claire was reassuring. 'I could sort of see where it was going.' Jess thought Claire was being a friend and followed her advice to the letter. 'I didn't tell anyone in the office – I didn't want to make the other girls jealous. I just got on with it.'

Three months into the job Jess's boss tried to kiss her. 'I stopped him – I was really taken aback. I didn't see it coming. And I didn't want it. He was nice enough about it.' At first. 'A couple of weeks later he tried again. I pushed him away. He told me to do my job properly.'

Claire was working at a legal practice which dealt with employment law, but still she encouraged Jess to keep quiet. 'I was typing all these letters about sexual harassment and stuff.

I knew what Jess should be doing.' But she didn't help. Claire's jealousy was out of control. And so was Jess's boss.

'It was late and I was the only person there,' says Jess, crying. 'I tried to leave but he wouldn't let me. He said I owed him a favour and grabbed my hand. I shook it off and shouted at him to let me go.'

Jess rushed to Claire, who finally admitted things had gone too far. 'I told her to tell HR everything.' Which is what she *should* have said from the start. Understandably, Jess phoned in sick. Next day she received a letter from her boss telling her she was no longer required. 'I couldn't believe it.'

Totally traumatised, Jess called Claire. 'She told me to stop crying and snap out of it. I couldn't believe how callous she was – she was supposed to be my best friend.'

Claire was pleased. 'I wasn't happy about how she lost the job but I am glad she did.'

Looking back Jess feels more hurt by what Claire did than the actions of her boss. 'He paid for what he did at the tribunal, but I still don't get why Claire treated me like that, I really don't.'

Claire does: 'I was jealous.'

Thankfully job envy is rarely so extreme or destructive. Claire had the worst case of all the twentysomethings I interviewed for this book. For most of us, job envy is a mild feeling experienced when we're not doing so great and our friends are. It's easy to imagine x is better than y when you're wondering why you did y in the first place. But job envy usually fades when things get better for us (or worse for them). Because it's often temporary, job envy doesn't get to us too much. You forget about being an astronaut and get on with being an accountant. Hopefully.

'Walking into work this morning I realised I am envious of every other job going,' says Sophie, 27, a marketing consultant. 'Having a London-based, office-bound job means I spend my days longing for other professions – even the weird ones. On a summer's day the thought of working in a park appeals. On hungover Tuesday mornings I want to be a *barista* in a coffee shop. On lazy Sunday afternoons I think it would be fun to work in a gallery. But I go to work every Monday and do the same things I do every day.'

Should she? Must Sophie be so quick to forget her fantasies? Could job envy be the first signal of a desire to make a positive change?

'I think I'm the typical victim of "grass is always greener" syndrome,' she says. That cliché just keeps cropping up. 'But when I really think about what I want to do, I'm stuck.' Like most of us. We aren't interested in the reality of other people's jobs – we want the fantasy. 'I once met a lion whisperer – he did, as the name suggests, whisper to lions – and reckoned that no job could be better. But, dull as it may sound, I am rather keen on seeing out 2003.'

Sophie's shifting desire to do something different or better is amazingly common among twentysomethings. We even share the same fantasies. 'When the weather is nice and it's springtime and I'm sick of being indoors I'm jealous of park gardeners,' says Jim, 23, a freelance journalist.

Sophie is aware of her job envy. 'I covet other people's jobs the same way I covet other people's partners, cars and homes.' Jim is too. 'The job I want changes with my mood, which changes lots. But I can't switch jobs every time I have a mood swing. Most of time I'm happy.'

Jim and Sophie are experiencing what I call 'positive' job envy. For all their gripes, they enjoy what they do. They're aware that they're happy most of the time, it's just that sometimes they fancy doing something completely different. Who can blame them?

'I reckon I'll stick to staring at computer screens and daydreaming,' says Sophie. 'To be fair, I like my job – just not all the time. Sometimes I'd rather be doing something else somewhere else.' You, me and everyone else. Jim became a freelancer because he had a staff job and hated it. 'I like being able to please myself and work where and when I want. But I sometimes think I'd love to edit a magazine – until I think about long lie-ins or a day off midweek. It's not realistic.'

Just because something is not realistic doesn't mean it's not real (look at Jordan's breasts). It's fine to dream of being a deep-sea pearl diver, but should you or shouldn't you take the plunge?

Positive job envy can be productive in three ways if you accept what it tells you about yourself:

1. As with Jim and Sophie, it can help you recognise you're actually quite happy with your job. (I know this goes against our antiwork ethic, so don't go round making people sick with your smugness.)
2. If you're happy most – but not all – of the time, think about what it is that pisses you off. Can you change aspects of your current job to make it even better?
3. If you're fantasising about a particular job, identify what it is that appeals and integrate that quality into your life, if not at work then at play. This might involve voluntary work, switching roles – or changing jobs.

'I enjoyed getting out of the office and working on stories,' says Jim. Changing the basis of his job from staff to freelance meant he never had to set foot in an office again. 'I had to quit my job and give up a lot of security, but I used those contacts to build my new career. It's all worked out now, just about.'

'It took me five years to leave my job,' says Jon, 29. For five years Jon worked in the music industry marketing bands. 'Basically I was the guy that made sure the posters were put up before the singles came out.' Far from drifting into the job, Jon interned through university and afterwards to get a toehold on the ladder to where he is now. 'It was a long journey. I think I was more focused on getting where I wanted to be than what I was actually doing.

'Music is my passion,' he says, pointing to the wall of CDs that passes for decor in his north London flat. 'I wanted to work with musicians and be a part of the scene, but not just a hanger-on.' Jon became a player. 'I had a department and a budget and I knew that the success of a record depended quite a lot on what I did to promote it. That was power.'

And there was money, too – lots of it. 'I was on £45,000 when I quit.' And he got all the free CDs and concert tickets he could ever have wanted. 'It would take years to listen to my whole collection.' So why quit, especially after working so hard?

At first he moved companies, attributing his growing sense of dissatisfaction with work to his old colleagues. 'I was happier in the new place, but I still felt something wasn't right.' Jon earned more than his friends and held a position much coveted by the many interns serving him, but he wasn't happy and didn't know why.

'To be honest, I was angry with myself. I couldn't believe it – I'd worked so hard to get where I was and I still wasn't happy. For about two years I was in denial about how I felt.'

Four years into his career he had a revelation. 'I took part in a project encouraging young adults from difficult backgrounds to make music. I enjoyed it more than anything I'd done in years. Then I knew what I wanted to do. I wanted to be more creative and constructive, but not make music. I was working with creative people and I was a "creative" in the marketing sense of the word, but I wasn't *making* anything. I was a salesman.' Jon suffered from job envy and job over-identification. 'I didn't want that project to end. I kept in touch with the people who ran it. The more I heard the more I wanted to do it.'

To do that he had to give up money, power and status and admit he'd got it wrong. 'That was tough. I had no trouble finding a job – the voluntary sector is always desperate for good commercial experience – but it took me a year to get it all straight in my head.'

When he told his colleagues where he was going, they looked at him like someone who'd just volunteered for peacekeeping duties in Iraq. 'They treated me like some sort of martyr and said they respected me. I think they thought I was mad, but by then I was sure I was doing the right thing.'

Jon's job envy was positive. It took him a long time, but he identified the missing ingredient in his work life. 'Working out why I was unhappy was the hardest part.' Rather than entrenching himself and becoming bitter, Jon made a move. 'But only when I worked out what I was going to do next.'

Had he stayed, Jon would have succumbed to negative job envy. We all have a friend who needs to leave their job. They sit in the pub and moan and whine, but do they ever take your advice? No. Instead, they revel in the misery caused by their boss/colleagues/office. You know they should quit. They know they should quit. If their job was a partner it'd be dumped. But negative job envy is all they have and so they cling to what they know and hate.

Positive job envy leads to a change of attitude or career. Negative job envy results in stagnation because you're consumed with resentment. Which are you managing right now? Find out by taking the test at the end of this chapter.

The all too popular belief that everyone else has a better job than you is mistaken. It just adds fuel to the job-envy fire. Is your job really that terrible? If it is, do something about it – make your job envy positive. If it isn't, shut up and get on with it.

What we do for a living now defines who we are. There is little we, as individuals, can do to change this. It has paralysed Elizabeth – she is terrified to become one thing at the expense of another. Hugh the bank manager's answer is to keep quiet about his job. The rest of us just have to try our best to make the gap between what we do and who we are as narrow as possible.

'I think the human condition is to be restless and never satisfied,' says Sophie. 'There will always be something else to tempt us round the corner.'

There certainly will. You just have to decide if you want to turn that corner or stay where you are.

The small print

Is your job envy positive or negative?

Remember: positive job envy should, ideally, lead to change (at least your frame of mind if not your job). Negative job envy ends in stagnation. You can go from positive to negative and vice versa. Only you can decide if, in the long term, you need to make changes to your working life. Never forget that you are more than just a job.

If you can say 'yes' to three or more of the following five statements, you have positive job envy:

1. I dream about doing something different.
2. Most days I am fairly happy in my job.
3. Sometimes I'd like my job to be a bit more exciting.
4. I wonder what exactly other people do all day.
5. Work isn't the most important thing in my life.

If you can say 'yes' to three or more of the following five statements, you have negative job envy:

1. I think everyone has a better job than me.
2. Every day is a bad day.
3. My closest friends think I need to quit.
4. I can't do anything else – this is the only job for me. My career is a mess.
5. I probably need to work harder.

Five ways to manage job envy:

Positive or negative, the following will help you manage your job envy.

1. Get real

Every single one of the twentysomethings interviewed for this book admitted suffering job envy, usually when dissatisfied with their job. You will almost certainly feel job envy at some point, so don't sweat it.

2. Be honest

Don't pretend you hate your job when you secretly love it, as this makes job envy worse. If you really are coveting another career, look into it but find out what's actually making you unhappy before doing anything drastic. Things could probably be a lot worse – you're not mining uranium with your bare hands.

3. Keep it to yourself (sort of)

By all means talk about it with your friends – misery loves company. But these are *your* feelings and you are responsible for managing them safely. Don't resent those you imagine have it better. And don't misdirect dissatisfaction with your own lot at your colleagues.

4. Fantasise

Imagine you're doing the job you think you want to do. What does it feel like? What are your colleagues like? Do you get paid more or less? Now have a look through the job pages. Is there any job out there that resembles your fantasy? Do you need to change the job you're in or switch jobs altogether to make your fantasy a reality?

5. Gloat

Secret smugness can help get you through those low moments. On a piece of paper write the things you love about your job –

your boss's arse, the smell of the photocopier, whatever. Make it a sort of 'good things about my job' mantra to be repeated when things get tough. Update it. Quit if you can't think of anything to write.

6

Fire Your Boss:

Tales of new workstyles.

'I can't imagine ever having a proper job again.'
Me – and just about every other self-employed person in the world

'I owe, I owe, it's off to work I go . . .'
Sarah, 27 – not as bitter as she sounds

It's 4.38 p.m. I woke up at 11.30 a.m. but only because the sun got too bright. After a wank I watched a repeat of *Trisha* on ITV2 having slept in for the early edition. The intervening hours were misspent buzzing around my flat doing everything but work. There's a cold cup of tea on my desk in the corner of my living room. I've just finished unloading the dishwasher while reassuring my editor on the phone. I am wearing my favourite pyjama trousers and a dressing gown which keeps flapping open. I have a deadline at 6.00 p.m.

Welcome to the world of the self-employed.

There are now 2.3 million self-employed people in the UK, according to the latest Labour Force Survey. That means people like me now account for 11.5 per cent of the total workforce. And there are more of me everyday. No wonder UK plc is in such good shape. Some theorists predict the end of the office – but they've been saying that since the first office opened its revolving doors.

Twentysomethings are increasingly keen to do their own thing when it comes to work. We are more likely than our parents to abandon traditional notions of work. There have always been self-employed workers – hookers, spies and foreign correspondents – but our generation is the first to go it alone en masse. And it's no accident that we are all Thatcher babies. Bosses are on their final warning.

Should you fire your boss? If so, why, when and how? What's it really like swapping colleagues for clients, pay for revenue and flexitime for all-the-time?

'I spent six years climbing the career ladder in London,' says Sarah, 27, formerly a cog in the great media wheel. Her reward? 'I was made redundant from my position as head of marketing for a TV channel. After that I decided I'd had enough of working ten-hour days for a salary I didn't feel was commensurate. I was doing these massive deals worth millions and my bonus was a few thousand, if that. I was knocking my pan out for what felt like nothing.' £50,000 a year isn't exactly nothing but the point is that, relatively, Sarah felt screwed. 'As well as working long hours I had to go to client events after work. I wasn't getting home till 10 p.m. Usually I was pissed or pilled so I felt fucked the next day.'

Sarah's job was so all-consuming she never got the time, or distance, to gain perspective on it. 'I was always working or thinking about work. I wasn't allowed to take more than a week's holiday at a time but it took me a whole week to calm down and come out of work mode.' Her friends advised her to quit. But Sarah kept going. 'I've never been a quitter. I don't give up. I thought that if I kept at it things would get better. Maybe one day I would be the one sitting in a boardroom wondering what to blow my millions on.'

Getting made redundant was the best thing that could have happened. But Sarah didn't think so at the time.

'I got an email from my line manager inviting me for lunch. He told me in the Ivy that I was one of the costs they were cutting. I felt totally betrayed. After everything I had done for them this was how they repaid me. I couldn't believe it. If I hadn't been in a public place I would have cried.'

Her things were in a box when she got back to the office and her security privileges had been stripped. 'I couldn't even email my friends to let them know what was happening. I felt like a criminal.' Security guards escorted her from the building.

Sarah had six months on full pay – 'they call it gardening leave' – to consider her options. Becoming her own boss was not option number one. 'I felt lost without a job. When people asked me what I did for a living I had to tell them that I was unemployed. I felt like a slacker. I've never not had a job.' It was a condition of her leave that she could not be hired by anyone else in the same industry for a year. 'I was going mental after four weeks. I even thought about getting a bar job just to give myself something to do.'

The stress of being out of work placed strain on her relationship. 'I was hanging around the house and getting depressed. I became obsessive about everything. If my girlfriend was late home from work and I'd cooked dinner I'd go ballistic. I was like a psycho fifties housewife.' Quality time it wasn't. 'Things weren't working. I suppose I had too much time to think. I realised I'd really neglected my relationship and forgotten why I was in it or what I got out of it.'

Within three months Sarah was single as well as jobless. 'By that point I actually felt free. I had some money in my pocket and only myself to worry about.' It was then that she began considering working for herself. 'I made a list of all the things I hated about my old job.' This included endless meetings, feeling ripped off, sucking up to senior staff, commuting and the architecture of the office building. 'I realised there was only so much I could control by getting a job in a different company. A lot of my problems were with having any job, not just that job. Basically I needed to bite the bullet and start my own business.'

The newly single and soon to be self-employed Sarah was spurred to transform the rest of her life. She moved to New York City. 'Running your own business is about being an entrepreneur and I don't think the UK is very entrepreneurial. I'd lived in the US before and I have family there.' A year on she is still in business. 'My PR and marketing agency specialising in music PR is established. I have three clients, a web site achieving 20,000 hits a week and I don't owe any money.'

The motivating factor to becoming self-employed is often becoming unemployed, either by choice (voluntary redundancy) or force (being downsized, getting fired or even becoming disabled). Would Sarah have chosen to be her own boss if her job was secure? 'I don't know. I was thinking of getting another job but I hadn't considered running a business.'

Only a fifth of the self-employed twentysomethings I interviewed made an active choice to leave their job. Many of those stuck in a job said they would go it alone if they could afford to.

Becoming self-employed isn't like starting a new job – it's a completely new workstyle. Vanquished are the irritating colleagues and forgotten are the fluorescent lights and freezing air conditioning. Gone is the suffocating bureaucracy and idea-phobic org chart, but with it the support of IT, accounts, marketing and admin.

'I set up at home,' says Sarah from her New York apartment. 'I factored workspace in when picking a property to rent. I have a dedicated office space so I can keep my work and home life fairly distinct. I've implied to my clients that I work out of an office and have several employees.' Already an accomplished blagger Sarah has stretched truth to new limits in an attempt to boost business.

'I had no experience in PR and no US contacts whatsoever. I pretended to know US DJs I'd never heard of. I made out like I had lots of journo contacts to my first client then went to Borders and made a list of names and contacts from the magazines. And I used campaigns that I'd worked on for past employers as client credentials on my own web site.'

Sarah admits it wasn't easy staying focused near a big-screen TV and fridge full of beers. 'Working at home with your partner, creature comforts and domestic chores staring you in the face provides much room for distraction. The chances of spending eight hours working in this environment are slim.'

Consequently Sarah initially spent more time 'off' than 'on'. 'I wasn't into working the hours I did in London. Part of the reason I set up on my own was to get a better work-life balance. I took pleasure knowing people were stuck in offices while I was watching TV at home. I value flexibility. I like knowing that everything I do is for me and no one else.'

But the self-employed suffer their own special problems, not least of which is deciding whether or not to get dressed.

'There is a lot of instability. Hustling for business has never been a favourite task for me, and harassing clients to pay isn't really my thing.' Gone is the monthly pay-packet, however meagre. 'Last month two of my three clients didn't pay, plus I was still owed $1,500 from a previous client so I was owed over $4K and I had a bunch of bills.' Not for the first time, Sarah had to dig into her savings to cover the grocery bill.

When she did manage to focus on her work Sarah found administrative tasks absorbing her time. 'I had to make invoices, chase payment, do clippings, buy software, fix the printer. And then there was all the household maintenance. All these worries are someone else's in the world of the gainfully employed.'

Although irksome, such practical problems are easily overcome. The most serious disadvantages are the least tangible: working in her basement was cosy but lonely. 'There's no one to bounce ideas off, discuss last night's telly with or take cigarette breaks with. It's too quiet.' As a coping strategy Sarah joined the gym and a local business group. 'I now associate with other similar businesses which gives me new leads, contacts, advice and support.

'It sounds crass, but I never appreciated how much self-esteem and confidence I gleaned from my status as department head. When you're the boss, with no employees, no company structure and no external hierarchy, you have no recognised status.' For Sarah, status is externally defined and bestowed by someone else – a boss. Lack of praise is her deal breaker. 'I love to please. I'm a real pat-on-the-head person. Pleasing myself just doesn't cut it. I need to be depended on in order to be really motivated.'

And that's why she's winding up her business, rehashing her CV and putting herself back on the job market.

'My business is a success but I'm ready to return to being an exec. I've proved I can make it work, but, for all I hated certain aspects of being an employee, I've realised that's what I am.'

Sarah made her business work but being self-employed didn't work for her. 'I don't think I've failed. And it isn't just a momentary doubt – I've been doing it for a year. I needed to do this for myself. I'll approach work with a different attitude this time. It'll all look good on my CV.'

The decision to become self-employed is clearly not irreversible. But it isn't easy returning to office-world.

'I know it will be hard. I've got used to doing what I want when I want. That's why I'm going to try and get some time working from home. Just because I'm becoming someone else's employee again doesn't mean things have to be as bad as they were.'

Sarah couldn't have known beforehand that she wasn't 100 per cent suited to being self-employed. No one does. It's a bit of a gamble, but you can consider the most obvious effects – on your finances, working hours, home life – before going ahead. Don't ditch the office if you can't live without the gossip.

Stuart, 28, has spent the last five years riding the ups and downs of the IT world. He's been a tech journalist and a tech PR. Now he's running his own business, doing bits of both. Unlike Sarah, Stuart chose to leave his job.

'People were being made redundant everywhere in the industry, but my job was secure. I just wasn't happy with it.'

For those who have jumped rather than being pushed, there is often a decisive moment when the shackles of wage slavery are thrown off. Mine came when I'd been made redundant for the third time. Stuart's wasn't all that dramatic. 'I'd been unhappy for months,' he says. 'I'd been weighing up the options. It got to Christmas and I thought, "Do I want to be unhappy for another year?". That's when I made the decision to set up on my own.'

The reason for his unhappiness was, like Sarah, partly to do with money. Or lack of it. 'I resented the fact that my services were being charged out for a lot more money than I was ever seeing in my pay cheque at the end of the month. I felt ripped off.' Stuart's work environment magnified this resentment. 'I got sick of being bollocked for being three minutes late. I was treated like a child. It was Orwellian – my time was measured out and my movements controlled. I had to get out.'

As with travelling, escape is a metaphor used by most self-employed twentysomethings. So is renewal. The phrases 'getting out', 'moving on' and 'fresh start' appear again and again. They're all connected to a growing sense of self-awareness. Sarah was one of the few self-employed people not to say 'I couldn't be a wage slave again.'

Stuart's spare bedroom is the base for his burgeoning business empire. His web site is run in collaboration with former colleagues and techie friends. 'Basically it's a second bedroom with no bed. I built the desk myself.' Furnishing the office was his sole set-up cost. 'I already had a computer and all the technology.' Expensive printed stationery has no place in the world of email. 'And I'm not having expensive lunches and stuff every day – my operating costs are a lot lower.'

Like Sarah, Stuart has to contend with creating a work-life balance, but for him it's about stopping, not starting, work. 'So far I've been happier. I work harder and longer than ever but I don't mind because I benefit directly from whatever I do.'

It's now 9.44 p.m. I'd like to be watching television but I'm not. Instead, I'm focusing on finishing this chapter. I could have done it earlier today but I went swimming instead – just because I could. All in all I will have worked at least twelve hours today; that's two hours more than your average employee. But if I don't do it nobody else will. Such is the blessing/burden of the sole trader. You have complete control over, and responsibility for, your work. There are no colleagues to blame.

'Keeping the money coming in is the biggest difficulty I foresee,' says Stuart. 'Building something from nothing is hard, but I'm doing it because I want to achieve something.'

Cash flow is a huge issue for the self-employed. You rely on other people paying you. They could go bust, deny receiving your invoice or underpay you – you're just another bill to be paid at the last minute, if at all. Last year I wrote off £1,000 in bad debts. Right now I'm overdrawn; thankfully, it's interest-free. If things get too tight I can whip out one of my credit cards and use it to cushion the blow. It doesn't matter how well you manage your money if you can't guarantee what's coming in. Sometimes I wish for a regular monthly wage. If the thought of such fraught finances gives you the fear, you're probably better off sticking with the pay-packet habit.

'Working for someone else is like paying rent for a flat,' says Stuart. 'It's the easy option. If something goes wrong someone else will fix it. But you're never building towards anything. You don't have anything to show for renting. Becoming self-employed is risky, but if everything goes to plan you stand to make more out of it.'

Stuart and Sarah both set up business in the sector they'd worked in. The advantages of this are clear. 'Maximise use of your past experience and contacts,' says Sarah. 'Prepare as much as possible before leaving your job – don't forget to take all the data you can.' However, such an inheritance can harm as well as help. Your boss might not bother that you've gone, but they won't be greatly pleased if you start poaching clients or colleagues. Hating your boss is a great reason for leaving, but don't take those feelings with you – leave them in a drawer in your old office. 'It's important to be professional, especially when dealing with people you used to work with,' says Stuart.

Starting up in a completely new line of business means at least you'll probably never clap eyes on your old boss again, but it also brings a whole new range of challenges. How do you switch convincingly from cooking meals to creating corporate web sites to designing clothes?

'My office is under my bed,' says Liza, 29, who qualified as a chef before completing an HND in Graphic Design and setting up her own fashion business. 'My dad built me this special plat-form bed with an office underneath, which means I don't have to hire office space or find a bigger flat.'

After quitting cooking, Liza worked full time designing corporate web sites for an agency for five years before setting up her web and clothing design business under her bed in Brighton. Her choice of office is unusual, but her decision to be an employee and run a business from home is not. Liza is part of a growing group called elancers. 'Being self-employed doesn't need to be all or nothing. I work part time for a company doing corporate web sites and run my clothing design business the rest of the time.' An elancer could be self-employed or a contractor working from home, a mobile consultant, or even a remote worker for a large organisation. Technology is key to their success. You can be an employee and be your own boss.

There are now around two million teleworkers in the UK – that's people who work regularly, if not entirely, from home. Thanks to the European Flexible Working Directive, which came into effect here in April 2003, you now have the right to negotiate a teleworking arrangement with your boss. On average we spend 7.5 weeks a year commuting to and from work. If we spent just one day a week working from home we'd claw back an astonishing ten days a year. A recent study by the Massachusetts Institute of Technology claimed that full-time workers will be in the minority by 2010.

Like Sarah and Stuart, Liza has become her own PA, technical support and office manager. 'Elancing can create stress as well as alleviate it,' she sighs. 'I don't have the stability I had when I was working for a company full time. I don't completely know what my income is going to be from one month to the next, but it's becoming easier as my client base grows.'

Staying inspired is especially important for Liza, who relies on friends to stimulate her design ideas. 'I miss the shared interaction at the coffee machine – you lose those chances to generate ideas when you work from home. It's very easy, without being aware of it, to become less creative and feel alone. I'm quite lucky as some of my friends work from home nearby so I can pop over and see them. I'd go mad otherwise.' Liza also uses chat rooms to communicate with other elancers. 'And I am always on instant messenger.'

Despite cash-flow concerns, Liza rates elancing as a positive experience. 'I can mix corporate work with funkier stuff and I can do what I want when I want. I love designing in my nightie.' But increased flexibility demands increased responsibility. 'It is slightly daunting,' she says. 'That's why I work a few days a week doing corporate web sites. I know where I am, what I'm doing and how much I'm earning at least some of the time. That bit of security is important for me. It enables me to take other risks.'

Henry, 29, graduated from Queen Mary and Westfield College with a B.Eng in Civil Engineering in 1996. 'My first job was with a firm of structural engineers and it was there I became a chartered engineer. I did that for five years before deciding to make a break.'

In that time Henry developed the concept and client base for his business. He now splits his time between working as a structural engineer for a firm in their offices and being sole employee of his own company at home.

'Leaps and Bounds Community Regeneration Ideas is a one-stop shop for community organisations seeking to improve their facilities and services. I work with people who run community initiatives, like youth clubs, designing their building projects and helping them access the resources they need.'

Like Liza, Henry works from home, although he makes frequent site visits. 'When I need to have a meeting I just use the client's office.' Like Stuart, Henry sometimes finds it hard to stop working. 'Finding a balance and creating new routines is difficult. All the boundaries are very blurred. I'm always contactable and my PC is always there making me feel guilty. I always feel I could be doing more.' Yet Henry couldn't elance without his PC. 'My business wouldn't exist without the web. The set-up costs of an office would have been too much for me to get off the ground.'

Whether you work six days a week, like Henry, or as many days a week as you fancy, like Liza, you must switch your focus from putting in hours to meeting goals. You become your own personal cheerleader. Yay you! Yay you!

'Working is not about clocking on and clocking off, it's about focusing on deliverables,' says Liza. For her, 'deliverables' are T-shirts, handbags and customised tops. 'It doesn't matter how you work or when you work so long as you get it done.'

As elancers, Henry and Liza are self-employed part time. Working as part-time employees gives them financial security and time off from stressing about their business. Both hope to become unemployed if and when they hit the big time. I don't doubt they'll succeed because they've made a business out of a passion, Henry, providing high quality buildings for needy organisations, and Liza making pretty things for pretty people.

If you're going to make a break from your old career you can do worse than consider turning a hobby or interest into a business. After all, what's the point of becoming a one-man band if you're just going to play the same old tune? Why shouldn't you become a florist if you love flowers? Business doesn't have to be cold and hard. Sure you've got to make a living, but why do you have to be miserable doing it?

Stuart and Henry plan, as Sarah did, to become big business. Liza doesn't. 'I enjoy having complete control over my designs. Right now people come to me and we work together to create the right garment or accessory for them. I wouldn't trust anyone else to do that. I'm not a control freak, I'm an individual. I want to get more business but I don't want to have employees and all the rest of it. I am my business.'

Counterintuitive as it may sound, non-growth can be a positive business strategy. There's nothing wrong with being small.

'I don't think I was more miserable than when I had mouths to feed,' says Dane, 26, a systems analyst. Like many in IT, Dane started out as a contractor. 'During the dotcom boom I moved from company to company upping my rate as I went to find the best work.' At that time, there was more than enough work to go around. 'I worked for two months straight on £300 a day. It was mad, really.' Hence his Lotus Elise.

After turning down several potentially lucrative jobs it dawned on Dane that he was missing a trick. 'There was work to be done and I knew people who could do it. I recommended them but I didn't get any money out of it.' After building a web site for a recruitment firm, Dane had the idea of setting up as a sort of cooperative – with him in charge, of course. 'Me and two mates got together. We referred work to one another and put the money into our business and took a share of the profits as a wage. I didn't think of it as a business. It was a cash cow. We didn't have to do anything – the money just came to us.'

Such was their success that Dane & Co. stopped working on-site. 'I took some offices in Farringdon – really nice ones.' Corbusier chairs, expensive flower arrangements and a receptionist soon followed. 'I took on another two people to meet our obligations to clients.' At that point the stress was finding, and keeping, the right people. 'Then it all went tits-up.'

When the boom went bust Dane was left with an expensive office to run, no cash reserves, and thumbs to twiddle. 'I had five employees. The rent was £2,200 a month. I worked out that we could keep running with the clients we had left provided we all took a rate cut.' Until then, Dane's most difficult business decision had been where to lunch. While things were good he felt unstoppable. 'I thought I knew what I was doing.'

Contractors were the first to go when the dotcom bomb went off. They remain under pressure. They're the most expensive and the easiest to get rid of. Rate cuts quickly followed staff cuts – many IT contractors now earn half what they commanded two years ago; some were quite mercenary and that put companies off using them. As a result, companies now have three or four candidates to choose from whereas they used to be lucky to find one. Companies can now afford to be choosy.

Through no fault of his own, Dane's remaining clients went bust. 'We had no work, except our *pro bono* clients which we couldn't afford to keep. I hated having to let them go.' But go they did. 'I knew what was coming.'

Sacking his mates was a nightmare. 'Of course I had to tell them; because I got them into it. They knew the story but I still felt bad having to say it. I felt like I'd let them down, even though plenty of other business went the same way. Give them credit, they didn't take it out on me. But it was bad.'

Dane didn't mean for business to get so big or so bad. 'If I'd stuck to being a contractor I would still have got burnt, but it would have just been me.' The gains, as well as the losses, would have been limited. 'I wouldn't have made as much money. It was a gamble and I won, for a while.' He hung on to the Lotus.

It's now 3.00 a.m. I have to get up at 7.00 a.m. – got a deadline to make for 2.00 p.m. But then the day is mine. I've just about finished this chapter. Doubtless I'll tinker with it over the next few days in between dusting skirting boards, pitching for work and chasing pay. Perhaps I'll buy some new pyjamas online.

The small print

Assessing your suitability for being self-employed

Needless to say, this is best done *before* you fire your boss. It may be that you need to focus on improving conditions in your current job or search for something new. Self-employment is not, as Sarah found, for everyone.

Top *five* benefits of being self-employed

1. Daytime television.
2. Flexible workstyle: work when and where you want to. If the sun is shining go outside.
3. Your pain, your gain: suddenly working hard seems to make financial sense. The beauty of claiming against taxes and reduced NI contributions.
4. An end to the office: kiss those cubicles and that photocopier goodbye.
5. Work-life balance: see your friends, find time to have sex again and develop interests outside work.

Top five traumas

1. Daytime television.
2. Flexible workstyle: opportunities for procrastination multiply out of control. Have you polished all the buttons on your clothes today?
3. Cash flow: where will it come from and when and why does it go so quickly? No occupational pension or insurance. Try getting a mortgage . . .
4. An end to the office: can you handle working from home? Where will you work? Who will you have lunch with?
5. Work-life balance: discover you hate your friends and your partner, realise your life is empty.

If you don't want to become self-employed but you do want to work from home, you're going to have to convince your boss it's a good idea.

Making a case for telecommuting

1. Be honest with yourself
Some people, jobs and tasks are not suitable for teleworking. Assess yourself, your working habits and your job (or parts of your job) and work out whether teleworking is viable for you.

2. Everybody benefits
Outline the business, personal and professional benefits of tele-working and present them to your boss. Point out that you'll be able to produce more work by not commuting. Surveys suggest teleworking can increase productivity by between 10 and 40 per cent.

3. Be professional at home
Make a list of what you'll need (computer equipment, fax line, phone line, extra insurance). Get your employer to pay, and ensure your home office meets health and safety regs. Keep

screaming kids out of hearing distance if you're on conference calls. Consider the tax benefits/problems of using your home for business. Don't forget to swap PJs for pinstripes when you do go into the office.

4. Offer your boss a list of 'productivity measurements'
Bosses fear you're going to sit around drinking tea and watching TV all day. You might do. But so long as you meet your deadlines, who cares? Set goals and meet them. Ask for a review period so you and your boss can assess your new way of working.

5. Be a guinea pig
Your employer might be convinced if they can use your experiences – good and bad – as a pilot for everyone else. It's an opportunity for them as well as you. Share your experiences with colleagues in an email newsletter, blog or regular meeting. Volunteer to liaise with other prospective teleworkers.

Two organisations were mentioned by almost every self-employed twentysomething. These were the Prince's Trust and Business Link.

- The Prince's Trust: 0800 842 842 or *www.princes-trust.org.uk*
- Business Link: 0845 6009 006 or *www.businesslink.org*

See *www.inbizonline.co.uk/theprocess.htm* for a good explanation of how to 'go' self-employed.

housing

get it together

7

To Buy or Not to Buy?

How we become house whores.

'Buying a house is just what you do.'
Rebecca, 27, nurse

'Property is now less affordable for first-time buyers than it
   has been for a generation, and rising deposit levels will
   inevitably make it harder.'
Andy Deller, Head of Banking and Insurance at Egg

If I watch another property show I'm going to beat myself to
death with a piece of MDF. I now know more about cheap
paint effects than I thought was possible. I can strip, lay and
sponge. I can even, to my horror, navigate the cavernous belly
of my local B&Q. There is a certain pleasure to be derived from
power tools and home improvements; but it's not sexual – it's
social. A battered plastic bag from a DIY store says much more
than a tote from Todd. It says 'I own my own home. *Do you?*'

Wall-to-wall property programming and an explosion in
homes magazines are symptomatic of our national obsession with
home ownership. This isn't just a passion for property, a harm-
less crush on bricks and mortar. It's an unhealthy bunny-boiling
fixation and I have to admit I've been successfully seduced. If we

pursued partners as madly as we hunt for houses we'd be jailed for stalking. Homes, formerly just a place to live, have become fetish objects, social barometers and pensions all in one.

Few nations are as obsessed by house buying as the UK. According to *The Economist*, our level of home ownership has settled in recent years at 67 per cent – just a touch above the US. In France, 54 per cent are owner-occupiers, The Netherlands has one of the lowest levels of home ownership at 50 per cent, and only four in ten Germans own their own *haus*.

But it's not all down to Thatcher's right-to-buy, when one million council homes were snapped up. Historically we have always been a nation of home owners. And at no other time have we been more obsessed by our homes: owning, adding value and obsessively comparing. Ironically, for our generation, it's never been harder to buy. If this moment in our twenties was an episode of *Friends* it would be 'the one where everyone but me has bought'.

For the first time ever, in February 2003, the proportion of mortgage lending accounting for first-time buyers fell below 30 per cent. According to the Council of Mortgage Lenders, only 29 per cent of all lending for house purchase was to first-time buyers, compared with a long-run trend of more than 45 per cent. Nervous are we?

You should be. According to the Nationwide Building Society, in June 2003 the average UK house price was £89,068. In London it was £160,635 – up 10.4 per cent on the same period for 2002. According to the Halifax, the average household income for first-time buyers like you and me topped £30,000. That means the average London home costs way more than five times the average household's annual income. By the time this book comes out it will be six or more.

Shit.

We have the misfortune to be catapulted into the market when there are more losses to be made than profits to be had. It feels a bit like buying tulip bulbs in seventeenth-century Holland or dotcom stocks in 1999. Right now our parents are getting drunk on leisure paid for with equity drawn from homes which have increased in value in a way it seems impossible for them to do again. We seem doomed to be poorer than our parents. While they indulge their middle-aged passions on painting holidays we struggle to find a paint that will cover the damp in our over-priced studio flats.

Where does this pressure to buy come from? Should you succumb? If so, how and when should you switch from tenant to owner? How does anyone afford it? And aren't there better things to worry about than dado rails?

'My parents own and so do my grandparents,' says Katharine, 28. 'They've all climbed the ladder to get a nice house. I really don't mind living in a shed so long as I can call it mine.'

It might very well come to that. Katharine feels enormous pressure to buy something – anything – just so long as it is hers. For her, there is a real stigma – and fear – attached to renting.

'At twenty-eight I feel a bit pikey to still be renting. Most of my friends have bought, though I'm not sure how. I hate to say it, but it's the Englishman and his castle instinct. There is a feeling of personal success and security when you can finally say "I own my house". It means you're managing to cover the mortgage and maintenance all by yourself.'

Rather than passing renting off as delightfully French and flexible, we've come to view it as something you do when you can't afford to buy. Ask someone who's renting about their flat. I bet they say, 'Oh, I'm *just* renting.' We have actually begun to apologise for *not buying*. Renting has been stigmatised. This is ridiculous. Repeat after me, *there is no shame in renting*. It's okay to rent.

But financially, emotionally and aesthetically, Katharine has had her fill of renting. Living in London, she fears she'll never be chatelaine of her own castle. She'll be lucky to get a wet studio flat in the Dungeon.

'Unfortunately, the merely reasonable salary attached to the London-based career I've chosen will never cover the megabucks needed to buy within the M25. I am utterly fed up with the mere mention of house buying. But I want my own place more than ever. My stress and jealousy levels go up every time a friend buys. The thought of renting in London with no end goal in sight sinks me into abject depression. Even if it takes me two years to buy a flat, it'll be worth it.'

Two years to raise a deposit, get a mortgage and secure the right property is actually optimistic for a twentysomething, especially one living in London. It took me three years and three attempts to buy a flat in Brighton (admittedly also known as London-on-Sea).

The decision to buy came when renting became oppressive and expensive rather than liberating and cheap – more on that in the next chapter. But finding the right place at the right time proved all but impossible. My first flat fell through because the vendor, a psychic, refused to relocate to a town with a graveyard. We waited six months for her to overcome her morbid fear of death but she never did. Aside from survey and legal costs we were hit by the intervening price rise. Not to mention the stress. Flat #2 fell through just before it fell down. The unscrupulous estate agent tried to discourage us from having an extensive and expensive survey done but I'm glad we did. I can't even remember why flat #3 didn't happen, but I remember crying about it. And I remember my partner and I rowed and talked about nothing else. When we eventually bought this flat it was hard to stop reading the property papers and find something else to row about.

'God, how much have I thrown away on rent!?' screams Katharine who has rented in London for seven years. 'I'm hitting thirty soon. I expect more for my money and maybe even to see a return on it. For me, I would rather invest in property than a pension as it is more likely to safeguard my future than some cowboy investment plan.'

This is a view widely held by twentysomethings: housing good, equity bad. (We'll get to that when we talk *Money*.)

The carpets in Katharine's current flat have been artistically nibbled by rats. Does her landlord care? Almost as much as when he forced her to pay for damage caused to a neighbour by water leaking from a washing machine he failed to repair.

'London landlords are a nightmare, ranging from the rude to the psychotic. My tenancies normally end in chains of long solicitor's letters trying to retrieve deposits. I'm a frequent caller to the Citizens Advice Bureau. I've now taken to withholding rent.'

In no way does buying your own place guarantee you complete freedom from hassle – there are leases, laws, by-laws and neighbours to consider. I can't have wooden floors in my flat for the sake of the neighbours below, (but I do have more control over my immediate environment). You replace a landlord with a bank manager (but a landlord's taste for your own).

Katharine feels that 'renting is brilliant when you first start out in a big city. But eventually it's money down the drain.' For a while she considered getting into one of the part-ownership schemes now being successfully run all over the UK by bodies like the Peabody Trust. These are often allocated to people on low incomes and those who might face difficulty finding affordable, safe housing elsewhere. 'They offer you a mortgage on 40 per cent of the property so you only pay rent on the remaining 60 per cent.' Sounds like a good deal. 'But property prices will keep rising and rising – that remaining percentage is never going to be affordable. I would forever be chasing the part I didn't own and end up very little better off.'

Having decided to buy outright, Katharine then had to find a deposit. This is without doubt the biggest challenge facing twentysomethings trying to buy their first place. It's nearly impossible to save money while coughing up rent and trying to have a life. 'I earn £31K,' she says. Sadly, not enough to buy the shiny knocker on the glossy front door of a ritzy flat in London.

'I had to revise my expectations down to ex-council level. The bank told me to start saving for a deposit big enough to offset my "lack" of income. It will take roughly five years of living on tuna and mayonnaise, by which time houses will have increased exponentially in price, *again*!'

Oh dear.

But Katharine is finally buying her own home. Only it's not in London. And she can't actually afford to live in it.

'I've come up with this probably hare-brained idea to do a buy-to-let on a house near Newquay. I want to live there eventually because I love surfing.'

She plans to rent the house out and scratch back a little bit of money every month. 'I have to ensure the property is always filled with tenants to cover the mortgage. I reckon I can let it to some US air force family for a good rent until I move down. Even if this fails I can sell higher, pocket the difference and be in a better position to consider a deposit on another house, possibly in London. This is the only way (apart from standing outside city bars stalking rich bankers) for me to buy. At long last I will have somewhere I can call home. And I can paint the bathroom the way I like it! Sounds frivolous, but I've had enough of living with other people's colour schemes.'

Katharine's parents are helping her with the deposit. A close friend of mine who has just turned thirty has gone begging to mummy 'for the last time' so he can finally buy his own place. He kept waiting for her to die so he could inherit, but she insisted on living. Many London estate agents report that so-called 'legacy buyers' now form the majority of first-time buyers in the twentysomething market. But what if your rich relative refuses to die? Or insists you stand on your own two feet? Or, like me, your family just isn't rich?

Don't go out, eat only what you find in bins, drink nothing but tap water and you might just save the deposit on your own bijou basement damp trap. Saving beats begging, borrowing and stealing when it comes to raising deposits. According to research done by property web site *fish4homes.co.uk*, just over half of first-time buyers aged twenty-five to thirty buying in London in 2002 managed to amass their own deposit.

Three-quarters of twentysomethings polled paid a deposit between 1 and 5 per cent. Half paid between £150,000 and £200,000 for their first home, which means they had to find a deposit of between £1,500 and £10,000. Two-thirds scrimped for two to three years. Those forced to save for four to five years cried real tears as rising prices destroyed their dreams of a spare room.

According to the Council of Mortgage Lenders, deposits have increased from an average of 10 per cent in 1996 to 21 per cent in 2003. That works out at £31,100 in London and £18,000 nationally. The lowest, £8,300, was in the north.

It's only going to get worse. According to Egg, deposits will reach an average of a staggering £32,000 by 2011 – that's 85 per cent of the £41,000 annual income a first-time buyer can then expect to earn. The average London property will cost £351,000 with a deposit of £74,000. Egg expect this will increase the average age of a first-time buyer to thirty-six.

Arrrrrrrgh!

No wonder so many of us are going begging to our families. According to *fish4homes.co.uk*, a third of twentysomething first-time buyers copied Katharine and raided the Bank of Mum and Dad. Taking an interest in your children is healthy, but what about taking interest from them? Loans from parents aren't always free.

Paul, 29, and Emma, 26, saved piously since graduating. 'I put away £100 a month for a deposit,' says Paul, a sales and events manager earning around £40K. 'Every time I thought I'd saved enough I'd look in the estate agent's window and everything had become unaffordable. I could've saved £100 a month for 100 years and still not had enough.' It didn't help that he wanted to buy in a posh bit of Ealing.

Saving seemed pointless.

'We rented for a year to test the area out,' says Emma, his partner. They loved it. Having found a desirable locale they then had to find the right property. In December 2001 they found it. But the price was wrong.

Spying an opportunity to help, their canny parents provided the £40,000 deposit necessary to secure the £190,000 two-bedroom basement garden flat.

'It was a loan, not a gift – we have to pay them back,' says Paul. 'Solicitors drew up contracts. We'll never enforce them, but it's important for everyone to have something on paper, especially as we're not married. We couldn't have done this without them.'

Before moving forwards, Paul and Emma had to go back-wards – all the way to Emma's childhood bedroom in Woking. 'Our tenancy ran out and we had six months before comple-tion,' says Paul. 'Emma's parents took us in.' And let them share a double bed. Very modern. Living rent-free saved them £1,000 a month. 'We used that to decorate the new place,' says Paul.

And the repayments? 'We'd rather borrow from our parents than a bank. We'll repay them with equity when we eventually leave London.' Too modern for me.

Increasingly, the Bank of Gran is offering favourable terms to favourite grandchildren. According to a study commissioned by the International Longevity Centre UK, around 17,000 twentysomethings received a windfall last year. The average amount was £20,000 – that's enough for a decent deposit. Granny is giving her cash to us because her own children don't need it. My partner's granny pulled a hefty stash from her knit-ting bag so we could buy (thanks again, Connie). Some call it generation skipping. I call it fair.

Even so, most of us have to do some saving. To me, saving means not maxing out my credit card. To others, cutting back means cutting up their cards. But hateful as it is, saving can be bearable if you have a goal.

Rebecca and Richard, both aged 27, are savers. When you and I had pets they had special edition piggy banks. Each saved £4,500 for the 5 per cent deposit on their first flat.

'We saw it in April 2002 and moved in August,' says Rebecca, a psychiatric nurse. An amazingly problem-free purchase. Their two-bedroom flat, in east London, cost £179,950. 'We bought off plan because we love the area. I grew up nearby, our friends are here and it's good for commuting,' says Rebecca. 'I don't want to live too close to work because of the nature of my job, but Richard's office is just half an hour away.'

The pair met in 1999 while backpacking in Australia and shacked up when they returned to London. Saving comes easily to Richard, an accountant. 'I did it because I had to, but Richard saved because he likes to. He's great with money.' As an accountant you'd hope he would be. They each earn around £25K. Rebecca worked extra shifts to raise her half of the deposit: 'I did agency work at weekends. It wasn't too bad, but I was glad when it was over.'

Why not rent the spare room and factor in the future income? 'We didn't want strangers sharing our home even if they were our age and nice or whatever,' she says. That's the same argument I used when a friend suggested I take a lodger. I can't imagine accommodating someone else's little habits in my home. Especially habits that smell.

Saving meant no summer holiday for Rebecca and Richard. 'We had no choice. If we hadn't bought when we did we wouldn't be able to afford anything – not in London, anyway.' After a year of austerity Rebecca went overdrawn and lived on her credit card for a few months. Same here. 'I wasn't stressed because it was short term. It was easy to extend my overdraft because I had a good credit rating, but it would have been cheaper if I had still had a graduate account. We didn't ask our parents for money because Richard couldn't and I didn't want to. This way it's all ours. I'm glad we did it on our own.' Especially as the flat is now worth £215,000.

But saving just isn't an option for many twentysomethings, especially those with scary student debts. Any spare cash is soaked up by student loans, career development loans, loans taken to cover tuition fees, credit cards and overdrafts. Oh, and drugs, clothes, booze, fags, food and fun. Which is why we're happy to take interest-free money from our family when we can.

For those with no chance of saving or borrowing the money for a deposit, 100 per cent mortgages are increasingly popular. Nearly 20 per cent of those polled by *fish4homes.co.uk* had a 100 per cent mortage; 80 per cent of them said they couldn't have bought otherwise.

'The longer we looked the less we could afford,' says Mike, 25. A quality control manager for a big food processing company he earns around £30,000. 'We saved £2,000, but that wasn't enough for a 5 per cent deposit. No one would give us a mortgage. We tried ten lenders and they all said no. We got depressed,' he says. 'It's very frustrating waiting an hour to see someone who looks at you for five minutes before saying they can't help you. We felt left behind by our friends. We desperately wanted to do this without our parents, but it looked like we might have to ask them.'

Finally Mike and his partner, Jo, 26, a self-employed aromatherapist, tried the bank they'd used as students. Forgiving them their fractious student finances, the Royal Bank of Scotland approved a 100 per cent mortgage. 'We couldn't have bought otherwise,' says Mike. 'And it meant our application was processed straightaway.'

Happily bemortgaged, Mike promptly bought a three-bedroom flat in Glasgow, leveraging his position as a first-time buyer. 'We had no chain which meant we could knock the price down from £150,000 to £135,000.'

Still, a 100 per cent mortgage comes at a higher price. 'We had to pay a mortgage indemnity guarantee,' says Mike. 'And we pay higher interest rates, but it's worth it to get on the ladder.'

Like Mike and Jo, you will probably have to pay an above-average interest rate for a 100 per cent loan. This covers lenders for the supposed risk they're taking. Lack of competition in the market explains the higher rate of interest, and you will almost certainly be charged a mortgage indemnity guarantee (MIG). This adds several thousands of pounds to your loan, which covers the lender, not you, should you fail to make repayments. You can pay this in cash or, if you can't afford to, lump it in with your mortgage. It's worth haggling over all these terms, but you have less choice if you're in the 100 per cent mortgage market.

'Things are a bit tight. The repayments are £650 per month and our rent was only £500.'

To make things easier Mike and Jo opted for thirty years rather than twenty-five. To make things more secure they opted for a repayment mortgage rather than interest only. 'Some of our friends are only paying the interest, hoping that the equity will pay off the capital. I couldn't deal with that stress,' says Mike. 'Until I had a mortgage I never understood why people were fascinated by interest rates – now I do. Our rate is fixed for three years.'

Their flat is now worth around £185,000. 'Soon we'll be able to switch to a 90 per cent mortgage.' Their rate will then fall.

Many twentysomethings stress unduly about negative equity, which is when the value of your home is less than the value of the remainder of your mortgage. A deposit acts as a buffer against this, and most of us pay some sort of deposit, but should you take out a 100 per cent mortgage you are immediately at risk of negative equity. If house prices fell just a bit, you would be hit with negative equity. *But* – this is only a disaster if you need to sell quickly or start finding it difficult to make your repayments.

Affordability is the key. My mortgage payments are fixed for five years and work out at around £600. I may not know what I'm doing from day to day, but I do know how much I have to pay each month to keep a roof over my head. My one-bedroom garden flat in Brighton cost £140,000. I put down a deposit of £41,000 because I could cope with owing five figures but not six. No negative equity for me! Anyway, the point is that my partner and I know we can always find £600 a month. No matter what happens, our mortgage will always be affordable. I can probably donate enough blood (and still live) to make up any shortfall. Going for a fixed rate, or capped, mortgage gives you security. But again, at a price.

'Getting the right mortgage advice is critical,' says Katharine, who is currently investigating buy-to-let packages. A fixed-rate mortgage would suit her as it would allow her to plan ahead financially. 'I'm not bothered if rates fall a little. I don't view that as losing out. I just want to feel safe against big rises.

'I've made the mistake of turning up to mortgage appointments and being quite flippant or casual. Be serious and go to lenders armed with knowledge so you can understand the language they speak. Don't let the bastards rip you off or get you down!' And wear a suit. (Of course, as with working from home, it doesn't matter what you wear if you do it online or over the phone.)

According to government figures, mortgage repayments swallowed 20.4 per cent of income for first-time buyers in London and 18.3 per cent for first-time buyers elsewhere in 2002. Compared with the seventies and early eighties these figures are quite high, but nothing like as high as during the last property boom. In 1990 first-time buyers in London sacrificed 32.0 per cent of their income in repayments (27.7 per cent for the UK as a whole). Don't stress too much. We'd need a rise in interest rates to 10.5 per cent for that to happen again.

All of which emphasises that buying is a gamble – albeit one we take in banks, not casinos, and chat about over dinner. More than a hundred people still lose their homes every week because they can't make the mortgage.

Despite the potential downsides, most twentysomethings still want to own their own place, but, given the continually rising costs of buying, it's no surprise many of us feel doomed to rent for ever. Over a fifth of twenty- to twenty-four-year-olds polled by Shelter said they didn't think they could ever afford their own home. Most of those who thought they would buy planned to do so in the next five years. Let's see how they feel after a few years of renting and trying to save a deposit.

The British Medical Association recently claimed that mortgages are bad for your health. They say the struggle to keep up with payments is making millions of people sick. Well, duh! Affordability isn't just about money, it's about time and emotion. Yes, you can work sixty hours a week to pay enormous repayments, but can your body take it, can your relationship, can your soul? The decision to buy should never just be financial, because your house isn't just about making money. (And, yes, I'm Cancerian.)

Symptoms of the ill effects of our national obsession apparently include drinking and smoking too much, general stress and relationship breakdown. We may even have more car crashes because we are so preoccupied. The report fails to mention unhealthy murderous urges brought on by dealing with estate agents.

Simply owning a house won't make you ill, unless it's built on a radon-emitting rubbish tip, but worrying about how to pay for it can. Twentysomethings count as some of the country's poorest owner-occupiers, yet there are no support networks available for us as there are for people in council or housing association homes. Then again, perhaps those lucky enough to buy should just deal with the luxurious stresses it brings.

Mark left home when he was twenty because he didn't get on with his mum's new boyfriend. He is now twenty-four. Since leaving home he has struggled to find somewhere safe and affordable to live. He now suffers severe anxiety and depression.

Initially, Mark's local council found him a flat because he was homeless. It was on a rough estate. 'I kept getting my windows put through, it was a really bad area.' Mark was working fifty-hour weeks in a toffee factory but was only paid for twenty hours. He got £70 a week. After complaining, he was told the missing money would appear in his next wage packet. It never did. Eventually he quit. 'Because my wages didn't come through I ended up £600 in arrears to the council. Then I got thrown out the flat.'

Since then, Mark has lived 'all over the place', sleeping on more floors than he can remember. He has slept in the street many times. The privately rented bedsits he could afford were awful. 'I was sharing with strangers. Many of them were alcoholics, they screamed and argued all the time.'

Eventually he found his current privately rented flat for £55 a week. Due to a restriction which affects all young people under twenty-five, Mark's housing benefit only pays out £39 weekly; he has to find the £16 shortfall from his other benefits. He's just had his Income Support stopped without warning, despite a doctor's note explaining he can't work because he's clinically depressed. The ever lovely Benefits Agency has asked for his book back. Mark has been given lots more forms to fill out but doesn't know if he'll receive more money. 'I don't even know why this happened.'

Mark rang Shelterline and is now being helped by a solicitor at Shelter's Housing Aid Centre in Manchester. The local council refuses to help and have excluded him from the housing register because he owes rent from his tenancy. 'I feel angry and wound up. I just want somewhere decent to live and it's not happening.'

As I said, it took me three attempts to buy a flat, but after meeting people like Mark I felt lucky to have the agony of choice. That doesn't mean it was easy for me – it just means I felt the appropriate level of middle-class guilt. You should too.

Ultimately, the decision to buy is not entirely yours. The economy, the European Union, your job, your physical and mental health, your partner, your family and fate – they all have a hand in it, as I discovered when I tried to buy a flat with my same-sex partner. 'It won't be a problem in sunny cosmopolitan Brighton,' I thought. Oh, but it was. Have you had anal sex? Have you had sex with someone from Africa or someone who has been to Africa? Have you ever been tested for HIV or any other sexually transmitted disease? Have you ever had sex with someone of the same sex?

These and other outrageously intrusive questions were asked by a very dull man in a very dull suit in a bank. I refused to answer. I was told that by doing so, I was, for the purposes of my mortgage, uninsurable. Had I answered the questions (yes, no, yes, happily) my insurance premiums would have sky-rocketed. As a gay man with a safe-sex habit I was told I would be placed on something called the Impaired Lives Register along with the partially sighted and those who have lost limbs in accidents. Appalled, I took my business elsewhere. There I found being self-employed was problematic. So off I went again. I am now fairly happily mortgaged up with the Halifax.

Women, too, can have problems getting a mortgage on their own. The average starting salary for a graduate in London is £22,000, but, outrageously, women's salaries are still lower than men's – by 20 per cent, according to the Equal Opportunities Commission. Yet, according to the Council of Mortgage Lenders, the number of single women buying their first home has doubled in the past twenty years. Although the average ratio of house prices to earnings has fallen, many women are still caught out because they get paid less. The answer, they've found, is to team up.

Clara, 24, an accounts assistant for a nursery, has teamed up with Jane, 27, a French teacher. Together they've bought a house in Durham. 'Everybody thought we were lesbians,' titters Clara. 'Not that I don't think Jane's pretty, but this is a purely financial union.'

'I didn't think I'd ever be able to buy a flat,' says Jane, who earns £17,000. Clara is on a similar wage. The pair rented together for two years after university; they got on great and had a brilliant time. 'But,' says Clara, 'we knew prices were rising.' When they started looking it became apparent quite how steeply. They went through the usual twentysomething desperation of scouting papers, begging banks and pleading with parents. To no avail. 'We actually argued about the whole house thing, and we never fight,' says Jane.

Jane and Clara were inspired to buy together by a couple they knew who bought a place together. 'We decided to do the same. Until then we thought one of us would buy and the other would just rent a room, but neither of us wanted to be the one taking the rent.'

Clara's parents eventually provided the deposit. 'We worked out how much we paid in rent and decided that's how much mortgage we could afford,' says Jane. 'We have two jobs – twice the income and twice the security,' says Clara. For once the bank agreed. The pair got a third bedroom which they let (to a guy they both fancy). 'He's our little bonus,' says Clara.

If, like Clara and Jane, you buy with a friend, make sure, as with a partner, you're protected in the event of a break-up. Mortgage Payment Protection Insurance (MPPI) will cover you if you lose your job, but it won't pay up if your relationship breaks down. Jane and Clara are essentially cohabiting. They got their mortgage on the basis of a multiple of their joint salaries, but if one decides to move out the other will be screwed and almost certainly forced to sell. This is different from marriage, whereby you both have a right over the marital home even if only one of you has paid for it. 'Neither of us could get back on the property ladder. We're in this together,' says Jane.

Money, or fear of lack thereof, is no reason to stay in an unhappy relationship. Protecting yourself and your partner sounds mercenary, but it's better for you both – especially if you can't or won't get married. Make sure you get a Declaration of Trust – a document witnessed by your solicitor which says who owns what and who gets what if you split.

Pressure to buy is, like the price of housing, only going to rise, and we will doubtless find ever more ingenious ways to join the legions of Great British Home Owners. We will continue raising ever bigger deposits. But we can't repeat the freakish good fortune of our parents, so let's not stress ourselves out trying.

Buying doesn't always make sense, though it should at least make more sense than renting. Ultimately we need to get some perspective. I've felt Katharine's desperation – we all have – but few of us have felt Mark's. Most of us are lucky enough to be able to make decisions about where and how we live. We must stop viewing our homes as cash cows. What does it matter what your property is worth, so long as you're safe and happy? No more buy-to-get. Buying your home is an investment in yourself. It's an emotional transaction. So it's not worth buying at any price. Especially if the decor isn't quite right.

The small print

Whether you're a buyer or renter, call the ShelterLine on 0808 800 444 if you're experiencing problems finding or keeping a roof over your head.

To buy or not to buy?

Five reasons to buy

1. No more money down the drain. Instead of paying rent you're putting money back in your own pocket.
2. No more landlords' decor. Finally, you can discover your own inner Lawrence Llewellyn-Bowen.
3. Take the long view. Tenancies are typically only a year long, but when you buy you buy for life. You can begin long-term planning – children, career change, whatever.
4. You might get rich.
5. Because you can. Interest rates are low, banks are feeling generous. If you're one of those people with nothing else to spend your money on, then go for it.

Five reasons not to buy:

1. Any money you make you have to shell out again next time you buy – unless you downsize.
2. DIY hell. Everybody thinks they've got great taste and that decorating is easy. You haven't and it's not.
3. Live for the moment. Rent, and if you don't like it you can move out with relative ease. Flexibility is good.
4. You might lose everything.
5. You're self-employed, single or in some way not beloved of banks, which means you're better off not buying.

How to (try to) buy a house in 12 (not-so-easy) steps

1) Home alone?
Are you buying on your own? Or with a friend/partner/sibling? Discuss one another's needs and come up with an ideal property, preferred location and realistic price. If you're buying with

someone else, make sure you're covered in the event that your relationship breaks down. Talk to a solicitor and get a Declaration of Trust, or something like it, drawn up.

2) Do the maths

Can you afford that Barbie Dreamhouse? Make a budget – a realistic one – and see how much you can afford to shell out each month. Remember: your payments could rise (depending on the type of mortgage you get). Now is the time to call in favours and debts – you need every penny you can get. Start saving your deposit.

3) Get a solicitor

You need one to handle the sale for you, liaise with 'the other side' and do all the necessary checks. They're the only person acting in your interest – forget estate agents, mortgage providers and, to an extent, surveyors. Try and find one near you so you can visit if need be. Agree a quote beforehand and don't pay everything up front. Find a solicitor at *www.solicitors-online.com* or call the Law Society's Records Office on 0860 606 6575.

4) Risk exposure

If you need to know what you're paying every month, go for a fixed-rate mortgage (beware: these can be hard to switch). Tracker, discount and capped mortgages mean your payments may rise or fall – can you cope with that emotionally and financially?

5) Get a mortgage

Easier than it sounds if you're self-employed or debt-laden (or both). Look at it this way – you're the customer, make the bank work for you. Ask them to match deals you've seen elsewhere. The cheapest deal may not always be the best. Take independent financial advice – find an IFA at *www.ifap.org.uk*.

6) Find a house

I looked at over fifty places and made around five offers. Don't be disheartened. Keep in mind your original goals. Don't be swayed by estate agents. And try to see the potential (where there is any).

7) Make an offer

You do this with the estate agent, who puts it to the buyer and gets back to you. Have an upper limit and stick to this – don't get talked into upping your offer if you can't afford to. If successful, you give your solicitor's details to the estate agent and they start making it yours. You can still walk away at this point.

8) Survey, survey, survey

The surveyor makes sure your building is safe to live and invest in. There are three kinds of survey: basic (valuation usually paid for by lender to make sure their money is safe), home buyer's report (reports on obvious defects and overall condition) and full, or structural, survey (recommended for very old or very dodgy properties). I went for home buyer's – it cost around £400 and satisfied my curiosity. Don't skimp – it's worth paying for peace of mind. Find a surveyor at *www.rics.org.uk* or call RICS on 0870 333 1600. Go with them to ask any questions you have as you can't ask them once they've prepared their report.

9) Long boring bit where nothing seems to happen

Searches are being done to make sure the council isn't building a sewage plant opposite your new home, that the managing agents aren't crooks, and that there are sufficient years on the lease. It's all very boring but very important. Make sure your solicitor is chasing stuff, and offer to go to local council offices or do whatever you can to speed things up.

10) Visit again

This will excite you all over again and remind you why you're going through hell. It will also ensure the vendor hasn't burnt it down or ripped out valuable fixtures.

11) Exchange

You swap contracts, pay your deposit and set a date for completion. *Only now* is the property yours. It would be very expensive for the vendor or you to pull out now, though this has been known to happen.

12) Complete

Your mortgage lender pays the vendor, you get the keys and you move in! It was all worth it. Wasn't it?

8

Bye-Bye Buy

Why it's okay to carry on renting

'No way am I going to buy. The whole economy is in the
toilet. Renting is the way forward.'
Jay, 25, graphic designer

How many of your friends have bought their own place? I
bet you know exactly how many. That's because the last
thing buyers do is keep quiet about their property achievements.
They're like parents with a newborn: well-meaning but ultimately smug as fuck. They carry photos in their wallets and
have obsessively memorised a detailed inventory of bedrooms,
radiators and light switches. Every conversation turns into an
update on their ever-increasing equity.

Renters, on the other hand, keep quiet about their accommodation. That's because there's no pride in renting.

As proven in the previous chapter, the pressure to buy has
never been greater. As we approach thirty it intensifies, and so
does the shame of renting. Somehow it's okay to rent at university and for a little while after, while you establish yourself, but
it's not okay much beyond twenty-five. Beyond your mid-twenties renting is perceived as a sign of weakness – financial impov-
erishment or an inability to 'settle down'. Either way, we assume

people rent only because they have to, not because they want to. Like ex-smokers, the smuggest buyers of all are those who've only just kicked the renting habit.

First of all, renters still outnumber buyers among twenty-somethings. This is not the case among other age groups. According to the Royal Institute of Chartered Surveyors (RICS), 46 per cent of under twenty-fives rent and 24 per cent own, whereas 80 per cent of forty-five to sixty-four-year-olds own and only 5 per cent rent. In our age group, buyers are the odd ones out, not renters. Remember that.

Contrary to what your smug twentysomething home-owning friends claim, the average first-time buyer is now thirty-three, according to the Halifax, and they're only going to get older. The proportion of buyers under twenty-five has halved over the past twenty years to 16 per cent, and a quarter of those are being forced to settle for shed-sized flats because houses are so amazingly expensive. That'll be everyone in London then.

The popularity of renting among twentysomethings is reflected in growing demand for rental property, currently at its strongest for two years, according to RICS. First-time buyers priced out of the market are taking advantage of cheap rents courtesy of all those buy-to-let properties, as are those who've sold hoping to make a profit before prices fall further.

Rents are rising everywhere except London – good news for landlords, bad news for tenants. The most notable increases are in the north, but the highest rents are still to be found in London, where the average rent for a decent two-bedroom flat is £1,619 per month compared with £714 elsewhere. Still, such increases are nothing compared to soaring house prices – in October 2002 the Halifax index recorded an annual house price inflation rate of 31 per cent. That's twice the rate of Spain, our nearest EU competitor.

Far from simply extolling the benefits of renting, this chapter also reveals the downside of living at the mercy of a landlord, be they friend, parent or stranger. What are your rights as a tenant? Does it pay to rent? When is renting a bad idea?

As I whizzed along Brighton seafront a month after graduation I fell in love with the creamy Regency wedding cake of Brunswick Square. I longed to lounge on the lawns and live my life behind the gracious Georgian windows. Given the fleet of Porsches parked outside and the general aura of expense it seemed an impossible dream. But, miraculously, a friend of a friend was ending her tenancy on the most amazing flat. Perching with seagulls on the roof it boasted sea views from every window. It had a roof terrace big enough for dinner parties. The square would be my garden. At £340 a month (in 1999) it was perfect, despite six flights of stairs and the dodgy 'ethnic' decor. And far less than I'd pay on a mortgage.

No sooner had we unpacked than friends began advising against the danger of renting. 'You're falling behind,' they said, while buying whole streets of investment properties with apparently no awareness that they were the ones driving the nails in my first-time buyer coffin. But my partner and I loved our flat and we loved renting. We'd just moved – why uproot ourselves again? Besides, we could never afford to buy a place as fabulous as that. So we stayed put for three years. Sadly, prices did not.

I saw the value of a neighbouring flat soar from £99K (affordable) to £160K (ridiculous). Asking prices became bottom lines. Even garages became unaffordable. But – get this – I am not bitter. Because my life isn't just about money. This sounds almost stupidly obvious, I know, but a central part of the logic used to justify the drive to buy is that properties are the new pensions. Renters are portrayed as profligate live-for-the-moment losers and buyers as cautious plan-for-the-future heroes. So if you're renting now you'll starve to death as a pensioner. Rubbish.

Our lives are about careers and friends and partners. And having somewhere beautiful, peaceful and safe to live (and work, in my case). *Whether you own it or not.* We'll answer the pension question when we talk 'Money' but suffice to say it's a distraction from the real debate about renting versus buying in your twenties. I simply wasn't ready to buy then. Renting enabled me to live in a fabulous seafront flat and sort aspects of my life which would have been neglected had I bought my very own overpriced coffin reeking of cat piss. I had a stable base and fixed payments for every month of every year I stayed, which is more than those who reel from every interest rate change can say. All right they rose from year to year, but not from month to month as mortgages can. Besides, the last thing I wanted to do after starving my way through university was put myself through further hardship, and that's what buying would have done.

'I can't stand this obsession with buying,' says Jay, 25, a graphic designer based in Brighton. 'It's all people want to talk about. It's so eighties!' So far so sadly true. But why is he so antibuying? 'It's so fucking boring.' True. 'And nobody knows what's going to happen to house prices.' Also true. But that doesn't totally explain why Jay, who earns around £35,000 and can afford to buy, would rather rent.

'I know I have to find £650 every month for the rent on my one-bedroom flat. That's probably more than I would pay on a mortgage if I'd put down a big deposit, which I couldn't afford to do anyway. But at least I know what my outgoings are. This way I'm not worried about my mortgage payments suddenly going up. I won't have to start a second career as a drug dealer to fund a house habit.'

Like most of the rest of us, Jay is a little fish in the big macroeconomic pond. Twentysomethings, all ambition and no resources, feel this particularly keenly. But surely a fixed rate mortgage could offer sufficient security in the medium term to make buying attractive?

'I suppose it would, but, like I said, I haven't got a deposit anyway so it doesn't really matter. You only get your twenties once and I don't want to spend them saving when I should be having fun and making the best of it.'

Jay works freelance. 'I had a full-time job but it ended up taking over my life, you know?' Oh yes, we know. Because he values flexibility, renting seems more attractive than buying. At least for now.

'Basically, I can give a month's notice and be out of here. I've seen friends trapped in flats they can't sell. They ended up hating the place. I don't want to do that. I like feeling free. If I want to go travelling or move in with friends I can. I don't need to worry about getting rid of some millstone.'

Equally, his landlord could give him a month's notice. 'It's not a big deal. A month is enough time to find a place – there's no shortage of flats to rent. I suppose I would be more attached to my flat if I owned it, but I don't, so . . .'

Certainty – knowing what he has to pay each month, and flexibility – living with a month's notice, are the main reasons Jay is renting rather than buying. These are the factors most cited by twentysomethings who choose to rent. Buying, to them, seems like a great big scary commitment that will lock them in or hold them back in some way. Simultaneously, buying would expose them to greater financial – and emotional – risk. Another reason for renting is love (or lack of). And almost as many men as women said so. So there.

'I am single right now,' says Jay. 'I don't know that I'd live on my own if I had a girlfriend. It would depend how serious it was. I'd keep my own place if we were just casual, but if we were serious we'd move in. I suppose we'd probably want to buy somewhere eventually. But not straightaway.'

Jay is single but not lonely.

'Apart from the steady stream of ladies I have coming through the door, I see my mates and have them over to stay. I like my life as it is. There's no reason for me to buy right now. None that I can see, anyway.'

Often the decision to stop renting coincides with the decision to stop screwing around and settle down. Stuart, the newly self-employed techie we met in *Fire Your Boss*, recently did the double whammy: 'I got married and bought a house in the same year.' He was twenty-seven, she was twenty-eight.

'Everything seems more secure now we're married as opposed to just "going out". It seemed like we should take the next stage in property as well as in our relationship. There was no point renting any more.' And besides, he needed a place to put all those toasters after the wedding. 'We got a cat, too.' (More on substituting children with pets in *Relationships*.)

Jay assures me that the question of him meeting the right girl is 'when, not if'. So how will his living arrangements change *when* he does?

'I'm not going to give up my own flat until I'm sure. I don't want to move in with a girl then find out she's a psycho. If I do move, it won't be into her place.'

Why? It has to be in better decorative health than Jay's darts and tarts palace.

'It's important to have a fresh start. I don't want to move in to her territory, you know? And I'm not bothered about leaving this flat, so it makes sense to get somewhere together. But we'll rent until we get married or have kids. Fuck, this is scary.'

Jay envisions following a similar trajectory to Stuart: renting alone until he's sure the relationship is right, then renting, and eventually buying, together.

Although renters form the majority of twentysomethings, Jay is in the minority of renters; he has *chosen* to rent rather than buy. Around two-thirds of the twentysomethings I interviewed rented because they *had* to, not because they wanted to. Jay made a choice, but twentysomethings forced to rent by scandalously high house prices have not.

Like Katharine in the previous chapter, Felicia, a 29-year-old charity fund-raiser, is unable to afford a home in London. 'I'm forking out £550 a month renting a room in Putney,' she says, 'and I resent every penny.'

Two years ago she could have picked up a two-bedroom flat for around £160,000, but at that time she didn't have the deposit or income necessary to afford such a big mortgage. 'Now I do, and it's really frustrating. I wish I could turn the clock back but keep the same wages and have my choice of flats.'

Despite living in London and loving shoes more than life itself, Felicia has managed to save a massive £10,000 deposit. 'Now the flats I was looking at cost £230,000 to £240,000. It's so frustrating. Right now all I could afford is a studio.'

But all is not lost. 'I know what happened ten years ago,' she says ominously. 'The housing crash.'

The last big house-price boom ended painfully for many first-time buyers. Stretched to the limit, they couldn't keep up with rocketing interest rates, especially with so many jobs disappearing. Repossessions hit record highs and prices collapsed. From that price trough in 1993 to 2001, house prices in London increased by 137 per cent on average, and much much more in some boroughs (Barking and Dagenham rose more than 25 per cent in 2002 alone). Felicia's praying for another crash.

'I know rates are at their lowest for forty years and all that – some of my clients are banks – but this just can't go on. My boss tried to sell her house in South Kensington and she couldn't, even after reducing the price. It won't be long before prices come down across the market.'

When they do, Felicia will be ready, deposit in one hand, paintbrush in the other. 'I'm holding on in the hope that I can one day buy a one-bedroom flat.'

Like Jay, Felicia is single. And she's sort of glad. 'I'd hate to be renting and in a relationship. I want to buy a place and settle down as soon as I find him. I don't want to waste any more time.' So would she buy while single? 'Yes. But I'd rather buy with the person I plan to share my life with. I think if you buy on your own you buy a house, but if you buy with someone you buy a home.'

Although she's unhappy renting, Felicia is in a clean, safe flat – which is more than many twentysomethings can say. Very few of us have escaped unscathed by nasty landlords as eager to keep deposits for the least infringement of their draconian leases as they are reluctant to make improvements to their crumbling properties.

David landed a great job in London almost without trying. 'It was the first job I applied for and they told me at the second interview that I'd got it,' he says. Still in his suit, David, 27, went out to letting agents to find a place near his new job as a carer for adults with learning difficulties. The job was in Wandsworth, so he hunted around SW15.

'I knew I really only had that day to find a place as they wanted me to start a.s.a.p. The same agent took me to see three places in Putney. I could really only afford a room in a shared house, but I was new in London and didn't have any friends, so I didn't mind.'

The first room was amazingly cheap. 'That's because it doubled as a living room during the day. Because I was only using it half the time I only had to pay half rent.' Unsurprisingly he didn't take it. 'Imagine having to wait until everyone has finished watching TV before going to bed? No privacy at all. I was shocked that the agent even showed it.'

Room #2 was more like Room 101. 'It was quite big but it didn't have a window, so you needed to turn the light on to see anything. It was on the top floor of the house, so it was boiling.' Perfect conditions for the mould he spotted flourishing behind the wardrobe. 'I pointed it out to the agent, who made a note. I don't know if he did anything, but I walked past that house about a month later and the room had gone.' At least it didn't double as a living room.

Third time lucky. 'The house was in a quiet road off Wandsworth Park and about twenty minutes' walk from my new job. I was sharing with four other people and they all seemed nice.' This room of his own came complete with a window and en suite bathroom. Thankfully, he was the only living thing in it. David paid his deposit and moved in over the weekend. The problems began on Sunday evening.

'I hadn't met the landlady but I paid my rent directly to the lettings agent, so I didn't think it mattered. I didn't know she lived around the corner. Anyway, my dad and I were taking boxes in and she came over with a cup of tea for us. We were well chuffed. She seemed so nice.'

Next day, David waved his dad goodbye and began settling in. His landlady popped by again that night. 'I thought she was being a bit overfriendly but she insisted on showing me around the house and telling me about the neighbourhood. I couldn't believe what she said. Ready for this? She told me she only took white people in the house and that she loved the area because there weren't many "coloureds".'

At first David sort of laughed, but a quick look at his white housemates – two of whom were South African – confirmed his landlady's boast. Shocked, but not entirely convinced she wasn't joking, he stayed silent. 'That was the first sign, really.'

The landlady lived nearby, which made it easy for her to drop in one or two or three times a day. 'I'd come down into the kitchen and she'd be there making herself a cup of tea. Sometimes she'd be watching television. I'd never rented before, but even I knew this wasn't on.' David spoke to his housemates, all of whom seemed too scared to do anything. 'I called the letting agent, who said they'd talk to her and ask her to reduce the visits.

'Next day she came round at 7 a.m and banged on my door. She was wearing her dressing gown! She started screaming that she knew I was trouble because I was Irish and that it was her fucking house and she'd come round when she liked. She said I'd be out if I complained about her again.' The visits continued. 'Sometimes she left notes about the washing up or the state of the flat – she was a hygiene freak.'

And she was often drunk. 'She reeked of booze but always acted so prim and proper. She wouldn't allow us to have parties and we weren't allowed to have friends over.' David found that out when he received an invoice for one day's rent. 'It was in an envelope under my door when I got home from work one day.' Puzzled, he asked his landlady when she came round that night. 'That's for the girl you had to stay the other night,' she explained. David was aghast. How did she know? 'She took me upstairs into my room and walked me to the window. "See that?" she said, pointing. "That's my bedroom window. I don't miss a trick."' From then on David kept his curtains shut.

For a few weeks things were fairly quiet. Summer passed, autumn came and his landlady's visits became fewer and fewer until it was only two or three times a week. But then came the last straw.

'We were having a barbecue in the garden. It wasn't rowdy but she came over to complain. She told us to extinguish it. We refused. She went into our kitchen and filled a bucket with water and threw it on the coals. She ruined everything and soaked one of the girls sitting nearby. That was it.'

David started looking for a new place – with a different agent. 'I was actually scared to hand my notice in because she wasn't all there, I don't think. On the day I planned to go round she came to us carrying an empty basket.' Going shopping? No. Harvesting. 'She went to the apple tree in our garden and started picking the apples. "You just rent the tree", she said. "I own the apples". I told her I was leaving. She said "good" and carried on picking.'

David then endured a month's notice. 'She came round every day and every night. She complained about everything. No one else seemed to care too much, but it really upset me. I can't have stuff like that going on at home, not when my job is so stressful. I spent a lot of time out with friends that month.'

The day before he left, the landlady jumped on her broomstick and popped over for a final inspection. 'Everything was perfect – better than when I'd found it.' But she found fault. 'She claimed I'd broken the toilet seat and that she'd need a new bathroom suite at a cost of £500.' The exact sum of David's deposit. 'I offered to buy a new toilet seat.' When she refused his offer, he bought one and installed it anyway. 'She said it didn't match and that it would reduce the attractiveness to tenants and that the £500 was partly to compensate her for loss of earnings.'

David walked away £500 the poorer but all the wiser for his nightmare experience. But what were his rights?

Legally, your landlord must give you advance notice – of at least 24 hours – of their intention to visit. If it is genuinely inconvenient, you can refuse and suggest an alternative date. David's landlady's visits were illegal as well as intrusive. What's more, attached to the contract he signed was an inventory detailing the condition and value of the fixtures and fittings. David admits he didn't check this before signing. Had he done so, he would have been able to contest the condition and value of the toilet seat. And he didn't have to put up with his landlady's racist remarks. 'She was always moaning about me being Irish,' he says. David could have complained about her to the CAB or the local council who could remove her from their list of approved private landlords. And he could have taken her to the small claims court to get his £500 back. But in the end, he just wanted to get away. I don't blame him.

'I was so ground down by the end that I never wanted to see her again. I fucking hated her. I couldn't believe the others were staying, but I think they were used to it. I'd never experienced anything like that and I haven't since. It was the longest six months of my life. I still work nearby, but I go out of my way to avoid that street. I've thought about pouring paint over her doorstep or putting shit through her letterbox, but it's not worth it.' He has since noticed that there is always a room for rent in that house which local agents continue to advertise. 'I think landlords should have to give references, not tenants.'

Perhaps the worst experience I had with a landlady (why is it that landlords don't seem quite so bad?) was in my first year at university. To cut a long story short, Jean started off well. In fact, she was on holiday when I moved in so I didn't meet her for the first month. I had the place to myself. When she got back she told me I couldn't use the living room or the dining room and that the kitchen was off limits outside meal times. I wasn't allowed anyone in my room past 11 p.m. and I wasn't allowed incoming phone calls. If I needed to call anyone there was a payphone nearby. She complained that I used too much bath water and constantly criticised my cooking. I later realised she'd been opening my mail. All this I could handle – but when I woke up to find her naked in my bedroom whispering that she wanted me, I had to get out. I broke my lease the next day, which cost me my deposit, but the really crazy thing was that, having driven me out, she was upset! I refused to speak to her for the week I stayed while finding somewhere else to stay. By day seven she was crying and begging me to stay. Scary. It was all I could do to stop my mother punching her when she came to help me move. Since then there have been several dodgy incidents, but nothing to beat Evil Jean.

For me, the decision to buy came when renting became oppressive and expensive rather than liberating and cheap. I was shelling out £650 a month on rent by the end of my three years in beautiful Brunswick Square. That would cover the mortgage on a very nice one-bedroom flat, even at current prices. A mortgage began to make serious financial sense – even to me. I began to resent renting. We were loathe to leave our beloved flat, but our time was up and we couldn't bear our landlady's pseudo-Mexican taste for another second. You try living with canary-yellow walls and fuchsia skirting boards. Nightmare. But, as I said in the previous chapter, finding the right place at the right time proved all but impossible. House-hunting is up there with fox-hunting as one of my least favourite pastimes – both should be banned.

My motives for buying weren't just financial and aesthetic, they were also emotional. As men still can't marry men in dull old England, buying a property together was the next biggest commitment we could make. Many straight couples who choose not to marry, and even some who do, say that buying a home together is the biggest event of their lives. So anyway, we went from renting a flat to buying a home. And we got plenty of toasters.

Buying usually makes more financial sense than renting over the long term (think 25 not 2.5 years), but, as we've seen, buying is an emotional decision very often tied to a relationship. Just as couples buy when they get together, so they sell when they fall apart.

Like so many twentysomethings, Jade has boomeranged back home. 'It's great. Mum does my ironing!'

Jade, a travel agent, left home at twenty-four but moved back in with her parents in Staines after splitting up with her boyfriend last year.

'It was so weird sleeping in my little single bedroom again. It hadn't changed since I left. My mum was really sweet and bought me a new quilt cover to try and update it a bit.'

The decor hasn't changed, but some things are different now than when Jade first lived at home. For a start, she's paying rent.

'It's only £250 a month. I don't mind. I know it's costing them to keep me in food and stuff. To be honest, I'd rather pay something because then I feel more like a tenant than a child.'

That hasn't stopped her parents from treating her like a child.

'It was hard to begin with. Dad wouldn't go to sleep until he heard me come home at night. I stayed at friends if I was out late and then I'd get the "you're using the house as a hotel" routine. We all had to adjust.'

Jade's rent is artificially low because her parents are cutting her some slack so she can save a deposit. 'And get out from under their feet.

'Losing my independence is definitely the hardest thing about living at home. It's weird when I'm out with mates and I have to ring my mum to let her know I won't be coming home. And I can't have guys back.'

But there are upsides.

'I don't have any responsibilities. Mum does everything for me: cooking, washing, ironing. Plus my rent is low. Renting from my parents has actually improved our relationship. I had lots of problems with my ex-boyfriend, and I didn't see them as much as I used to. We've got closer again. We're all adults now, which is nice.'

So where is the incentive for Jade to get her own place?

'They've said I can stay as long as I like. I save a bit every month but I do go out a lot so it's never very much. Anyway, prices are so high now that I don't think I could afford anything. I might rent somewhere with some friends. Or maybe I'll find myself a rich man!'

Jade is waiting for a rich man, Felicia is praying for a crash and Jay is living month to month. For different reasons, they're all renting: single, skint and emphatically free.

Work, and the pursuit thereof, is another key reason for renting. How many of the people living in London were actually born there? Not very many. Hardly any of the twentysomethings I interviewed in the capital started life there. The main reason given for moving there was work. So many Dick Whittingtons, so few streets paved with gold.

'I looked at about ten rooms before taking this one,' says Jo, 23, a still-fresh graduate who moved from Glasgow to London last year. 'I can't tell you how minging some of them were. I went to one place and they showed me the room. It had hooks in the ceiling and a pulley above the bed. I wouldn't have minded, but I asked if I could move them and the land-lord said no.'

Marketing degree in hand, Jo took the brave step of finding a place before finding a job. 'Based up in Glasgow it was expen-sive to keep coming down for interviews. I started off flying down, then I got the train, and last time I caught the bus.' A dear do indeed. 'And I wanted to be near the action. I'd been to London but I didn't really know it, so I couldn't chat confi-dently about bars and stuff. I thought if I moved here I could get established and make myself seem less like someone from the provinces.'

Within weeks, Jo had a suitably cool mullet-style hairdo and plans to take moped lessons. 'But I was kipping on a friend's floor and she was getting sick of me.'

Some flatmatemares at uni put Jo off sharing. 'I wanted my own space. Moving to London was part of a strategy of doing things for me. The last thing I wanted to do was move in with a complete stranger and have to think about their needs and worry about their dirty dishes.'

A quick look at *Loot* cross-referenced with her almost non-existent savings confirmed the worst: Jo was going to have to rent a room in a shared house.

'I didn't want to go back to living like a student again. I hate all that shared milk stuff. I want to be able to watch what I want to watch on TV and not worry about staying on the phone too long. I was really gutted that I couldn't afford my own place.'

Minimising the number of flatmates seemed sensible. 'Two-bed flats are generally more expensive than five-bed houses, but I was willing to pay a bit extra for fewer people.'

Looking for a house and a job at the same time wasn't easy.

'I went from interview to viewing, which was tiring, but at least I always looked professional when I turned up to see places. A couple of times other viewers thought I was the estate agent.'

Jo found a room first.

'It's in a flat in an ex-council block – that put me off at first but I've realised I was being snobby. It's nice and light and two minutes walk to Exmouth Market. The rent is £500 a month. I phoned my mum to tell her and she nearly died when I told her how much it was. Back in Glasgow I could get a whole flat for that. I was a bit taken aback at first but now I think it's a snip.'

And the flatmate?

'She's great – she's Scottish too, which is why I think we get on. I don't think English people are racist, but sometimes they sort of clam up when they hear your accent. That, or they ask you to say words like "murder", which is kind of boring after a while.'

Then came the job, a ten-minute walk from her flat. 'I don't have to get the tube, thank God. I've got an entry-level position with a direct marketing agency. So far I love it.' Even if the job doesn't work out, Jo plans to keep her flat. 'I've got a base now.'

Does she plan to buy eventually? 'Not in London. I couldn't afford to, but I don't think I want to, either.' Like an increasing number of twentysomethings, Jo has come to London to gain work experience, not equity.

'I can work on projects here that I wouldn't get a chance to work on in Glasgow. I'm making contacts all the time. If, in a few years, I go back home I could probably work freelance for an agency down here. I don't want to buy in London because I would feel tied to it. When I buy a place I want to stay there for a long time.'

Jo plans to cash her experience in and save enough money for a deposit on a flat back in Glasgow. So why not rent in

London and buy-to-let in Glasgow? Over 230,000 buy-to-let mortgages were advanced by lenders between 1998 and 2002, according to RICS. Suddenly it seems everyone has a property portfolio.

'I wouldn't want to rent my home out to strangers. A house is personal for me – it's my space and I want to know who's in it and what they're doing. I couldn't trust anyone else to take care of it like I would.'

Although she doesn't plan to buy immediately, Jo aims to buy eventually. Only a handful of the twentysomethings I interviewed planned to rent for ever. Even Jay plans to buy. Buying your own place is now up there with finding the perfect partner and landing the ultimate job. We all have different ideas about what we want to do for a living and who we want to do after a hard day at work, but we have surprisingly similar views on property. Generally speaking, the more bedrooms the better and a dining room would be nice as well as some outside space (at least big enough for smokers to congregate in at parties). Paradoxically, this is the reason many twentysomethings rent: nobody can afford to buy their dream pad.

I spent last night at a party in a swanky flat in Arsenal which has three – count them – bedrooms and two bathrooms (one en suite) and a thing called a 'wet room'. Best of all, the roof rolled back at the touch of a button. And the beautiful couple who live there rent it. I did just the same, renting my amazing seafront flat rather than buying something grotty on a street I wouldn't stop to piss in. Prices are going up for them just as they did for me, but they don't care. 'We're happy here and now. We'll cross the buying bridge if and when we come to it,' says the lady of the must-have house.

If only we were all so relaxed. Jay has approached the accommodation question deductively – he has a set of circumstances and needs which, considered together, means he's opted to rent. When he finds a girlfriend things might change. Felicia, on the other hand, is eaten up with resentment at being unable to buy. Her inductive logic – 'I must buy a flat' – is not fitting in with the facts of her life. And she is suffering for it. Too many of us are.

I regret the time I wasted feeling bad about not buying. I don't regret the time I spent renting. And neither should you.

The small print

Your rights as a tenant

You have far more than you think you do. For example, your landlord cannot – as David's landlady did – drop by whenever they feel like it. You have responsibilities as well as rights, and these vary *lots* between Scotland and England. Visit *www.shelternet.org.uk* for a full list or call 0808 800 444 if you have a specific problem to discuss.

Test: Should you buy or should you rent?

Don't feel bad about not buying – remember, buyers are in the minority at our age. Ask yourself if you agree or disagree with these five statements to find out if you should carry on renting:

1. I need to know exactly what I'm paying every month.
2. I couldn't give a shit about the wallpaper.
3. I think I might go travelling soon.
4. Property price movements scare me.
5. Living alone scares me.

If you mainly agree, you should probably stick to renting for now. Like Jay, you value flexibility – living with a month's notice, and certainty – knowing exactly what you have to pay out each month. And you like having other people around.

If you mainly disagree, you should think about buying. Fixed or capped rates will offer the security you're after, and you can finally stop moving around and start building your own little nest (and possibly even a nest egg). No more annoying flatmates (unless, of course, you rent rooms out). It's okay to be scared at this point – you're on the verge of the biggest purchase of your life.

9

Home Alone?

Home is who you make it

'A house is not a home . . . I'm not meant to live alone.'
Burt Bacharach

'I'm sick of living on my own,' says India, 28. 'It's just no fun doing everything for one and it's harder. I really never thought I'd say this, but I'm lonely. How embarrassing is that?'

Twentysomething in loneliness shock! Like many of us, India misses the days of wall-to-wall people – flatmates, fellow students and friends. Since graduating five years ago she has lived alone watching cable television and developing a close relationship with new best friends Ben & Jerry.

'Even when I had my own room in halls of residence there were always people about – in the kitchen, the bar and the library, not that I went there much. There was always someone to talk to. I was never really on my own. Now I am.'

When she's not at work, India drifts around her two-bedroom flat near Clapham Common. 'I've done so much DIY there's nothing left to fix. I'm even bored of my flat.'

Perhaps a flatmate would make things more interesting?

'When I moved to London I looked at shared houses, but they were, without exception, horrible. I don't want to live like a student any more. I'm earning a good wage and I want my lifestyle to reflect that. I'd get a flatmate but I don't want to live with just anyone.'

India doesn't want to be home alone. What she wants, more than anything, is a flat-share with friends, but they're scattered all over the country, and those that live in London have shacked up with partners or new friends. 'I feel like everyone is settled and having fun but me,' she says, currently the only singleton in her group.

Sounds familiar?

Twentysomethings aren't supposed to feel lonely. Our lives are meant to be one long *Sex and the City* episode with friends and lovers competing for our attention as we bounce from party to party. Our diaries should bulge with beautiful people who'd take a bullet for us and always say the right thing at the right time. Our evenings and weekends should be the envy of everyone.

But, as India has found, our twenties just aren't like that.

For a start, we're usually far too busy working to play. The fun half of the work hard/play hard cliché is dumped in the rush to forge a career, buy a house and generally reach perfection before thirty. Week nights are a no-no as we're too knackered and/or skint to go out. Saturday is chore-riffic while Sunday is dominated by Sunday syndrome as we prepare for, and dread, the events of the week ahead.

Although we're working longer and harder than ever, it's a bit too easy to say we're too busy to have fun. Going out is like going to the gym – you can always find time if you really want to. India works until 7 p.m. most nights. She admits she doesn't always need to.

'When I started I had to make a good impression, but now I could probably leave on time if I wanted to.' So why doesn't she? 'What's the point in going home? There's no one there.'

We don't want to admit we're not having as much fun as we thought we would once the degree was done and the wages came rolling in. India makes me swear not to tell her friends she spent Saturday night manicuring her nails in the company of Carrie Bradshaw.

India is trapped in a Catch-22. She doesn't leave work till late because there's no one at home for her to return to. There is no one at home because she spends all her time at work. She spends all her time at work because there is no one waiting for her at home. And so on.

Her loneliness is complicated and compounded by feelings of jealousy ('Everyone is settled but me') and guilt ('I'm embarrassed to admit I feel lonely'). She feels bad about feeling lonely. This is a lot like job envy. India is convinced everyone is having a better time than her and that she is the only person in her peer group who feels lonely. That's because, as with job envy, nobody wants to admit they're anything less than ecstatic 24/7. This group denial magnifies any feelings of loneliness, making it hard for anyone to step out of line. India is actually one of a crowd of lonely twentysomethings.

Tim works seven days a week every week as a surveyor. 'I know the security people and they let me in on weekends. My boss thinks I work from home.' Saturday and Sunday whizz by as he prepares surveys done during the week. He's been busy during the housing boom, but Tim plans to work like this boom or bust. 'I'd rather work, you know?' He's by no means the total saddo he sounds. Although not a model, he's decent looking and he doesn't smell bad. There is no obvious reason for him to spend all his time sitting at a computer when he could be propping up a bar or at home lounging on his sofa. 'I've always worked this hard,' he says.

This might explain why his wife left him. Married at twenty-four and divorced at twenty-seven. Not exactly a happy marriage. 'I married her because she got pregnant and refused to have an abortion. I didn't want to change my life, she forced me into it.' Angry with his wife and uninterested in the child he didn't want, Tim spent more and more time at work. Home was a hate-nest. He didn't take a holiday in the three years he was married. Now he's divorced he still has no plans to get away. 'Who would I go with?' The friends who attended his wedding have drifted away because Tim is never around to do anything. He's always working.

'I hated going home. I dreaded six o'clock coming because I knew I'd get grief as soon as I walked in the door. She begged me to spend more time with her and the baby, but the more she did that the less I wanted to see either of them. To be honest, I was going to leave her. She just got there first.'

In some senses Tim had already left. 'My work is my life now. I've no time for friends. I get on with the people I work with and we go out for drinks and that, but I'm not interested in anything more. And I don't want another relationship.'

Isn't he lonely?

'Yes and no. I try not to think about how things were before I got married because it upsets me. It didn't need to be this way. But you can't turn the clock back. Work is consistent. Home is like a hotel for me now.'

Tim stayed away from home *because* he had someone to return to. He has rerouted his social ambitions into work and is making a great success of it – unsurprising, given the hours he puts in. When he thinks about it long enough he admits to feeling lonely. India stays away from home because its emptiness magnifies her loneliness. When I tell her about Tim she is shocked by his lack of concern about his seeming social failure. 'I'd be mortified. I'd hate people to think of me like that.' India is proud that no one knows she's lonely. 'How sad would that be?'

Like Tim and India, those anxious to avoid home, for whatever reason, often hide out at work, but there is also a whole bunch of twentysomethings hiding out at home. Call it cocooning if you must: more and more of us are spending more and more time back at base. Staying in is the new going out. In reality, the closest many of us get to Charlie is an episode of *Casualty*.

Lack of time and money for leisure partly explains why we're now so focused on our domestic lives – our televisions, games consoles and music. (Not to mention our beds – do you know anyone who gets enough sleep?) We simply can't afford to live the idealised twentysomething lifestyle of parties, holidays and expensive fun, but it isn't just that we're skint and tired; we're getting to the age where we start to focus more on a smaller circle of people – our friends, best friends and partners. We're realising that how we live – whether we rent, buy or squat – is not as important as who we live with. Home isn't so much about how or where but *who*.

We've established that those who choose to rent are usually single. Twentysomethings rarely buy on their own, mainly because they can't afford to. India is a well-paid exception. And couples who rent tend to be in the early stages of a relationship – they're saving for a deposit and waiting for things to get serious enough to buy. But there are many more designs for living than alone or with a partner. You could kip in a commune, manage a *ménage à trois*, share with friends or, like Jade in the previous chapter, boomerang back home. Living alone needn't be a grim litany of ready-meals and late-night TV. In each instance the twentysomethings we're about to meet are focusing not on how or where they live, but on who they live with, and finding an arrangement that works for them.

Jack, a 27-year-old barman, lives with his partner, Madison, a 29-year-old-teacher, and their toddler, Arizona, in a small family community in Wales. The community (they don't like the word commune) has existed on and off for around twenty years. It's a farmhouse with ten bedrooms and lots of living space, enough for the three families who share it.

'We live here because our politics prevent us from buying and selling property for personal profit,' says Jack, a good old-fashioned socialist. 'I don't think where you live should be about what you can afford. It makes me very angry to see houses standing empty when there are people sleeping on the streets. We should all have equal access to the best possible accommodation available.'

Prior to living in the community, Jack and his family lived in student accommodation in Manchester. 'I was finishing my teacher training,' says Madison, who took a year out to have Arizona. 'It was quite equitable. We shared kitchens, laundry facilities and bathrooms.' Far from being put off by this experience of shared living, Jack and Madison were inspired to look at how they could continue it after their student days.

'Arizona was just a baby, but we wanted to raise her in a community which reflects our principles,' says Jack. 'We don't want her to grow up hearing the same messages we did.'

They heard about the family community through a friend in the local Green Party who'd gone to a party there ('great people, great weed'). After a visit they were interviewed to ensure they fitted the profile of the group. They were then invited for a trial weekend to assess their suitability for communal living. A year and a half later they're still there.

'There's no landlord and we make all decisions jointly. We contribute to the upkeep and split the bills, it works out well for everyone.' Jack and his family rent two rooms and have a year-long lease subject to renewal by a majority of the community. Each week everyone has to work for a day on the house or grounds.

Meals are cooked and eaten as a community, but there's no penalty for being late and you can eat on your own if you want to. Meat is allowed, but most members are vegetarian. Everyone has a normal job. Madison teaches Arizona and the other junior school-aged children at home. The only qualifications for living here are ideological – nobody Right of the Left is allowed, not that they'd be happy anyway, but it's not part of any wider political organisation.

'We love being surrounded by people like us, and Arizona has made lots of friends,' says Madison. 'We're all working towards the same goals and supporting one another. It's the only way to live.'

But surely there are problems?

'It's like living with any group of people,' says Madison. 'There are certain individuals you clash with, but you've got to sort issues out because you live together. You can't let things fester. You have to be accommodating and tolerant.'

If an issue can't be resolved by the parties concerned, someone from the community acts as a mediator. But this happens rarely.

What if they want to leave? Could they ever climb on the property ladder?

'Money was never the issue for us – Madison inherited enough from her father to buy a place in London if we wanted to. But we don't.'

If they ever did buy it would be a house big enough to contain their own community. Right now they're consulting the 'Buildings at Risk' registers which every local council must maintain. The lists contain information about the state of repair of properties ranging from architectural follies to country houses, some of which are for sale. 'We'd love to build our own community,' says Madison.

If their dream becomes a reality, it will be tough to leave, emotionally and practically. 'We have a year-long lease which we cannot break. I wouldn't want to leave the others in the lurch anyway.'

Jack, Madison and Arizona have removed themselves from conventional society as far as possible. They don't want to disappear entirely – Jack enjoys his bar work – but they are selective about their degree of engagement. Where they live is important

– they won't leave the UK because they want Arizona to see her grandmother. *Who* they live with is the key factor in their decision to live as part of a community. The other families reflect and reinforce their political beliefs, providing support and inspiration. And they can all share lentil recipes. It's the people, not the place.

Mick and Chris have lived together for five years. They met when they were both twenty-two. For the last two years Paul has spent weekends at their home in Blackpool.

'It started out quite casual,' says Mick, 27, a fireman. 'We met Paul at a party and we all clicked,' says Chris, 27, a nurse. The licking came later.

'I thought they were great,' says Paul, 25, a painter and decorator. 'A mate told me they had an open relationship, but I wasn't putting myself forward or anything. We didn't sleep together for ages.'

After swapping numbers at the party, Mick and Chris had Paul over for dinner with friends. 'I didn't want to admit that I found him attractive,' says Mick. Neither did Chris. Although they had an open relationship, the rules they'd established banned sex with someone both partners found attractive. It also banned sex with friends. 'We don't shit on our own doorstep,' says the reassuringly northern Mick.

Three tense months ticked by. 'One night it was just the three of us. We got drunk and fell into bed. It was amazing, I'd never had a threesome before,' says Chris. Paul stayed that Saturday. And the next. And the next. 'I didn't move in but I didn't want to go home because I enjoyed being with them,' says Paul. 'I think we took so long to get around to doing it because we all knew it wasn't just sex,' says Mick, who admits to initially feeling threatened by the new arrival.

'Mick and I talked about what to do after about a month of Paul staying for weekends. I mean, we weren't seeing much of our friends and questions were being asked. We had to make it sort of official or cool off.' Despite Mick's jealousy issues, the pair agreed to out themselves as a trio.

'I haven't been gay for very long,' says Paul, who lived with a girlfriend for three years after leaving school. 'I'm not ready for a full-on boyfriend, so weekends suit me.'

And so, at a party for twenty of their closest friends, Mick and Chris and Paul went from having a threesome to living in a *ménage à trois*. The reaction was mixed.

'A lot of people just laughed,' says Paul. 'They didn't take us seriously.' Several friends approached Chris and Mick afterwards, concerned that Paul could split them up. 'It took some convincing, but most people accept it now,' says Chris. They haven't told their parents.

Paul arrives on Friday nights after work and the three have dinner together. 'Paul has his own room,' says Mick. 'We only sleep together in the same bed if we're having sex. At the start, Chris sometimes went in to sleep with Paul but I got jealous, so now we don't do that.' They usually go clubbing on Saturday and spend Sundays together at home. The weekend is over when Paul leaves for work on the Monday morning.

Although they have sex, their relationship isn't just sexual. 'If it was we'd kick him out at the end of the night or get a different guy every week,' laughs Mick. 'We're really close and it helps having three different points of view.' I would have thought that was complicated, but . . . 'We do row,' admits Chris. 'Everybody does, but usually one of us calms the other two down. The three of us haven't had a fight, and I hope we don't.'

Mick and Chris never imagined they'd end up in a *ménage à trois*, but now they have they can't see an end to it. 'It's just better – it's hard to explain,' says Chris. 'We all love one another in different ways. It's a bit like seeing yourself in two mirrors and looking good, but different, in each one.' Let's hope the mirrors never smash.

Again, as with Jack and his family, Mick and Chris and Paul have set up an unconventional home. They have rejected monogamy, building their lives around a trio rather than a pair. Their home is just the space that their lives take place in. It's important – they need that spare bedroom – but it doesn't matter if they rent or buy. And it doesn't really matter what other people think. Such lack of concern is refreshing.

Flat-sharing is the more conventional option and still hugely popular with twentysomethings, but, as India said, the older you get the harder it is to put up with other people's habits. Dirty dishes are fine at nineteen but not at twenty-nine – not when you're trying to grab breakfast before running to catch the train. I can barely live with myself. Put me in a flat with other people and it'd be a competition to see who killed who first.

'I know The Girls are there for me,' says Laura, 24, a trainee systems analyst. The Girls are Nat, 26, a customer services manager and Perveen, 25, a dental hygienist. The three share a flat in Sheffield.

'We've shared for two years,' says Nat over a glass or five of Pinot Grigio. 'We're like a family.'

Indeed they are. The rent and bills (except phone) are split equally. Straws were drawn for the small third bedroom – Perveen lost. 'I don't mind,' she says. 'Nat has three wardrobes so I use one of them.'

Before moving in together Nat lived with her boyfriend, Perveen with family and Laura with flatmates. Not once have they looked back. So how did they meet?

'Pure luck,' says Perveen, who spotted an ad for the flat in her local paper. 'I stayed at home till I finished studying. I couldn't afford my own flat, but I could manage if I was sharing.' After three months of looking at properties trashed by Sheffield's exuberant student population, Perveen found the perfect pad – only she didn't have anyone to share it with. 'So

I wrote a Lonely Hearts type ad and put it in the paper where I found the flat.'

Nat, having finally decided to dump the boyfriend from hell, found Perveen's ad while looking for a place to recoup her relationship losses. 'I didn't want to go back home because my parents couldn't understand why I was leaving my boyfriend, and I didn't want to be on my own.' Nat's friends split evenly between those who thought he was a wanker and those who were pleased he was now single. 'I needed a fresh start.'

'I was sharing with flatmates from uni,' says Laura. 'They both got jobs in London so I needed to move. I wasn't bothered about staying in the house – I'd been in it three years and I didn't really like the landlord.' She responded to the ad and agreed to meet Perveen and Nat in a pub near the new flat. 'I don't remember drinking or laughing so much,' she says. And they haven't stopped.

Nat's break-up provided an instant rallying point for The Girls. 'I know I could have got through it without them, but I'm glad I didn't have to,' she says. But worse was to come. Less than a month after moving in, Nat discovered she was pregnant. 'It was his. I knew straightaway I didn't want it.' That same week she was accompanied to a clinic with Perveen on one side and Laura on the other.

'I couldn't tell my mum and I didn't want to get into it with my friends 'cos they knew the father. I don't suppose we all knew one another that well, but they were there for me when no one else was, and I'll never forget that.'

Since then events have been less traumatic – a couple of minor break-ups, a lost job not much liked anyway, and a missed flight on a group holiday to Ibiza. Together, The Girls are getting it together.

'We're more than just mates,' says Laura. 'I can tell them anything and I know they'll listen. When you see someone every day, you learn to read their signals. Sometimes we know before one another if something's wrong. That can be annoying – having someone tell you how you feel – but it's good to know you're being watched. I don't mean that in a bad way. We just keep an eye on one another.'

The Girls have different jobs and different schedules, but they make time for one another. 'We stay in on Friday nights,' says Perveen. 'We watch telly or get a DVD and have a takeaway and some wine. It's a good way to end the week.' And a great way to catch up on gossip and sort out the bills.

'We turn our mobiles off and unplug the phone,' says Laura. 'We're busy on the weekends: Nat usually has to work, Perveen visits her mum and I go out with mates from work. So Fridays are our time.'

For The Girls, the benefits of sharing a flat are clear: constant companionship, shared expenses and shared understanding. But what about the disadvantages?

'We only have one bathroom,' says Laura, who gets up early to have her share of the hot water. 'So mornings get a bit frantic.'

Perveen wishes she had a bigger bedroom. Nat also sometimes feels a bit cramped – but emotionally, not physically. 'Sometimes I just want the flat to myself, you know? I don't always feel like talking.'

Basically, there are no problems unsolvable with bigger bedrooms and some en suite bathrooms. The Girls make their arrangement work, supporting one another through their quarterlife crises. And, like the other less conventional twentysomethings, their success is down to putting people first.

'If one of us moves in with a guy or something, the rest of us will need to move out,' says Perveen. 'But until that happens we're sticking together.'

India's loneliness persists. She remains convinced everyone is having more fun than her. To an extent she's right – The Girls are. But, as with job envy, India could make herself feel better. She could accept she lives on her own and celebrate the freedom this gives her. She could leave work at a decent hour and cultivate some friends. And, contrary to her fears, there are decent flatmates to be found – she could become one of The Girls.

No one living arrangement is categorically better than another – Mick, Chris and Paul probably wouldn't have a lot of fun in the commune. But in each household – commune, *ménage à trois*, friendfest – twentysomethings are focusing on people. We can be more creative in our living arrangements. The secret of success is who, not where or how. Renting, buying, whatever – it's all a means to an end. And it's okay to live alone, so long as that's okay with you; you'll never have to queue for the bathroom or fight over the remote control.

The small print

Living on your own, sharing with friends, shacking up – which is for you?

The best things about living on your own:

1. You can be as messy as you like.
2. You can walk around naked.
3. You can control your bills (and use them to build up credit for yourself).
4. There is no one around to tell you what to do.
5. You don't have to share a bathroom/kitchen/whatever.

The worst things about living on your own:

1. You're being as messy as you like and you bring someone back/get a surprise visit from your mum/get lost in your own bedroom.

2. You're walking around naked and you realise everyone on the top floor of the double-decker bus at the stop outside your house is enjoying a good look.
3. You get lonely sometimes – talking to yourself gets boring.
4. It's more expensive than sharing.
5. It's too easy to be very lazy – your own little routine becomes a rut.

The best things about sharing:

1. There's always someone around to talk to.
2. You can borrow someone else's milk/money/clothes/booze.
3. You can share the bills.
4. If your friends are boring, you can always play with theirs.
5. You won't ever get locked out.

The worst things about sharing:

1. It's very hard to have space/time to yourself.
2. Magpie flatmates who steal everything you own.
3. Having to be the responsible one who works out the bills, chases payment and makes up the shortfall.
4. Enduring your flatmates' hideous boyfriends/friends/family.
5. Feeling like you're still living like a student.

The best things about living with your partner:

1. Sex on tap – no more late-night cabs.
2. You develop a day-to-day intimacy and grow closer.
3. You can road test them as potential husband/wife/life-partner material.
4. He or she is there for you at the end of every day.
5. You can build a home together.

The worst things about living with your partner

1. Sex on tap – suddenly you don't want it so much.
2. The magic disappears and you realise they grind their teeth.
3. Three weeks after giving up your own flat you realise this definitely isn't the person for you.
4. The row you had in the morning is waiting for you after work.
5. His crap fights with your clothes for wardrobe space and it turns out you each despise the other's 'taste'.

If you fancy setting up a commune or moving into one, try contacting Radical Routes, Rootstock, the Triodos bank or the Ecology Building Society. See *www.diggersanddreamers.org.uk/ links.htm* for more details.

If you and your mates fancy rescuing a ruin and making it your own, try the Buildings at Risk Registers: *www.doorsopen days.org.uk/bar* for Scotland and county by county for England – find details on local council web sites.

get it together
money

10

Life Is Expensive

Twentysomethings on the focaccia-line.

'If I don't sort my finances out soon I'm going to be eating cat food and sleeping in a skip.'
Charlie, 27, project manager

'Life is cheap. London is expensive.'
Missy G., 27, PR account manager

A well-meaning friend recently bought me a copy of the money management programme *Quicken*. My heart stopped as I unwrapped the package. What had I done to deserve this? Why did she hate me so much?

There can be no more inappropriate gift for a twentysomething than a pedantic computer programme which requires you to honestly account for your daily spending. It takes a braver man than me to confront a financial situation bleaker than that of Argentina's. I'm afraid to say it's lying unused beneath a pile of credit card receipts and angry red bills. I considered some creative accounting, but it's no fun embezzling from yourself. It's a sign of my fiscal incompetence that I haven't even exchanged it or got a refund. I'm ignoring it: which is the principle applied to all financial information placed before me. I am just as likely to forget to pay a bill as I am to bank a cheque. And I'm not alone.

For once, the stereotypes are sort of true: twentysomethings are generally shit with money. Of course there are exceptions – and we bow to them – but on the whole we just don't do money. Mainly because we don't have very much. Yes, wages are higher than ever before, and starting salaries for graduates are especially good at £13,422 (more in London), but we've graduated into more debt than any other generation – £12,700 on average and nearly £15,000 in London. That's before top-up fees. So when your parents next tell you that you've got it good, you know what to say.

So what are all the hidden expenses which conspire to financially cripple us in our twenties? How does our attitude to money, or lack of it, change as we approach thirty? No more nasty financial surprises: go forward forewarned and forearmed!

In case you've forgotten, money is that tradeable currency you fantasise about. It's the stuff you find in dreams that eludes you in nightmares. Money is what you use to buy things and pay off debt. It's what you're promised in abundance when you graduate. And it's something you don't really encounter till you hit twentysomething and start earning in earnest.

'When you're at school you don't think about money,' says Lars, 26, a garden landscaper. 'You live with your parents and they take care of everything. I got an allowance and I worked Saturday mornings, but that was all fun money. I didn't really think about money till after university.'

Even when things go wrong, our parents try to shield us from financial matters. As children we know nothing about money (it's the stuff that falls from birthday cards) and as teenagers we know just enough to get what we want. Yes, there are piggy banks and post office accounts, but we're not managing an income or stemming the flow of outgoings. Having been kept in the dark about money, it's no wonder so many of us go off the rails when we get to university. I remember my grant, £1,892, seemed like riches beyond measure. It was supposed to last a year but disappeared in three months.

'I still don't exactly know how much debt I'm in,' says Lars. Worse still, he doesn't know how to find out. I could at least make the calls and write the letters and wait for the debt-laden missives to reach me. Not Lars. He thinks he might have a store card or two. 'Anyone could tell me I owed them money and I'd believe them. Not that I have anything to pay them with.'

Lars went travelling after university. His year-long sojourn was almost entirely funded by flexible friends. 'I got two credit cards with a £10,000 limit,' he says, 'and maxed them both out.' Lars has student loans – but he doesn't know how big they are. His parents won't give him any more and his friends are sick of forking out. Like most returning travellers, his tan was his greatest asset. 'I had nothing.' He lived with his parents until they got on his nerves and he got back on his feet. 'It took six months.' Now he's sharing a flat in London and doing bar work while mulling over his next move in garden landscaping. He can't believe the cost of living.

'I share with friends but my rent is still £500 a month. People say it's low, but that's half my wages. And then there's my travelcard to get to work. Food, drink, going out, gym. And all the bills. What the fuck is council tax for?' (We've all asked that question.)

Although he's lived away from home for years – university and then travelling – this is the first time Lars has had to deal with the full horrors of complete financial independence. At university his key costs, accommodation and fees, were taken care of by his parents. As students we don't have to worry about council tax. Income tax isn't really an issue as few of us earn above our £4,615 personal allowance. Utilities, like water, are part of our rent. All Lars had to do was make sure he had enough money to get drunk. Now people around him are talking about pensions while he scrapes a living on his hardly generous barman's salary.

'It's like I got left behind. When I went travelling everyone was in the same boat. Since I got back I feel poorer than my friends. I don't understand how they seem to have so much all of a sudden. I was only away for a year.'

We all know a Lars: a total debt-ostrich who spends with seemingly little regard for the financial future. We think he's mad, but we also envy him a little – why are we trying to be good when he's spending his way around the world? Life is expensive, that's indisputable, but nobody told us just how cataclysmically costly it could get.

Let's get some perspective before we doom ourselves out. Firstly, if you have a degree, your earning potential exceeds that of the people from your school who didn't go to university. You're potentially better off than most people. Secondly, however bad things are, you're probably not as poor as you were when you were a student. You might think you are, but you're not. Gone are the days of shopping at the bargain corner in the supermarket. No more dented tins. Never again will you eat instant mashed potato or those longlife meals with ancient dehydrated carrots in. You're off the breadline and on the focaccia-line. It's not easy, but it's easier.

'I never, ever envisaged I would spend so much money on sundried tomatoes, mozzarella, olives, balsamic vinegar and fine wine,' says Monkey, a 26-year-old animal behaviourist. Well, someone's got to keep the dogs and cats of Britain under control. 'I used to be quite happy sharing a portion of chips and a bottle of Thunderbirds with friends.'

As a student, Monkey thought Lambrusco was a luxury. Then came Chianti, and now . . . if it's not *premier cru* Chablis it's not getting in the door. It's not just that her tastes have improved; her standards have risen. And with them her bill for everyday living.

'I earn more than ever, but I still feel really poor. The more I make the more I spend, but I don't honestly know where it all goes. I think I've got too used to catching cabs and drinking wine in restaurants.'

Can you imagine saying that as a student? Remember when cabs were a luxury to be shared by five people? When the only wine you drank in a restaurant was some bilge you brought yourself? When you ate bread instead of a starter?

Somewhere around twenty-five, earlier for some and later for others, we stop living like students and start living like adults. Not sure it's happened to you yet? Here's a test: imagine trying to live now on the budget you subsisted on as a student. If you're scared, you've passed. If you're still serving spaghetti Bolognese in a wok at your dinner parties, you've failed. Bang goes all the nice booze, swap coke for speed (if you're lucky) and get charity shopping for a new look.

Our attitude to money changes as we earn more. For a start, our standards rise: we simply must have and do nice things all the time. Luxuries – cabs, good wine, quality cosmetics – become basics. We're tired of waiting for the good life and watching other people enjoy it; we all want instant gratification which is anything but cheap.

Secondly, we talk less about it. We assume that's because we don't want to be the lowest earner. There is some truth to this – it's not nice being the poor friend – but it could also be because we don't want to be the highest earner. Too much money can be equally divisive. At university we were all pretty much as skint as one another, but suddenly you're a lawyer and your best friend is a teacher and they can't afford to eat at the same restaurant or go on holiday with you any more. Or vice versa.

'My flatmate has caviar in the fridge,' says Sue, 29, a human resources manager. 'I have some eye gel that I need to keep cool, and some milk, and that's about it.' As with jobs and property, we covet the cash of others. 'I see people in the street and add up the cost of their outfits and I'm amazed they can afford it all. I don't have a single item of clothing – apart from a coat – that cost more than £50. Of course I'm jealous!'

Sue earns £25,000. Her flatmate earns £30,000. 'That's not much more than me, but she has such a better lifestyle. She eats nicer food, wears nicer clothes – I don't understand how.' (We'll find out how in the next chapter, *Debt: Can't live with it, can't live without it*.)

Money gets serious in our twenties. It's when we begin to make big purchases – cars, homes, drug/shoe habits. We may only be buying small flats and secondhand cars, but they make a gigantic impact on our financial lives – anyone saving for a deposit knows this. Mercifully, these are rare events: you don't go shopping for a two-bedroom flat every week. It's all the little day-to-day expenses that really change the way we spend and how we live. The cabs, the takeaways, the non-sale rail clothes – these are the things that immediately improve our quality of life. Enjoy now, pay later.

'You could just get up, go to work and come home,' says Angus, a 27-year-old lawyer from Australia living in London, 'but to go travelling, to eat out, to entertain, to go drinking or to go to the theatre you have to spend money. These are all the things that really make life worth living.'

Angus takes this one step further: 'I've begun to think more in terms of how my money can work for me and how/where I should be investing it. Compare that with a couple of years ago, when cash was only a vehicle for my entertainment and a way to keep some pubs in business.'

His finances reflect his attitude: he lives in the black. Sue lives in the red: 'I still think of money as something to enhance my life in the moment, not as something I need to invest for the future.'

Charlie, 27, a project manager, has a wardrobe bursting with handsomely tailored tweed suits. 'They do look good,' he says. They certainly do. 'But they're not cheap.' Not at £500 a pop (excluding shirts, ties, socks, pants and shoes). 'And I have some really nice cameras.'

Work clothes are one of the great unexpected and unfair costs of our twenties. There's something galling about shelling out for clothes you can only wear 9–5. Charlie's response is to buy suits that make him feel fabulous whenever he wears them. As you know, my working-from-home wardrobe consists mainly of pyjamas.

Men can get away with wearing the same suit Monday to Friday and alternating shirts and ties, but not the ladies, oh no. She who wears the same skirt twice in one week is a dirty bitch that cares not a jot for her appearance. Women have to spend far more than men on clothes for work.

'I spend a fortune on outfits for the office,' says Missy G., a 29-year-old 'PR girl' based in Chelsea. Last year the sartorial total was £4,000. Admittedly, looking good is a big part of her job.

'I spend way more than my male colleagues. I think women are expected to look good all the time. That pressure comes as much from other women as it does from men. And it costs lots to look great – it's competitive. I view it as an investment in my career, but I wish men would spend as much on suits.'

Hair (cut, colouring, style and products), nails (manicure, pedicure, polish), body (gym, moisturisers and other sundries, boob-job fund) and clothes (work, boudoir and going out) absorb most of Missy G.'s disposable income. 'Undoubtedly, it costs more for women to maintain themselves than it does men,' she says. These costs are multiplied in London. 'I have friends who go to New York for the weekend to get their hair and nails done and buy clothes because it's cheaper than London.' Monkey agrees: 'Even our car insurance is more expensive. And men don't have to buy tampons!'

Life seems to cost less for men, due in no small part to the disparate beauty maintenance factor. I know that sounds sexist, but if you want further proof of this just ask your female friends, then imagine spending that much on your appearance. Beauty costs. (For the record: I have a manicure every now and then as a treat, and sorry, boys, shaving doesn't count – it's not as expensive or painful as intimate waxing.)

Charlie is a well-tailored exception. Like me, he's fairly relaxed about the hideous cost of day-to-day living. 'If you want life to be fun it has to be expensive. Worry will do you more damage than any debt ever could, unless you get kneecapped by a loan shark. I don't let it stress me out. A lot of my wealthy friends are actually as miserable as sin.'

Monkey and Lars are both distressed by the rise in cost of living experienced when full-on adult life hits. Lars has lost track of his debts. Monkey wishes she could forget hers. 'I'm at the end of my overdraft every month – all my wages do is take me back to zero. I have £100 in savings that my granny gave me when I graduated, and that's it. When I think about the future I get freaked out. I mean, how am I ever going to be able to buy a house or start a family? I can't imagine ever earning enough.'

Even Angus finds he has to fork out for unimagined eventualities. For him, broken bones are an expensive fact of life. 'I have an uncanny ability to hurt myself doing sport,' he says. Rugby doesn't cost much, but the repairs do. 'I've had one knee op and loads of stitches, hurt both my shoulders and broken a couple of bones.' When Angus lived at home, in Australia, his parents covered the cost of private medical insurance. Here in the UK he's on his own. 'I tend to use my policy quite often, which means my premiums are high. They're about £60 a month.'

Whatever kicks we spend our cash on, it's accommodation that's the killer.

Charlie's house is the biggest purchase of his life so far. 'I kept meaning to buy, but I took years to get round to it. There always seemed to be something better to spend my money on than a house.' Like snappy suits, boys' toys and fine whisky. 'Of course, prices went up massively while I was off on big holidays playing with my new cameras.'

Charlie is currently doing hard domestic labour, sanding floors and stripping wallpaper. He can't afford to get someone in to do it for him because 'that would soak up what fun-money I have left'. Months on he's still reeling from the hidden costs of becoming a home owner.

'Stamp duty. Nobody ever told me about that. I thought it had something to do with the Royal Mail when I first heard about it. It's 1 per cent of the purchase price – that's a fuck-load of money to be hit with at the last minute. It's a total rip-off. More money for the government. What do they spend it on?'

Bang went the dregs of his savings and any chance of a summer holiday. 'There are so many little expenses that just mount up. Before you know it you've paid thousands in fees for this and that. The worst of it is that you don't get any tangible benefit for most of the costs. When I got the keys to my own house, it just felt like I'd been to the world's most expensive key-cutter.' (The total borrowed was £152,000.)

Anyone buying a house will encounter these unexpected and unwelcome expenses. I've detailed all of mine for you at the end of this chapter, so you won't suffer the nasty surprises I did. Buying is never going to be cheap, especially in London. 'Everything costs so much more here,' says Charlie. 'Solicitors, surveyors, estate agents, removal people.' And, of course, the bricks and mortar. 'It all adds up. Friends who've bought in Newcastle, where I went to university, can't believe how much it's cost me. They don't understand how I can afford it. To be honest, neither can I.'

The cheapest place to live in the UK is, according to the Halifax, Abertillery in Wales. Needless to say, it's grim. High-fliers flock to Esher, England's most expensive town and replica of the Stepford Wives set. It's prim down south. The majority of us live between either extreme, but wherever you are, keeping a roof over your head sucks up the greatest proportion of your income in your twenties. Especially if you live in London – currently the seventh most expensive city in the world, and easily pricier than New York City.

'It's unbelievably expensive, even if you're a dullard who stays in all the time watching the box,' says Monkey. 'All the basic costs are higher, but salaries don't match. London weightings are a joke.'

Aside from his new home and his little luxuries, it's day-to-day London living that saps Charlie's bank balance. Even though he earns almost £40,000, Charlie still has to be careful with his cash. 'I am completely convinced you can't live in London and not be in debt,' he says.

This is the only sentiment shared by every twentysomething in this book. We disagree about all sorts, but every one of us believes that if you live within the M25 you're in the red at least some of the time. Our attitude to debt might vary, as might our strategy for clearing it, but we're all in it. At least, that's what we think. (As you'll see in the next chapter, some twentysomethings manage to live in the black. Strange, I know. But true.)

'My theory about London is that you live there because you want to do all the lovely London things,' says Missy G. 'I love going to gorgeous bars and restaurants and seeing amazing stuff at the theatre.' Surely you could catch Shakespeare in Preston and maybe even have a glass of something nice after the show? 'London is amazing and unique in that it has the best of everything – that's why it's so expensive.' Tell that to all the twentysomethings who've fled to the country or gone travelling because they're so sick of the city. London remains an irresistible lure for thousands of Missy and Mister G.s. 'You can wear to-die-for shoes out in the sticks, but what the hell is the point when there's no one to see you in them? That's what I say!'

Missy G. manages to have a ball and not be spectacularly in debt. 'I am only £1,000 overdrawn – a snip.' But she has no savings, no pension and no property. Every penny of her income goes on her lifestyle.

'I am living for the moment. I sure as hell don't want to be in the smoke for the rest of my life, so I may as well maximise my going out and generally do *everything* and spend way too much money on overpriced vodka cocktails now, as I'll be gutted when I'm sat in a semi in Reigate with a child on each hip and a Labrador slavering at my ankles.'

Like Charlie, Missy G. is chilled about being in the red. 'Don't worry about debt as it's going to happen – you can't avoid it. It will all come out in the wash. One day you'll suddenly have money and you'll wonder what all the fuss was about.'

Charlie's monster mortgage and Lars's proportionately scary rent show that keeping a roof over your head is the biggest expense in your twenties. There are big costs and little costs associated with this, but, as with most expenses in our twenties, we meet them financially and emotionally unprepared. Pocket money is insufficient training for university which, in turn, does not prepare us for a life of what Monkey calls 'endless pointless bills for everything'. These costs vary depending on location: London is the biggest cash vortex.

All the twentysomethings in this chapter have at least one degree. Their earning potential is greater, but somehow the money coming in is never enough. Charlie and Missy G. share high expectations about their quality of life, but Charlie has a better chance of realising them. Why? Men still earn disproportionately more than women – on average 20 per cent. Charlie earns around £8,000 more than Missy G.; they're both twenty-seven, work in the same sector and have broadly comparable experience. It's this disgusting inequality, much more than the outlay on leg waxes and work outfits, that makes life more expensive for women than men.

'I worry more about money,' says Monkey, 'but I have more than ever. How does that work?' The same way it does when you worry about your flat being too small or your job being crappy. As we get closer to thirty our expectations become punitively high.

Relax – we can't all be millionaires. The fear that everyone is richer is a key feature of the quarterlife crisis. We must stop judging ourselves against false standards and comparing ourselves unfavourably with our peers. Instead, we should focus on ourselves as individuals and savour what we do have instead of lusting after what we don't. There's nothing wrong with living for the moment – just don't forget you have a future too.

By the way, you're probably thinking that, as a hugely successful writer, I'm very rich. I don't need to start using the financial management programme my friend gave me to tell you that I'm not. At the time of writing I'm sinking into overdraft (thank God it's still interest-free) and my savings – £10,000 – are all earmarked for the tax man. Let's not talk about my credit cards (note the plural). Feel better yet?

The small print

COMPLETION STATEMENT
PURCHASE: **One-bedroom flat, Brighton**

Purchase price	140,000.00
Add	
Tennant and Knight's costs plus VAT @ 17.5%	552.25
Stamp Duty	1,400.00
Land Registry fee	200.00

Bank telegraphic transfer fee at £16 plus VAT @ 17.5%	18.80
Local Authority Search	150.00
Drainage Enquiry	40.54
Environmental Search	29.38
Land Charges Search	2.00
Land Registry Search	4.00
Landlord's Notice of Transfer and Charge	35.25
Indemnity Insurance – BR approval	44.00
Stamp Duty Declaration of Trust	5.00
	142,481.22
Less	
Mortgage advance	98,970.00
	43,511.22
Deposit	14,000.00
Less	
On account of costs	250.00
Total required to complete purchase	29,261.22

Why life is expensive: top ten unexpected costs

1. Work

Who knew it cost so much just to haul yourself into an office and be miserable? Travel, clothes, professional memberships, endless birthdays and leaving dos.

2. Bills, bills and more bills

Worst offenders: water bills and council tax. If you're working you have to pay your dentist and your optician.

3. Getting around

Car insurance is punishing for under-twenty-fives. Then there's parking, MOT, petrol, cleaning . . . Is it better or cheaper than the tube? Kiss your Young Person's Railcard goodbye!

4. *Communicating*
Mobiles – texting hurts bank balances as well as fingers. Land line and Internet. Travel to see friends from uni now scattered all over the world.

5. *Student loans*
The interest is low but the payments start as soon as you hit £10,000 (that's just £833.33 a month). Beware.

6. *Overdrafts*
No longer a student? They might no longer be interest-free.

7. *Housing*
Renting or buying, it's all going to cost you – on average about a third of your wage. Stamp duty is the one most of us don't know about.

8. *Getting together*
Moving in, getting married or living apart but staying together – relationships cost. You can't get a good wedding cake for under £200.

9. *Splitting up*
Moving out or getting divorced – splitting up also costs. There are legal fees to pay, possessions to fight over and contracts (tenancies, marriage licenses and mortgages) to be broken.

10. *Pensions*
Should you get one or not? The sums we're expected to squirrel away seem ridiculous. (More on this in Chapter 12 where I reveal why you'll never retire.)

(11. Kids)
(Let's not go there – yet.)

11

Debt

Can't live with it, can't live without it

'This is the first generation to experience almost comprehen-
   sive debt. For most people in their twenties debt is now
   a fact of life.'
Carl Bayliss, National Debtline

'Debt is inevitable, partly reflecting the increased costs of
   further education.'
Wendy van den Hende, Personal Finance Education Group

Oxygen and carbon are the two elements essential for life
on planet earth. Without them, our world would be a
lump of cold rock spinning silently in space. There would be
no trees, animals or people. But on planet twentysomething
there is a third element without which life would be impossible: debt.

Judging from the record number of calls to the National
Debtline, red is the new black for twentysomethings. More and
more of us are reporting ever bigger debts. According to mortgage firm the Mortgage Lender, twentysomethings believe a debt
of £3,000 is totally acceptable. That's almost twice the debt
over-55s are willing to get into.

Credit records are becoming more like debt profiles. Here, for your delectation, is my current dp:

- Credit cards: about £5,000
- Store cards: £0 (I keep them because they're good for non-sale discounts)
- Student loans: now about £2,500 (I've paid half off)
- Overdraft: varies but I regularly hit the £1,000 limit

So what's that – about £9,000? Give or take £500. Of course, that doesn't count my £105,000 mortgage. Eagle-eyed readers will notice it's gone up – that's because I've had to borrow more to pay for a very swanky writer's shed. By the time you read this it could be even more (if I've swapped my crappy car for a new one) or less (if I've started selling my sperm on the Internet).

£9,000 seems like a lot to me, but according to the Consumer Credit Counselling Service, I am less in debt than most twentysomethings. In 2000 they estimated we each owed an average of £12,452. This rose 28 per cent to £15,891 in 2001. A year later it hit £22,520. I shouldn't take pleasure in the misery of others, but that makes me feel better. Admittedly these figures are for individuals contacting the CCCS and they are more likely to be more in debt than the rest of us, but whether we owe more or less, we can't imagine life without credit. And credit, unless you're very good or very rich or both, equals debt.

I'd rather chew both my little toes off than cut my credit cards up. Without them there would be no shopping, holidays or days/nights out. I swipe them more than my debit cards, so often that the signatures have almost worn away. I don't carry cash because I know I'll spend it, yet I'm happy to flash plastic. Each month I slip in and out of overdraft, the interest-free facility cushioning unexpected or ill-advised expenditure. Like most twentysomethings, I don't even count my student loans as debt – they're a low-interest investment in my future. It's my mortgage that's a pain in the arse.

Wages are higher than ever, so how come more of us are more in debt than ever? What, as our parents constantly ask, is going on with our finances?

It's very clear that life on the focaccia-line is far from cheap. Housing, as we've seen, is the biggest cost and one we shouldn't compromise on. We're getting into debt to finance a vaguely decent quality of life while struggling to build our careers and relationships and run a house. The more shameless among us have turned to cyberbegging.

$20,000 in debt and sinking, Karyn, a twentysomething television production assistant and self-confessed shopaholic from New York, built a web site begging for money.

When *www.savekaryn.com* launched on June 23, 2002 Karyn was $20,221.40 in debt. Twenty weeks later, on November 20, she was in credit again. She received a total of $13,323.08 from 'nice people'. But not everyone approved of her strategy, hence *www.dontsavekaryn.com*.

'There's no need to send me hate mail,' she says. 'I created a fun, campy web site that is light-hearted. I'm not the devil, nor am I the most horrible person to ever walk the earth. I am simply a girl who spent too much money buying clothes. If that's the worst thing I did, then that's not too bad.'

Save Karyn is the best-known cyberbegging site – it has inspired a book and there's even talk of a movie – but it's not the only one. There are now so many cyberbeggars that Yahoo has created a special search category for them. I love The Society To Prevent My Employment (*egomania.nu/causes/indexsoc.html*), run by Princess Natalie. Look out for *SaveDamian.co.uk*.

The reasons for getting into debt are as varied as the strategies for getting out. In this chapter we'll look at who owes what and why and show how obtaining credit can be as much of a problem as managing debt. We'll also explore our changing attitude to debt and consider responses to it, like budgeting (the very mention of the word makes me shudder).

When I interviewed him, Charlie, the project manager with the nice suits from the last chapter, had £500 in the bank, no savings and a mortgage of £165,000, having finally bought a modest house in London. By the time you read this he'll have chipped a bit off his mortgage, and his savings, decimated by the deposit, may have recovered a little. But his basic debt/asset ratio won't have changed.

'Your lifestyle expands to match your earnings,' he says. 'I earn about £40,000 but I have always lived exactly the same percentage beyond my means regardless of my income. I did it when I was a student, I do it now and I'm sure that I will continue to. Don't get me wrong, I would like to get out of debt. Like Mao, I have a five-year plan – mine is to settle down and live within my means. But it's more likely that I'll just get a better paid job.'

Are we all just living beyond our means? I certainly am, and so are most of the people I know. The thought of living within them is just grim. It's like the speed limit on the motorway – only the old and clinically cautious stick to 70 m.p.h. We know we shouldn't go faster but we do. Some go at 80 m.p.h., others cruise at 100 m.p.h. Usually it's okay – nobody gets caught or hurt – but sometimes there are consequences.

'I was declared bankrupt just after my twenty-third birthday,' says Nina, now 29 and solvent. Nice present.

'It was a combination of things. Growing up, I never had pocket money – cash was just given to me whenever I asked. In some ways, it never meant anything to me.' Although still in secondary school, Nina was given her own credit cards and bank account, with debit card, by her parents. 'I never checked the balances. My parents put more in when my account was low.'

Nina's supply of ready cash continued at university. 'My parents didn't allow me to work at first, so they gave me a lump sum of spending money each month. They paid my rent and all my bills.' In her second year Nina's parents let her get a part-time job. 'It was less than twenty hours a week, but that money was on top of what my parents gave me. I was doing quite well.' Certainly better than most of her slightly envious friends.

Nina got a good degree and everything looked peachy. With no debts to pay off there was no pressure to find work. She was considering travelling. 'Then, a month after I graduated, my father was laid off.' And the cash stopped coming. 'I was on my own.'

Like most of us, Nina struggled to get a job straightaway. 'I eventually took a couple of different jobs, but they weren't great. I wasn't thinking about my career at that point. For the first time in my life I had to pay all my own bills.'

After a few months Nina realised she couldn't keep track of her bills, let alone pay them all. 'I was working ninety hours a week, but there were still too many.'

That's when she started shopping. When she was most depressed, usually after another twelve-hour shift in one of several shitty jobs, she'd hit the mall, plastic in hand. 'I went on huge sprees and the bills mounted. I wasn't even buying things I needed – I was just shopping to make myself feel better. Things were incredibly tough. I didn't really know what to do. I couldn't ask my parents for help because they had their own problems. Rather than seeing a financial counsellor, I just pretended things were fine and kept spending.'

Nina started noticing purchases she couldn't account for. 'It wasn't just things I hadn't bought. There were items from shops in places I had never visited.' But in the full throes of a finan-cial meltdown, these blips were eclipsed by bigger concerns – like not getting evicted. Only when the credit card company served notice on her did the TV-movie-style truth transpire.

'My mother had opened a credit card account under my name, maxed it out and defaulted on the payments. She'd also been using my credit card. I had no idea.' Totally out of credit and betrayed by one of the two people that could save her, Nina filed for bankruptcy. 'It really was my only option but, to this day, I still regret it.'

Nina was given more than her peers in all respects but one: responsibility. 'I never really learned to budget. And I had already developed very bad habits. Money wasn't real to me.' What her parents called generosity I call financial abuse. The real damage was done long before Nina's mother made her bankrupt.

Nina's story is extraordinary, but the factors contributing to her debt spiral – redundancy, inability to budget, refusal to accept reality – and her reaction to it are all too ordinary.

'I felt helpless and hopeless and alone. I was too embarrassed to tell anyone.' Nina wouldn't seek help because she was mortified at losing 'little rich girl' status. 'Previously I could have everything and anything I wanted, then suddenly I was poor. It was awful. I couldn't bear it.'

On top of feeling poor, Nina felt unloved, not only because her mother had betrayed her but because she was raised to associate money with affection and approval. 'My parents were not warm, cuddly people but they gave me plenty of things. Early in my life I started associating money with personal worth.' That was all right for her when she was rich (though bad for all the nice, but poor, people she snubbed). 'I hate to say this, but when I met someone I judged them by their bank balance or the economic status of their family.' Suddenly poor, Nina suffered the double whammy of loss of status and realising she'd been a real rich bitch.

'I am ashamed of how I was. I now realize that the money a person has, or doesn't have, tells me absolutely nothing about who or what that person is.'

Nina is right to blame her parents for their failure to attach responsibility to the resources they rained upon her.

'I just never understood what it takes to pay regular bills. I did not know (or want to know) how to become financially responsible. I had to learn a really hard lesson.'

Despite the fact that her mother helped force her into bankruptcy, Nina retains the strongest criticism for herself.

'I deserved it. It all boils down to one thing – I was stupid, stupid, stupid. I should have known better. I should have sought help before things got as bad as they did.' But she didn't. 'I just buried my head in the sand and hoped it would all go away.' But it didn't. It never does.

So, how much debt do you think Nina was in? Four, five, six figures? 'Actually I only owed £10,000.' That's just £1,000 more than I owe now. But Nina's salary was only £15,000, even though she was working 2.5 jobs. 'It wasn't a lot, but I just couldn't make the repayments.' And she couldn't, or wouldn't, curtail her lifestyle. That's when good debts become bad.

'The worst part of being bankrupt is the stigma. The world treats you like a pariah. My life was over for about five or six years. I couldn't get a credit card or anything.' Her father had to act as guarantor when she bought a car. 'Nobody trusted me. I felt like a loser.'

Six years on, Nina has repaid the debts that bankrupted her. She is fully functioning financially. Not only does she know her means, she stays within them, unlike me and Charlie and most other twentysomethings.

'Sad to say, bankruptcy was likely the best thing that happened to me. I truly learned the value of money. And I now know I don't need money to make me feel good. I'm happy as long as I can pay my bills and do a few fun things for myself.' She even has credit cards again. Isn't this a little like an alcoholic having a minibar? 'No. I keep them at home so I'm not tempted – they are for absolute emergencies only.'

Here are some of Nina's tips for debt management.

The Seven Debtly Sins and how to avoid them

We're all guilty of at least one of these. Personally, I've done 1, 3 and 7.

1. Going boozing with flexible friends
Taking your cards to the pub and putting them behind the bar is the worst thing you can do. Take cash instead.

2. Leaving on a debt plane
If you're going travelling, save as much as possible before you go and appoint someone to keep your accounts in order while you're away. Use a debit card while you're away and take a credit card for emergencies. Insure everything.

3. Taking shit from your bank
Your bank needs you! Challenge them to meet deals – mortgages, overdrafts, whatever – you read about and threaten to switch if they won't. It's really easy to move money around, so don't be deterred by paperwork.
N.B. Consolidating. Lots of companies offer to bundle all your debts into one payment. This might seem easier but it could very well be more expensive and could put your home in danger – get help checking it out.

4. Debt-nial
Don't pretend it isn't happening. Seek advice from any of the people listed below in 'Never Pay for Debt Advice' (p. 197). Talk to your friends, parents, anyone – don't be embarrassed.

5. Cover me!
Lots of companies offer cover if you lose your cards. If you go for this, insure them centrally with one policy – don't duplicate expensive insurance. Make sure, for instance, that you aren't already covered by your home insurance. Also, consider how you'd pay debts if you lost your job (insurance is rarely any good for self-employed people).

6. Neglecting key costs

How much do you need to stay alive? Take the Reality Cheque at the end of this chapter to find out. Prioritise your key costs and make sure you can always meet them.

7. Favouring good over bad

Student loans are low interest and therefore should be at the bottom of your list – they're good debts. Credit cards should be at the top – they're bad debts. Make sure your key costs are taken care of, then pay your bad debts first.

Despite everything, Nina still gets into debt, only now she pays them off in full every month. She admits she can't live without credit, 'but I now know how much debt is reasonable and how much debt is dangerous. My life is now as expensive as I want it to be.'

Had Nina owned her home it would have been repossessed. Thankfully, bankruptcies and repossessions are at record lows. During the first six months of 2002, 6,860 homes were repossessed compared with 16,980 after the first six months of 1997, according to government figures. This is mainly because interest rates are lower than they have been for fifty years, which is also why home owners are going crazy with mortgage equity withdrawal. But when rates start to rise, debt becomes less affordable and things get tough – especially for twentysomethings struggling to get started.

I am not setting myself up as some sort of financial guru – I have tried and failed to budget. Knowing exactly how much I shouldn't be spending just made me feel worse. But I do have financial priorities – setting aside enough for the tax man and making sure I can pay my mortgage. I live on what's left over and go overdrawn if I need to. I know things are bad when I'm getting cash advances on my credit card. Budgeting is like exercise: I know it's good for me and I know I should do it, but somehow I can't. (I really hope my accountant isn't reading this.)

Most of us have tried budgeting at some point – usually the first week at university. Most give up by the second term. But not all.

Camilla, 23, is a committed budgeter, the sort of girl Gordon Brown would be proud of. 'I've always done it,' she says. As a child she saved a proportion of her pocket money. 'And when I was fifteen I had enough to buy half of my horse.' Her parents bought the other half to avoid Damien Hirst-style antics at the Pony Club.

'It's how I was raised. I didn't think there was anything odd about it until I got to university and realised most people just don't bother. I saw friends getting into terrible problems. It wasn't so much that they didn't control their spending, they just didn't consider how they were going to pay it all off.'

Camilla spent Sunday evenings revising her budget. 'I reduced my party money for two terms in my second year so I could go travelling that summer.' She still spends one evening a week balancing her cheque book and keeping a tally of her financial comings and goings. While you're doing your nails or catching up on TV, she's totting up receipts.

Although Camilla budgets, she's far from being a money-obsessed freak. 'I do it so I don't have to think about money. I talk about money far less than my friends. I suppose that's because I've got everything under control. I do get teased a bit for it, but to be honest I think a lot of people are jealous because they couldn't do it themselves. It's scary when you start, but once you've got a system going it's easy.' That's exactly what the well-meaning friend who bought me that scary money management programme said!

At university, even Camilla's best friend mocked her prudence. But not for long.

'She lost her part-time job in the final year. She was gutted and penniless – no savings, nothing. And her parents couldn't help. It looked like she might have to take a year out and save up to come back. I knew she probably wouldn't come back if she left, so I loaned her two-thirds of my emergency fund.' That saw her through the next three months. 'She got a job after graduation and paid me back straightaway. Now she's budgeting too!'

Camilla did go overdrawn in her final year – proof that she's human – but she managed to get a nice interest-free deal that the bank has since extended. 'So I don't go into debt while I'm getting my career started.'

Sarah, 25, is another budgeter. 'I do all my banking online so I know exactly what's where. I keep all my receipts and type them into a spreadsheet and put in my salary information. It's not very complicated, but it predicts what goes in and out each month so I know what I've got to play with.'

At the start of each month, 15 per cent of her salary goes into an easy-access savings account 'in case I need to run away'. Unlike Camilla, Sarah regularly goes over-budget. 'My overdraft is for big nights out. It's too easy to spend when you're drunk, I don't think bars should be allowed to do cash back. I'm never very much in debt – say £300. If I wanted to clear it I'd just do an extra special budgeting drive for a month.'

Budgeting is one response to debt. Nina's shopping-fuelled denial fest is another. Clear financial limits don't constrain Camilla. On the contrary, they free her from worry. Sarah keeps the books (she just doesn't bother balancing them). And I am living proof that, providing you keep key expenses under control and your bank manager sweet, you can live without knowing exactly how much you do or don't have.

As credit replaces cash, we've become fascinated by how much people owe. We even boast about our debts – 'I owe more than you'. There's a perverse glamour in Elton John's enormous flower bill (£293,000 on flowers in twenty months) or Posh's hair extension expenditure (she pays £500 every six weeks to keep her extensions lustrous). Conspicuous consumption is okay if you're a celebrity – you can pay it off – but look what happened to Nina. Nonetheless, spending is much more interesting than saving (more on that in the next chapter).

For most of us, debt, or at least a big chunk of it, is a hang-over from our student days. How mundane.

When Susannah, 28, a contestant in TV's *Survivor*, was asked what she would do if she won the £1 million prize, she said she'd pay off her student debts. Mercifully, I got through the system before fees of any kind were introduced. The prospect of top-up fees of up to £15,000 per year for the Russell Group universities, like Oxbridge, would certainly put me off studying now. Again, our parents, for whom education was as free as the air they filled with psychedelic music and patchouli fumes, got it good.

'When you get your first job it's easy to lose perspective and think you're loaded,' says Kate, 27, a 'new media whore'. 'You're not. It's just the difference between no cash and a little. When you see a salary advertised it looks like lots, but you have to think about tax and pensions, healthcare schemes and the long queue of people waiting to take your money off you.' Thanks for that reminder.

But it's true. No sooner do you start earning than *bang*, the student loans company demands the blood from your veins and your bank manager writes politely requesting the marrow from your bones. The sense of financial euphoria experienced upon receiving your first pay-cheque is short lived. So we get credit cards to soothe the pain and make it all better.

'All I can say is absolutely under no circumstances get credit cards, they are the devil's playthings and will get you into real shit,' says Kate, who has a Visa card. 'I only have one so I can buy stuff online! And I always pay it off straightaway.' Kate actually earned interest on her bonus introductory fee.

These days it seems hard *not* to get a credit card. In 1993, US credit companies like Capital One landed on our fair shores promising low-cost credit for all. To make this dream/nightmare a reality, they brought with them new credit-scoring techniques. Previously unsophisticated, these tests now give plastic to people who may have defaulted on past debts or had county court judgments. Debt for the masses – hurrah! But, crucially, these credit cards are secured – which means you could lose your house if you can't pay up.

Few twentysomethings have fabulous credit records, especially in our early twenties. We haven't been alive long enough to amass a lengthy credit history – how many sofas did you buy at twenty-one? If you're living at home, you don't have a mortgage and the utilities are in your parents' names. If you're in halls you might as well not exist as far as most credit card companies are concerned. Twentysomethings with credit histories often have nasty glitches from living in student houses that have been blacklisted. The first thing on your file is information taken from the Electoral Roll. This will identify any addresses at which you've been registered. The debts, like the socks you find down the backs of radiators, might belong to a previous tenant, but as far as credit reference agencies are concerned, they're yours.

Jim, 22, has no plastic. But he'd like some. 'It's a pain in the arse – I have to use my Switch card but I don't always have enough money in the bank.' A trainee accountant, Jim knows everything there is to know about money. 'I get paid £12,500 – I'd earn more if I had a degree. I don't plan to spend a load, I just need some flexibility. And it's embarrassing. When I bought my stereo I had to put it on my flatmate's credit card and now I'm paying him back. He's all right about it, but I hate owing him money.'

Most of us need some form of credit to get through our early twenties. When we're getting started we're shelling it out far faster than we can rake it in. I lived on my overdraft while waiting for my first pay-cheque to clear and got a cash advance on my credit card for my rental deposit.

So why doesn't Jim just get some plastic? Especially now it's so easy.

'I can't. Basically, I grew up with my mum and, for one reason or another, she has a bad credit record. I only moved out of her house last year. When credit companies check you out they want to know your addresses for the last five years. I think that's why I get turned down every time.'

Although the number of people falling into credit difficulties has declined, nearly eight million people in the UK still find it difficult to get credit, according to Datamonitor. Like Jim, more than one in five UK adults are defined by banks as 'non-stan-dard'. This is because their income is either too small, not substantiated or too irregular for banks to take a risk. Self-employed people are typically 'non-standard'. This doesn't mean you won't get credit, it just means it's harder.

Jim can wait five years or he can get a copy of his credit record now and fix any errors (see 'The small print' at the end of this chapter to find out how).

Twentysomethings with plastic, and that seems to be most of us, are intent on spending. In June 2002, card issuer Morgan Stanley recorded yet another fall in the number of people planning to pay their cards off – from 61 per cent six months ago to 56 per cent. This lack of urgency could be because low interest rates mean credit is cheap, but the credit card rates are nowhere as low as the basic rate. Twentysomethings don't seem to care – just 38 per cent of us aimed to pay our bill off within three months. Of course, two-thirds of over-50s planned to clear their credit cards as soon as possible.

Our comparative unwillingness to pay debt off reveals the widening gulf between us and our parents. For them, debt is a terrible thing to be avoided at all costs. It's shameful, dangerous and unnecessary. Doubtless some twentysomethings feel that way too – Camilla does. Nobody likes debt. But for the vast majority of us, debt is a fact of life. Yes, we'd like to pay it off, but we won't if it means compromising our quality of life.

And why should we?

Despite what our parents and those who revel in a stern approach to personal finance say, debt is not intrinsically bad. It's only not being able to pay it off, as Nina couldn't, that fucks you up. Luckily, few of us are in her state or likely to be. So long as we differentiate between good and bad debts we shouldn't feel bad about being in the red. Debt is a fact of our lives and, for better or worse, desensitivity to debt is a defining characteristic of our generation. We should be honest with one another about how much we owe, and give ourselves some credit – but not too much.

The small print

Take a reality cheque

It's important to know just how expensive your life is. I'm not proposing you keep a tally of everything you spend – that would be ridiculous and scary. Instead, make a list of all your key costs. (Booze doesn't count.) Here are mine (per month):

Mortgage £580
Council Tax £50
Building Maintenance £40
Water £18
Gas £20
Electricity £35
TV £10
Telephone £80
Mobile approx £40
Internet £25

Money set aside for tax 20% of income
National Insurance payments £10
Food £250
Clothing £50
Student Loan payments £120
Minimum credit card payments £200
Work expenses (inc travel) £250
Car £150

Review this expenditure monthly.

So, I need to spend about £2,000 each month. That's without going out, buying birthday presents or doing anything fun. Clearly, that's not realistic. But I know how much I can survive on in the event of a catastrophe. I try to have £2,000 in an easy-access savings account so I know I can survive for one month should I not be able to work or need to take time out. I recommend you do the same.

Would you credit it?

Every time you apply for credit (a loan, mortgage or credit card) the lender checks your credit record with a credit reference agency. There are two agencies in the UK, Experian and Equifax (see below). Each holds slightly different information about you, so you should contact them both. It costs £2.

Don't suffer like Jim – find out what your credit record says about you. If you find mistakes, tell the agency. They will take it up with whoever gave them the information. And hopefully you'll be sorted! As Jim's credit-unworthy family are the problem, he can ask for a Notice of Disassociation separating his credit information from theirs.

Easy ways to keep your credit record blemish free:

- Ensure you are on the Electoral Register (check by contacting your local authority). Lenders need confirmation that you live at the address on your credit application.
- If you miss credit repayments, try to make them up quickly. Long-term non-payment goes on your record and stays there for six years.
- Don't make too many credit applications in a short space of time – it suggests you're overstretching yourself or being repeatedly turned down.

Experian Ltd Consumer Help Service, PO Box 8000, Nottingham NG1 5GX. Go to *www.experian.co.uk* or call 0870 241 6212. Experian also run the Unclaimed Assets Register – for £18 they will tell you what happened to that forgotten savings account (I checked, but sadly I didn't have one.)

Equifax plc, Dept 1E, PO Box 3001, Glasgow G81 2DT. You can call them on 0990 143700 or go to *www.equifax.co.uk*.

Never pay for debt advice!

There are lots of approved agencies who will help you for *free*.

The Consumer Credit Counselling Service helpline is open 8 a.m. to 8 p.m., Monday to Friday, on 0800 138 1111, or go to *www.cccs.co.uk*. If you want to talk face to face, visit one of the CCCS debt counselling centres.

CCCS can help you set up a debt management plan. A DMP is an arrangement whereby CCCS help you reschedule debt repayments with creditors at a level you can afford. You make a monthly payment to CCCS and they pay the agreed amount to your creditors. CCCS can help renegotiate payments if your circumstances change.

Other places to get help:

- Citizens Advice Bureaux: visit *www.citizensadvice.org.uk*
- National Debtline: 0808 808 4000 or visit *www.national debtline.co.uk*
- The Money Advice Association (England and Wales): 01476 594 970, or visit *www.m-a-a.org.uk*
- The Money Advice Association (Scotland): 0141 572 0237, or visit *www.moneyadvicescotland.org.uk*

12

We're All Downshifters Now

Why you'll never retire

'I'll never stop working.'
Stephen, 29, lecturer

'I have to admit, I'm relying on bagging a rich husband.'
Sacha, 27, photographer's assistant

According to the TV advert I just saw, I should start a pension right now. If I don't sign on the dotted line straightaway, I'll spend my retirement huddled around the single-bar electric fire that heats and lights my bedsit. I'll fight stray dogs for scraps from bins. Grown adults will faint at the sight, and smell, of me. And all because I didn't start a pension the second I graduated.

Bollocks.

For a start, if I am impoverished in my dotage I won't be on my own. According to a report by Egg, at least one in seven twentysomethings are set to 'jeopardise their retirement'. And how are we doing this? 'By postponing starting a pension and diverting all their spare cash into saving for a deposit.' Oh, how reckless we are, buying homes to provide shelter in the here and now instead of planning for still distant futures.

The scare tactics of the insurance and pensions industry are nothing new. It's their job to put the existential frighteners on us – the freshness of youth is soon replaced by the pallor of death, blah, blah, blah. They did it to our parents and they'll do it to our children, if we can be bothered to have any. Death – or more accurately, the fear of it – has always been a growth industry. What's really changing is our attitude towards retirement.

'I would rather invest in property than a pension as it is more likely to safeguard my future than some cowboy investment plan,' says Katharine, the 28-year-old would-be home owner we met in Chapter 7.

I think just the same thing: my four walls are my pension. I've seen the ads – I know I can continue living at home spending equity until I die. Okay, if I have kids they won't be left with much, but hey, that's their problem. Property is tangible – even if house prices crash we're still left with a place to live. And we know that prices will eventually recover. Whereas pensions, although they're subject to the same market forces, seem risky. We know all too well that the value of investments can go down as well as up. Equitable Life, Enron and all those other nasty number-crunching scandals have left us feeling financially fragile. Perhaps that's why we're more into flats and houses than stocks and shares.

Life is expensive (and it's not getting cheaper). We're all in debt (and falling deeper), so what's the point in saving? More to the point, who the fuck has cash to save? It seems we'll never be able to afford to retire. In this chapter we'll debate the whole pensions versus property issue – does it have to be one or the other? We'll reveal why many twentysomethings will never really retire and help you decide if downshifting is right for you.

It's tempting to say we're the 'live now, pay later' generation, but we're not. Yes, we're in debt, but we have to deal with it each and every month. We're already paying higher taxes to take care of parents and grandparents who are living longer than they probably should. Like the tights we'll all be wearing sooner or later, the state is straining to support us. Retirement homes are filling up while classrooms empty. It's a simple equation: there are more and more older people and fewer younger people to support them. According to government figures, this 'support ratio' – the number of workers to pensioners – is expected to fall from 3:4 today to 2:4 in 2041. In 1900 it was 14:4.

'I have no faith in the government pension being anything more than the cost of a trip to a futuristic suicide-centre in the year 2020,' says Stephen, 29, a university lecturer (philosophy, seeing as you asked). 'I think we have to be responsible for ourselves. It's not selfish, it's just realistic.'

Stephen owns two properties and rents one to students. He also has a private pension. 'I started paying into a plan as soon as I could afford to.' Why, especially as he already has a nice property nest egg? 'I know I can't depend on the government and I don't want to be solely reliant on the housing market or the stock market. This way I spread the risk.'

The government is currently trying to raise the retirement age to seventy. This is great news for those who want to work longer, and it should help combat ageism in the workplace. As with the current cut-off, seventy won't be compulsory – it'll still be up to employers to decide how long we can work. This fairly obvious way of boosting the Treasury's coffers means our generation will be kept on the work treadmill.

'I believe we should have a state pension, I just don't think there will be one, or much of one, by the time I retire,' says Stephen. 'Concepts of retirement are already changing radically.'

In Chapter 6 we met many twentysomethings successfully managing different workstyles. We're job-sharing, running businesses and employing ourselves like never before, and those of us who remain in full-time work for a single employer are unrecognisable – we're telecommuting, wireless intrapreneurs. We're also job-hoppers, with an average five job changes per career and three career changes per working life (expect both figures to rocket).

The next generation will benefit from our pioneering moves. Meanwhile, we're suffering a gross mismatch – we're being forced to buy conventional retirement products no longer appropriate for our increasingly unconventional workstyles. We don't want carriage clocks.

The Dilbertian parody our parents played out is now just one of many different workstyles, albeit still culturally dominant. There are still plenty of pod workers, especially in low-paid service industry jobs and the manufacturing sector (yes, we do still make things). But few of us aspire to this. The way we work directly affects the way we earn. This, in turn, affects when and how we will 'retire'.

'My home is my workplace,' says Liza, the Brighton-based clothing designer with the office under her bed. 'I bought my flat to give me more security personally, but also because I wanted a base for my business.'

When Liza left her full-time job in corporate web design she lost her occupational pension, not that she had much of one anyway. 'It didn't seem worthwhile or important. I transferred the contributions to another pension which I put a bit into every month.'

How, with a mortgage and a fairly erratic income, can she afford regular pension payments?

'It's only £40 a month. I'm never going to miss that. And it comes out on a direct debit so I don't have to make payments or anything. It's easy.'

Although she has a pension, Liza, like Stephen, isn't sure what she'll get from it. 'My parents forced me to keep it, but they've had lots of problem with theirs. It's basically a gamble. The big funds want to make profits from me not for me. I also have an ethical issue because they invest in nasty companies.' There are, of course, green pension products available, but these have higher costs attached; a conscience is an expensive business.

Liza's biggest investment is her flat. It's her workplace, pension and personal space all in one. 'I plan to continue working from home. It has its problems, I know, but it's getting a lot easier. In twenty years I'll be an expert!'

She knows property prices can't continue rising. 'But I'm not stressed about it. I'm here for the long term. I just hope they're high when I start working less.' Her flat enables her workstyle – without it she'd have to hire studio space or work in-house for an employer. 'Right now, I can't imagine working any other way.'

So what will Liza's £40 a month buy when she hits pension age?

Not much. I hate doing this, but it's time for a quick history lesson.

Final salary schemes offer a guaranteed income based on length of service. These are what our parents got. You can still get them – John Lewis has one of the UK's best schemes – but almost all employers now offer money-purchase schemes. This is where you set aside some of your salary into a fund managed by your employer or someone appointed by them. How much you get depends on (a) the amount you put in (b) how much your employer contributes (c) what the fund invests in and (d) whether or not your boss embezzles everything.

Liza's parents experienced a problem caused by an overreliance on overvalued equities. When the FTSE crashed from its peak of 7000 in 1999, thousands of people like them lost millions of pounds. Partly in response, the government created a minimum income guarantee whereby they top up private pensions to an agreed level, currently £102.10 a week for a single person or £155.80 a week for a couple. Hardly lavish.

History lesson over. So what does this mean for Liza?

She's done well to start so young – as the scary ads remind us, the sooner you start the better. But she isn't contributing enough. She can't afford to retire at sixty-five, not in any conventional sense. The government's plans confirm our fear that we'll have to work for longer than our parents. Although deprived of the chance to spend her twilight years caravanning around Wales, Liza will also be earning for longer. So will she be richer when she's older?

Only if she pops every spare penny (and a few that aren't) in her pension piggy.

My financial adviser suggested the following stepped payment plan: £200 a month by twenty-eight, £500 by thirty-five, £750 by forty, and £1,250 by fifty. Needless to say, I laughed the mad laugh of a man being told the guillotine will tickle just a bit. Assuming average annual growth of 7 per cent (ambitious, considering the stock market now), this would give me a fund of £592,000 at sixty. That's an annual pension of £38,477 (£21,000 in today's money). He scared me so much I bought a flat.

Liza's £40 a month won't cover the cost of her false teeth. Stephen is a little better off – he pays £150 a month – but he has no plans to increase his contributions: 'I'd rather pay more off my mortgage.'

The worst is yet to come. Suppose you won £1 million tomorrow. You'd be sorted for life, right?

Wrong.

If you lived for another sixty years – and most of us will – and shoved that cash in a 4 per cent best-buy savings account, you'd have £40,000 a year to live on. But thanks to inflation, that's not the chunk it seems. Over time, your pound (or euro) will buy considerably less. If inflation stays at 2 per cent, your £1m will erode slowly. But if it rises to 4 per cent, your £1m will eventually be worth just £200,000. It's hardly worth buying a lottery ticket.

Despite its ups and downs, the stock market is widely predicted to grow at its average rate of 12 per cent over the next forty years. So if you put £10,000 in the market now, you'll have a fund of more than £100,000 in thirty years. Nice, but who has £10,000 kicking around?

Even for job-hoppers it seems final salary pensions remain the best option. So, if your employer runs such a scheme, join *now*. Saying no would be like turning down part of your salary.

But what if, like Liza, you don't have an employer? Or, like me, you have more than one? Or, like Stephen, your employer no longer offers a final salary pension?

Pile into property. But we're hedging our bets there, too.

'I only pay the interest on my mortgage,' says Max, 28, a soon-to-be GP. Fine, loads of people do that; but Max is one of a growing number of twentysomethings who, to the horror of bank managers and parents, isn't saving cash for the capital.

'I pay out £200 a month as opposed to £800 or something like that. That leaves lots to play with.' And play he does. 'I've been on four holidays this year and I'm planning another. I don't let my mortgage control my life.'

Although he earns around £40,000, Max is in debt. 'I put everything into the deposit.' Which meant living on credit cards and pasta for three months. 'Things are settling down now, though.'

But what happens when the bank comes for its cash?

'Twenty-five years is a long time. I'll buy and sell several times before that happens and I'll use the extra equity to pay some of the debt off each time. I'll make a profit.'

Max is confident about his plan. So why does it make me, Mr Repayment Mortgage, nervous?

'I'll still be okay, even if prices don't rise like they have.' Unlike most of us, Max has a big fat occupational pension to fall back on. 'But that's for me to live on, I won't use it to pay my mortgage off.'

Nicola is another interest-only gambler. 'I am the first to admit I don't have a plan,' she says. Currently jobless, she returned from travelling with a guy she met backpacking. They moved in together. It didn't last. 'So my mum gave me a deposit and I bought this place.' She sleeps in her living room and rents the other two bedrooms out. 'Mum would freak if she knew, but I need the money.'

Isn't she worried about paying her mortgage off?

'No, I've enough on my plate working out what to do with my life. I'm not sure I want to live here. I might move out and let the whole place or sell it. George W. Bush could blow the whole fucking world up tomorrow, so I'm not wasting my energy worrying about a mortgage.'

Fair enough.

Providing the world remains intact, Nicola can expect a handsome inheritance. 'I reckon mum's worth about a million,' she says, rather coolly. That's more than enough to clear her mortgage and debts from travelling and studying. She might have an exceptionally wealthy mother, but Nicola's sense of entitlement is not unusual. We all expect a little something from our parents. I do – although all I'll get from them is a strong stomach and a good head of hair.

Research from Marks & Spencer Financial Services claims that two-thirds of twentysomethings expect cash from beyond the grave to fill their retirement shortfall. No surprise there. But there's more, sadly. Inheritances are shrinking because (a) our stupid parents insist on getting divorced, (b) they're spending it all now – especially the equity, and (c) they're living too bloody long. All of which means we could be forced to work until our debts, and possibly even theirs, are cleared. I'm just glad debtors can get buried in normal graveyards these days.

Max plans to stop working at sixty. His pension – not his parents – and his property will provide for him. 'Medicine is more of a life than a job. I'll have earned my retirement.'

But for Liza, Stephen and me, the old 'work-save-retire' routine isn't working. Liza knows she'll still be designing clothes in her sixties. 'I want to stay creative but I know I'll need the money too because I'll stop working when I have kids.'

Stephen isn't planning a family but sees no reason to retire when his employer says so. 'I'd like to get paid to pursue a passion.' Even with two properties and a pension he doesn't think he'll be able to afford to stop working. 'I don't want my standard of living to fall. And who knows what illnesses I might get and what state the NHS might be in by then?'

Working for longer but steadily doing less and spending less is fast overtaking the traditional retirement concept. It's called downshifting.

Downshifting is about simplifying your life, identifying what you really want to achieve and changing your workstyle. For many, it's a response to redundancy or similar betrayal by an employer who expects 110 per cent from you but isn't prepared to give anything in return. But increasingly, downshifting is an allergic reaction to the increasing stress of everyday life. We're all too busy dealing with an ever-increasing flow of information from endlessly proliferating platforms – phones, mobiles, PDAs, digital TVs. We're weary of choice, burnt-out by options. I am no Luddite – I couldn't live without my online diary – but technology complicates as it simplifies, stresses as it soothes.

According to Datamonitor, 1.7 million of us downshifted in 1997. Last year that figure soared to 2.6 million. It's expected to reach 3.7 million by 2007. It's not surprising considering the average 'lunch hour' in British offices is now twenty-seven minutes. Half of us are too frightened to take our full holiday entitlement, and, at forty-eight hours a week, we work the longest hours in Europe. You can downshift at any age, but twentysomethings seem especially attracted to a non-9–5 life.

I downshifted after being made redundant for the third time in 1999. I used my pay-off to fund a workstyle change and go freelance. That money was vital when work was stuttering in – it covered the bills and gave me breathing time. I still make less than I did, but I'm better off in other ways: no more four-hour commute, no more office politics, no more early starts. I have time for my friends, energy for my partner and space to relax. It's a trade-off I'm happy to make. But it will impact my so-called retirement.

Dan, 27, and his wife Tara, 28, sold their two-bedroom flat in Stoke Newington for £280,000 at the end of 2002. They made £90,000. 'We knew the housing market wasn't going to hold up,' says Dan. 'It seemed like now or never.'

They took the equity and planned to run. But where? 'We just knew we couldn't stay in London,' says Tara. It wasn't about making money. 'It was about making a change.'

'I only planned to do the London thing for a year,' says Dan who moved south from Sheffield four years ago. Until he met and married Tara. 'We didn't plan to end up there, it just happened.'

So many twentysomethings say exactly that. One minute you're twenty-two and starting out, the next you're twenty-nine and wondering where your twenties went.

'As soon as we decided we both wanted a change, we sold the flat,' says Tara. 'It was important to get money in our pockets before making plans because the sale could easily have fallen through.'

While they were thinking about what to do next they took a holiday in Scotland – and found their future.

'I'd never been before,' says Tara. They stopped in Callander, a pretty little town on Loch Lomond. 'I couldn't believe how beautiful it was.' Dan was also smitten. 'It has such a great feel – it's small but not scary and Glasgow is close by.'

They stayed in a B&B and started house-hunting. 'We were shocked at what we could afford,' says Tara. Their small two-bedroom flat in London morphed into a microcastle with five bedrooms and walls thick enough to withstand midges, cannon-fire and Scottish weather. But it needs work – Dan's been on a DIY crash course.

'We'll have enough space to start a family when the house is finished,' says Dan. 'It feels safer and cleaner here. Even though we're English, the people are so much nicer.'

So what are they doing for money?

Tara, an illustrator, has gone freelance. 'I took my favourite clients with me. Most of it can be done online and over the phone.' This brings in £1,500 a month. Dan isn't earning. 'I'm saving us money by doing a lot of the work on the house.' He earns interest on his savings. 'But not much.' And he's about to start a new career. 'I know it's a cliché, but I think I've got a book in me. I want to expose the whole London thing and make everyone there realise they're throwing their lives away.'

Supposing Dan never finishes his book (he's barely started it), he's still successfully changed his life for the better by down-shifting. As has Tara. 'I'm not as tired as I was, and Dan and I get on a lot better.' Things are great now. But what about when they have children? How will they afford the nappies, nannies and nervous breakdowns kids demand?

'Well, we won't need a nanny,' says Tara, 'because we're both working from home.' Good job too. A survey by *Nursery World* found that a live-out nanny in London can easily cost £1,500 a month (about £1,100 elsewhere). But even without a nanny, it costs about £2,500 to kit out a newborn – that's without the Tiffany teething ring sported by Baby Beckham.

Children are ferociously expensive but Dan and Tara aren't deterred.

'We can always take on more work or get help from our parents,' says Dan, 'but I don't think we'll need to. Life outside London is simpler and cheaper. We're not drinking cappuccinos all the time and shelling out £100 for dinners that aren't even all that special. If we make a family our priority, then it'll happen and it'll be okay.'

Patrick, 28, recently swapped his £100,000 banker's salary to earn £12,000 as a care assistant for children with special needs. Is he mad?

'No,' he says. 'I went to the City after graduating from Cambridge and, outwardly, I was doing really well.' Inwardly, he was stressed, tired and depressed. 'After work I flopped in front of the TV and that was it until work the next day. I had plenty of money but no time. I was too tired to do anything. My life wasn't what I imagined it would be.' Neither was his body. 'I put on weight because I didn't have time to cook healthy food or go to the gym.' Ah, man-tits – so late twentysomething.

Patrick tried to arrange a more flexible workstyle – as it was his legal right to do. 'My manager told me I'd be better off leaving if I wasn't committed.' He wasn't. So he left. And he is. Why become a carer?

'I wanted to do something worthwhile. This way I make an impact on someone's life that isn't measured by profit.'

And he has more time and energy. 'This job is hard, but I feel good when I get home – I'm not permanently exhausted.'

Money isn't an issue thanks to savings amassed while slaving in the City. 'I've bought about three years of freedom.' What happens when the money runs out? Patrick's lifestyle – nice car, smart flat – is not very voluntary sector. 'I won't be able to keep it up, but I don't want to. I'm not part of that world any more – it doesn't matter if I am not wearing a £1,000 suit.'

In a few years he probably couldn't get back into that world even if he wanted to. His contacts and industry knowledge will be out of date, as will his suits. 'But I can't imagine wanting my old life back, I'm over it.'

Downshifting isn't easy – you have to adjust to a new work-style and a more moderate lifestyle – but rejoining the rat race is all but impossible.

'I hated being a smaller fish in a smaller pond,' says Michelle, who gave up a career in law to run a boutique with her sister.

'Things were good for the first three months when we were finding premises and hiring staff.' But when the new, quieter rhythm got going Michelle fell asleep.

'I was bored shitless. I love my sister, don't get me wrong, but it was just me and her and the customers day in, day out. I felt like someone from a Victoria Wood sketch. It was surreal.'

This was in direct contrast to her life in Birmingham where it was all go. 'In the countryside I couldn't even get a signal on my mobile. I realised you can have too much peace and quiet.'

After six months she had to get back to the city.

'My sister understood, she saw it wasn't me. She was living with her husband so she didn't need to find a new place or anything. She got a manager in to replace me.'

Michelle broke the lease on the cottage she was renting. 'I never want to live in anything that was built more than a hundred years ago again. I don't know what I was thinking.' She'd rented her city-centre flat out, which meant staying with her parents till the tenants moved out. 'Six months of hell. I was desperate to get back into my own flat and have my things around me.'

She then tried to get her old job back. 'I called one of the partners. They didn't sound too surprised to hear from me, which bugged me; it's like they expected me to fail.' She was invited to interview. 'I was chatty with them because I thought it was just a formality, but they were stand-offish. It was awkward.' Michelle was rejected. 'I couldn't believe it. They said I'd broken their trust.'

She had her flat and her friends back but she didn't have a job. 'I interviewed at a firm I'd dealt with before, but they'd heard from my old boss and that was that. Everybody thought I was going to run off to the country again, even though I'd come back to the city.'

In the six months it took Michelle to find a job, her savings evaporated. 'I am back on track now. I tried downshifting, but it wasn't for me.' Had she sold her flat, Michelle would really have been in the shit. As it is, she was lucky.

Downshifting worked for me and Dan and Tara. But Michelle regretted it and, painfully, reversed her position. Should you downshift? Take my test on page 214 and find out.

Finishing this chapter I feel less worried about my financial future. Not because I've suddenly won the lottery (though we now know even that's no guarantee), but because I'm not panicking. I can't predict interest rates, property prices or stock prices any more than Gordon Brown can smile. So why bother trying?

Liza and I earn less than our peers but we're happier than many of them because we're doing what we want to do. We're lucky – we have dreams and the opportunity and confidence to chase them. I have my flat, my skills and my support network – friends, partner and family. I am starting to realise that *who* I have is almost more important than *what* I have. Dan and Tara chose one another over London; but they, like me, will never fully retire. 'There's no point retiring rich if you've worked so hard your whole life you've no one to share it with,' says Tara.

Everything else is a gamble, but you can be sure of one thing: you need people and a pension, whether your money is in property or stocks. I know I won't retire rich. I won't retire – I'll just keep downshifting until I'm underground in a cardboard coffin. But in the meantime I guarantee I'll have plenty of people happy to huddle around that electric fire with me. I might even stretch to two bars.

The small print

Three things my accountant always says:

1. Pay off – don't save up

Savings income is almost always dwarfed by credit rates; pay off bad debts first. Currently, a basic-rate taxpayer would have to find a savings account returning 38.37 per cent to make saving more worthwhile than paying off a debt on a store card charging 30.7 per cent.

2. ISA, ISA, ISA

These are a way of legally getting one over on the taxman. I put away my tax money in an ISA which means I actually make some money on my taxes – and I can't be taxed on it either. You might not think you earn enough for taxes to matter, but ask an Independent Financial Advisor – you'll probably be surprised. Which brings me to the third and final nugget of advice:

3. Always pay for advice

Advice is never free, and if it is it's because they want you to buy something from them (which probably isn't right for you).

Stuff about pensions

All money stuff is deathly boring. I'd rather spend money and have a good time in the here and now than save for an old age I may never reach. And I know I'm not alone in my irresponsibility. However, there comes a time when the future must be considered, and sooner is better for pensions.

You need independent advice, especially if your company has recently changed its policy on pensions. Go to *www.ifap.org.uk* and find someone who will look at your circumstances and help you make an informed choice. Explain your full situation and be honest about what you want to achieve – a small nest egg, a guaranteed weekly income, a vast fortune for your grandchildren to waste?

The government web site, *www.pensionguide.gov.uk*, provides a good overview of the whole situation, but they're not impartial (Gordon Brown wants you to save hard).

Talk to the pensions authority if you think your employer is spending your pension for you: *www.opra.gov.uk*.

Should you downshift?

If you answer yes to at least three of these questions you could safely consider going down a notch or two. But remember, it's a lot tougher getting back on the property ladder, shinnying up the greasy pole, *insert another cliché of your choice here*. If you answer mainly no, you should probably continue as you are – but remember, you can downshift at any time.

- I think I could live on less
- I have sufficient savings to live for three months without working
- I'd rather feel happy than important (whatever important means)
- Having a career isn't as important as having a life
- Risk doesn't scare me – it excites me!

The next step is to decide what you want to do – create a new career, start a family, build a house, go travelling, open a café . . .

These people can help you start a business:

The Prince's Trust, 0800 842 842, *www.princes-trust.org.uk*
Business Link, 0845 600 9 006, *www.businesslink.org*

relationships

get it together

13

Fuck 'The Waltons'

Redefine your family

*'I might as well be an orphan and they might as well be
   childless. I've got my mates.'*
Dan, 27, hasn't spoken to his parents for years

'I don't think I could cope without my mum.'
Louise, 26, speaks to her mother every single day

The day, dreamed of by me and dreaded by my mother, finally
dawned. It was time to go to university. Of course I hadn't
packed. But I was ready. I didn't want to take anything, apart
from some photos and my clothes. My parents, sodden with
sentimentality, somehow crammed the contents of my room into
the car. 'Don't forget home,' said Dad. It was the first time I'd
seen him cry. Next day I binned everything they'd forced me to
take and forgot my childhood home. I had a new home now,
and, although I didn't know it, the nucleus of a new family.

Wings, long-clipped by parents, are finally spread at university. For most of us it's our first taste of independence. We really
can do what we like, when we like, with whom we like. Hair
goes pink. Bits get pierced. Everything changes. I loved it. But
not everyone does.

Two friends I made in the frenzy of Fresher's Week didn't survive the first term. They rushed home every weekend and, after the holidays, they didn't come back. Here is the complete text of the Christmas card sent to me by one of them:

Dear Damian,

Thanks for the prez – it's great!

I feel bad about saying this after all our talks, which is why I am writing it down instead of phoning you (coward, I know). I am dropping out.

Please don't be angry with me. I will miss everybody. But it's not for me, you know that. My academic counsellor agrees.

I am not like you – I really miss my family! Especially my sister and my mum. I know I can talk to them on the phone but when they came to see me I wanted to go home with them. I can't handle three years away from them, especially as my sister is finally preggers (that's a secret). I know people will laugh at me but I don't care. I'll do my degree near home so I can live-in, it'll be cheaper too. And I'll come and see you – promise!!!

Love,

Amanda.

xxx

I never saw Amanda again. I don't know if she finished her degree or not. I received a similar card from another friend citing the same reason: family.

I didn't get it. Family was what drove me to go to university. All right, my parents loved me, but I didn't exactly have an easy so-called childhood. It seemed bizarre to me that, given the choice, Amanda wanted to spend some of the best years of her life with people she already knew everything about. I wanted the excitement of strangers. I wanted freedom. I wanted a new family.

That's not to say I ditched the family I grew up in. Well, not all of them anyway. I chose to stay in touch with my siblings, my parents, the odd aunt or uncle and one set of grandparents. As far as the rest were concerned – and, thanks to the miracle of Catholicism, there were lots of them – I couldn't care less. An accident of biology had brought us together that moving away would fix. Sounds harsh, I know. Of course, I didn't bargain on the whole emotional and physical distance thing – I'd never been far away enough to know you can still feel close whether you want to or not.

Leaving home – to go to university, start a career, pursue a partner or just get a life – is the catalyst for a change in the way you feel about your family and the way they feel about you. Amanda couldn't wait to get back to hers. I couldn't wait to get away from mine. But family was important for both of us. I was sick *of* home, but I wonder how many students there are who drop out every year because they are sick *for* home?

Love them or hate them, most of us have some kind of family and our relationship with them is one of the most enduring and important we'll ever have. In this chapter we'll chart how that relationship changes in our twenties. Does growing up mean growing apart? How can you be an adult when your parents still treat you like a child? For many twentysomethings, friends are the new family, so we'll look at families of choice – best friends, buddies, soulmates.

'I haven't spoken to my parents since my first year at university,' says Dan, 27. That's seven years of silence. 'I talk to my brother and we see each other, but that's it as far as family goes.'

What happened? Are Dan's parents evil? Is his family talk-show material?

'No, my brother still lives at home. It's just me they don't talk to. Basically, I didn't do as I was told. They wanted me to be a lawyer and I didn't.'

When the time came, Dan applied for law courses to please his parents. 'My dad actually checked my form to make sure I was doing what he wanted.' To be fair, Dan had never actually told his parents he didn't want to do law. 'I tried, but every time we talked about it they just went on about how it was right for me and how they were proud of me and all the rest of it.' It didn't help that his uncle is a barrister. 'I felt trapped. There was all this pressure.'

A model student, Dan got into Durham. But, without telling his parents, he switched his subject. 'Loads of people change their major. I tried law but I just couldn't get into it, it was so boring.' English Lit. appealed more.

'I was going to tell them I'd changed after the first term when I was sure I'd made the right decision. I knew something was wrong as soon as I got home. My mum picked me up from the station and I thought someone had died.' They drove home in silence. Dan's father was sitting at the dining table holding a letter from the university. 'It was a note from a tutor in the English department and my results.'

It didn't matter that Dan had done incredibly well. 'My father told me to switch back straightaway. I tried to calm him down and explain why I'd changed, but he wouldn't listen. I told him I was never going to do law. He said he wouldn't pay for an "artsy-fartsy" degree.'

Dan returned to halls of residence that night. His parents withdrew all funding. And he hasn't spoken to them since. 'They made it so hard for me. I had to work through every single holiday and I have really big debts now.' It wasn't just the money that stopped. Dan tried calling but they wouldn't speak to him. His letters were returned unopened. As a last ditch attempt at reconciliation, he invited his parents to watch him graduate. 'It took a lot for me to do that.' They sent the tickets back.

How does he feel now?

'I'm still angry. They cut me off because I wouldn't do as I was told. Now the shoe is on the other foot – if they contact me I'll ignore them. Why should I listen to them? I'm sick of them punishing me.'

Dan's little brother is now approaching university age.

'They're doing the same to him. It's like they haven't learned their lesson. I've told him I'll help him out if he wants to do something else. I won't see him go through what I did.' It's almost like Dan wants his brother to hurt his parents. 'Put it this way, I'm not bothered about what happens to them. My brother is more important to me than them.'

I don't know if Dan and his parents will make up. Neither seems willing and both seem childish to some extent – the parents more so, of course. Dan put himself through university, and he paid the price for that – emotionally and financially. 'I used to feel left out when other students got visits and stuff from their parents, but I got over it.' I'm not convinced he has. I think Dan might secretly love a visit from his parents – if only so he could slam the door on them.

'They don't have a role in my life any more,' he says.

'I don't think I could cope without my mum,' says Louise, 26. 'I can't bear the thought of anything happening to her. She's my life, you know?'

I do know. I also know that, as much as I love my mum, I can cope without her, though I wouldn't choose to. Like Dan, I put myself through university but, crucially, I did it with the emotional support of my parents. Louise's father died when she was ten, which explains why she feels so strongly about her mother.

'He'd had a massive stroke. I found him. We all thought he was upstairs reading, so we didn't bother him.' For years Louise was tortured by what-ifs. 'I know there was nothing anyone could have done, but I still wish I'd been with him.'

Louise's older sister had already moved out when her father died. 'She moved home after the funeral, but eventually she went back to her boyfriend. I saw how much it hurt Mum when she left.' She doesn't blame her sister. 'She didn't mean to hurt Mum, I don't even think she knows she did. She was just getting on with her life.' Like my ex-friend Amanda, Louise stayed at home while studying.

'I've got the rest of my life to move away, I don't need to do it now.' What about the phone, letters, email? 'We call and text but it's not the same. I want to go home at the end of every day.

'Mum and I grew very close after Dad died. I don't want her to be alone. And I don't want to be without her. I know it sounds sad, but she's my best friend.' So will she ever leave? 'I can go any time I want to – my mum would never stop me. If I find the right man or the right job I will go for it, but I want to stay close to home, no more than an hour away.'

They even holiday together. But, like all best friends, they argue. 'Of course we do. But we sort it out really quickly. If something happened and we'd had a row I'd never forgive myself.' The spectre of death forces this unnatural state of permanent cheer upon them. Louise is scared to say 'I hate you' in case they're the last words her mother hears. Would they have stayed so close for so long if Louise's father was still alive?

'I don't know. We've always been a close-knit family. I think that just made us much closer.' So would she have gone away to university? 'Maybe I would've if he was still alive, but I can't answer that question because he's dead. My sister went. I don't think they would have stopped me.'

Parents play a huge role in our lives, even, or especially, *in absentia*. Dan and Louise occupy opposite ends of the same spectrum, but despite their polar differences, each remains in thrall to their parents. Dan devotes as much energy to hating his father as Louise spends loving her mother. Both have very clear – and real – reasons for doing so, but neither is truly happy or, come to think of it, grown-up. They would both be better off if things were different – if Dan forgave his parents and they accepted his choices, and Louise started living for herself. Maybe that's asking too much, especially of Dan.

Dan was very resourceful in supporting himself. 'I started off as a barman and by the end of my degree I was part-time bar manager.' He got by financially, but how did he cope emotionally?

'Mates. There's nothing I wouldn't do for them,' he says. And he means it. 'They were there for me all the way. I remember feeling completely alone after my parents cut me off. I felt like an orphan. They didn't expect me back and we had a sort of surprise party. I didn't tell them what happened but I think they knew. I got bladdered.' Sometimes that's what friends are for.

Dan finally came clean when he had to find work. 'They wanted to know why I needed a job so I told them. I don't think they believed me at first. Honestly, I still couldn't take it in myself.' At that time, Dan didn't foresee the current complete lack of contact. 'Their reaction made me realise my parents had actually been quite extreme.' For real. Abusive, I'd say.

While trying to repair the relationship with his parents, Dan relied more and more on his friends for advice and support. 'We were all in halls together so we could sit up and talk.' Why didn't he get therapy? 'I've never had it and I'm never going to get it – I'm my own therapist and my mates are there to support me when it gets too much.'

Like when his parents refused to have him back in the holidays. 'I was gutted. That really was it for me. My own mum and dad didn't want me in the house I'd grown up in.' He was amazed, and embarrassed, when both his best friends offered him a room at their parental roosts. 'I felt like a bit of a charity case but, as they said, it suited them not to be stuck with their parents. I saved on rent and I was working, so it worked out well.' He spent one summer in a tent on a friend's back lawn 'because his mum didn't have enough room'.

Since graduating, Dan has returned the favour by putting his mates up at his flat in London. 'They're welcome to crash on my sofa any time. It gets a bit much after a while, but it's cool doing something for them for a change.'

Dan's friends are his family of choice – they give one another shelter, support and, although they wouldn't say as much, love. Why should such relationships be reserved exclusively for those related to us? Especially when, as in Dan's case, they don't deserve them.

I know my twenties would have been all but impossible without my fabulous family of choice.

As you know, I dropped out of university after my first year because I hated my degree. Where did I stay while I was working out what to do with my life? On my best friend's sofa. How did I live? On my best friend's salary. Who could I not have done it without? My best friend.

John and I were born within weeks of one another. We went to the same school, got into the same trouble and had the same issues. I went to university while he skipped education and got a job. I chose to live with him, rather than my mother, because I knew he wouldn't judge me. He supported me unconditionally. That's not to say my mother would have been a bitch, but I needed space and she couldn't give me that because, well, she's my mum. It's their job to fuss.

John didn't survive his quarterlife crisis. After several attempts he succeeded in killing himself aged twenty-three. Hanging. And when I got the call telling me I fell to the ground and passed out. The pain I felt was more than that of every 'family' loss combined. To me, he was more important than the family I was given. He was the family I chose. And the grief was all the greater.

I am not saying families of choice are perfect – they're not. John shouted at me every day for cluttering his immaculately tidy flat and I resented him for having a job, an income and a partner. We had to work at our relationship, especially when I went on to university (again) and he didn't (again).

The physical distance we achieve in our twenties from those we've grown up with – friends and family – gives us space to get perspective. (Helen, my therapist, once likened it to a Persian rug: up close it's just a load of swirls but, from a distance, you discern patterns. Of course, you might not like what you see. I didn't – that's why I started therapy.) A whole ocean, half a continent and a ten-hour flight from my family I realised I wasn't happy about a lot of the things that happened to me while I was growing up. I'm not going to get all *Angela's Ashes*, but it wasn't good. It was bad. I needed perspective to see that, and my family of choice to help me through it.

Ann is my big sister. She's thirty-five. We're not *actually* related. My older sister died when she was a baby (she'd be thirty now). Without meaning to, Ann filled a gap in my family. Living in the same halls of residence at the University of Texas, we saw one another every day. I made lots of friends there – hey, they're nice people – and I'm still in touch with a handful of the most delightful, but Ann's the only one I'd count as family. I am there for her and she is there for me, despite the distance between us.

At first, it wasn't easy keeping in touch. Letters took days to arrive and phone calls were costly. But cheap and easy technology – I don't know how I lived before instant messenger – means we now 'talk' every day. However, frequency of contact is not what makes someone a member of your family of choice; it's commitment, love and helping someone to be who they want to be – it's what Dan and his friends have.

'I couldn't care less about my parents,' says Dan. 'As far as I'm concerned they're dead.' But he'd do anything for his two best friends. 'And I know they'd do anything for me.'

Again, I'm not making a big judgement – your family of choice can be just as complicated and challenging as the family you were born with – but the point is, you aren't stuck with either. Just because you've been friends with someone since you were ten doesn't mean they're closer to you now than the colleague you see at work every day or the man next door. Similarly, our closest relatives – parents and siblings – aren't always those we're closest to. A good friend of mine speaks to his great aunt every day – far more often than he calls his father.

'I hated doing it,' says Laura. 'But it was over.'

That's the language of dumping, quitting and walking out. So which was it?

'We were "best friends" for as long as I can remember,' says Laura. 'We met in the first year at university and lived together until we graduated. After that I moved to London.' Then the problems started. 'She wanted to move into the flat I was sharing but there was no room. She asked me to move into another flat with her but I couldn't break my lease.'

Aisha, Laura's then best friend, was upset but she got her own place and everything seemed okay. 'We met up every Friday night for drinks. It was a laugh – we always had a good time.' But with different flatmates and different jobs, they had less and less in common. 'I realised that all we really talked about, apart from the other people in the bar, was the old times.'

Laura also noticed that Aisha was reluctant to meet her new friends. 'She's not shy. I couldn't think why she was being so weird.' Then, when she got a boyfriend and Aisha didn't, it became clear. 'She was jealous.'

'At uni we did everything together and saw one another every day. We were really close. When I only got a 2:2 she helped me with my appeal, and I went with her to her granny's funeral. We were like sisters.'

But away from the intensity of campus life, they had little in common. 'I realised that we were actually very different. And I didn't like how she was. I can't stand jealousy and insecurity. She expected me to jump when she called and do anything for her because she would do that for me.' Laura no longer needed, or wanted, that kind of relationship.

'I tried not calling or emailing, but she didn't get the message.' It was time for a carefrontation.

'We went out for a drink and I told her I didn't want to see her any more and it was horrible. I felt like a total bitch. But our friendship wasn't good for either of us. It was all about the past. It took me a long time to realise this – and she didn't see any of it. We were both crying.' In the end, Laura was brutal. 'I got up and left and I haven't seen her since.' Because Aisha pointedly didn't integrate with Laura's friends there have been no awkward moments. (We'll consider 'best friends' in more detail in the next chapter.)

Aisha and Laura grew apart, which is perfectly natural. But Aisha couldn't accept it, just as Dan's parents couldn't understand why he didn't want to be a lawyer any more. For them, growing up meant growing apart. Families can safely anchor us through our stormy twenties, but they can also drag us down. Families of choice can do just the same.

No matter how far you go from your family, they can always reach out and get you – phone, email or tendrils of guilt. Why haven't you called? We haven't seen you for years. They casually remind us that they're hurtling towards death so we feel even worse about not spending every day by their side, or at least by the phone waiting for them to call. Christmas becomes a hellish choice, especially if you have a partner. Which set of parents to offend? Five Christmases later and my mother has finally stopped begging me to come home. As much as I love her, I choose to be with my partner. If you're really assertive or good at thinking up big lies, you can get out of most family things, but not all. There are those occasions when we are forced to get close. Like funerals. Few of us get to thirty with a full set of grandparents. So far I've lost two, which, as Oscar Wilde would say, is careless. But our families grow, too – siblings and cousins reproduce.

There are weddings and christenings. Suddenly you get your own invitation (which means buying a separate gift). As your twenties roll on you get further from your family, but you never really get away. You might not want to.

Of course, we do reach out to our families, especially when we need money. Remember Katharine from Chapter 7 who went begging to Mummy and Daddy for a deposit so she could buy a house? Or Harriet from Chapter 2 who got a cash advance from the Banco de Mummy to go travelling?

But we have to accept that big cash gifts – even loans – come with expectations. They might be helping us on the road to greater independence, but, along the way, we have to take a detour down Kinder Street. Such transactions remind us that, however old we get, we're still their children. It would be easy to say they love this reminder and we hate it, but that's not quite true. For a start, plenty of parents who can afford to help their kids just don't. When your parents loan or give you money for a place, it comes with ties – you're going to have to send them pictures, show them around and put up with comments on your style. Giving them a stake in your home gives them the right to comment, and maybe even intervene, whether you like it or not. And not just on the decor – they might want to know who you share your new home with. Sadly, we can't have it all our own way (though there's no need to display the hideous house-warming gifts they give you).

'It drives me mad,' says Angela, 28. 'I couldn't have bought my house without money from my mum and dad, and I'm grateful.'

So what's the problem?

'My parents live in the country and I'm in town. They come to see me every Saturday before and after their shopping trip.' Often their dog comes along for the ride. 'I'm expected to look after it and take it for walks.' She just leaves it in the garden – no nasty accidents on her nice new carpets that way. 'I feel forced to see them and go through everything they've done and bought. It's so tedious.'

Her parents rarely clear off before 6 p.m. – if they do. 'If Dad's had a drink with lunch, he won't drive and Mum can't drive, so I'm stuck with them. At least they don't expect me to stay with them.' Angela's spare bedroom has been rechristened 'Mum's Room'. 'She even bought one of those little door plaques – she keeps asking why I haven't put it up.'

Angela has already put up with too much. The weekly visit is made worse by her mother's forensic approach to housework. 'She snoops everywhere and touches everything to make sure it's clean. She thinks I'm "filthy". Dad doesn't care – he looks after the garden, which I don't mind. But Mum does my head in.' Then there are the phone calls. 'I am seriously thinking about changing my number. I got an answerphone with caller display so I don't need to talk to them.' It's passive-aggressive, but it works.

'The worst thing is, they have keys.' Given for use in an emergency, Angela's parents clearly have multiple crises all the time. They've let themselves into her life. 'If I'm not in they just make themselves at home – in my home. I can't relax in my own space. I'm terrified that they'll come in and find me naked on the floor with my boyfriend.'

Angela's parents are having problems accepting their child has grown up. She isn't really helping matters, but she should be able to accept financial assistance while retaining emotional and social freedom. This is a trade-off we all have to consider. Perhaps if Angela had a loan, rather than a gift, her parents would hang around less? 'They'd probably visit more, to see how their investment is doing.'

You'll never have a greater opportunity to make friends than you will in your twenties – through university, work, sports, whatever. You have more disposable income (credit cards) and time (no babies yet) than you ever will have again. You're probably still pre-3 Ms: marriage, mortgage and monogamy. So make the best of it. Take the best of your family and dump the rest – they aren't worth having just because you share the same genes. Ditto for your friends – just because you share a lot of history. But be nice about it if you can – you could be the one getting dumped one day.

You can choose the best of the family you were given *and* have a completely new family of choice. Both require maintenance, but the support they can give through the toughest decade of your life is not to be underestimated. Nor is the grief. Start redefining them, if you haven't already. We don't watch *The Waltons*, we watch *Friends*. And doesn't it show: Good night, John Boy.

The small print

Ten must-have carefrontations for every twenty-something

1. *Approval*
It's no use screaming that you don't care what your best friend/parent/whoever thinks of your flat/job/partner if you actually *do*. Think about who you're living for – yourself or them? Approve of yourself.

2. *Independence*
You really can accept a loan or a gift without accepting the grief that goes along with it. Take what you want. If you can't do that, don't take anything at all.

3. *Don't cut your nose off to spite your face*
I'm very guilty of this. Basically, you have to make some concessions at some point – your twenties cannot be one big self-actualisation romp. Decide what's important – like getting your parents to accept your choice of job – and concede the rest.

4. *Grow up*
Moving back with your parents is not an excuse to become a

child again, tempting though this may be. Negotiate sensible boundaries. Maintain maturity in the face of all opposition – it will make the real world re-entry that bit easier.

5. You can wear what you like
You really, really can. Unbelievably, some people still get dressed up/down to go home.

6. You smoke/drink/generally misbehave
Oh yes you do. Respect your parents' wish not to do it in their home, but don't lie about it – be an out and proud whatever!

7. You have sex
Again, maybe not under their roof unless that's what does it for you. (Just put a towel down first and keep it quiet.)

8. You're financially irresponsible
Okay, maybe you're not, but your parents probably think you are. The world isn't the same as when they were our age, but it's not your job to make them realise this. If they can't accept the way you spend, just lie – it's probably easier. This may make getting a loan from them hard. See carefrontation #2.

9. Wedding bells are not ringing
Again, the world has changed. You're living in sin and they need to deal with it. If they want a big white wedding they can pay. You'll decide if and when you want to get married.

10. Tiny feet – I can't hear any, can you?
Your parents probably want to be grandparents. Well, they can want. Solutions: claim to be infertile, pay a sibling to get pregnant and have a baby. If your parents want you to procreate, they're going to have to pay. You'll make more of you at your own pace.

14

Insignificant Others

Juggling the most important people in your life

'People who need people,
Are the luckiest people in the world . . .'
From the song 'People' by Barbra Streisand

Clea, Alan, Rebecca and Louise meet every Friday night for drinks. Lots of drinks. The merry foursome bonded bumming round the slopes in France. They now manage to keep close while chasing success around London. I joined them for a boozy catch-up and took my tape recorder along for the ride. I got so drunk I lost my hat. This is what I heard.

Louise announced that she fancied Alan (he'd already guessed). Clea (nickname: the Virgin) confessed to masturbating at least once a week. Alan, sales manager, came out as a wannabe teacher. Then, very quietly, Rebecca said she'd had an abortion just a few weeks before. Clea started crying. Louise started shouting. And Alan looked lost. I fumbled for my hat.

Just another night out for a bunch of twentysomethings.

Clea, Alan, Rebecca and Louise aren't especially screwed up. Fancying your friends, a surprise sexual habit and a secret abortion are all par for the twentysomething course. They have jobs and plans to quit them. And flats they dream of buying. Right now, despite their eventful evening, their relationships with one another are the most stable and important they have. Obviously there are other people in their lives – colleagues, flatmates and partners – but they always come back to one another.

'My boyfriend gets a bit jealous of us all going out every week,' says Rebecca. He's had to learn his place – as just *one* of the most important people in her life.

'I love him but I love my friends too – in a different way, obviously. I neglected them at the start of this relationship so I'm lucky they're still there for me. But it's not easy balancing everybody. A lot of people expect a lot from me. Sometimes I feel pulled in different directions.'

As children we would die without our parents – it's then we need them most. As teens we consider dying just to spite them. In our twenties we lurch between extreme adulthood (running off to Thailand every five minutes) and extreme childhood (moving home to save money). The importance of your family, friends and partner (or need to have one, if you're single) varies with your needs. Different people are important at different times and in different ways. Your mother won't give you frank advice about your blow-job technique, but your best friend might. Actually, my mother might.

In your twenties the pressure to have a cast of successful friends, a supportive family and a stunning partner is huge. Like Rebecca, we have too many people competing for our attention. We get stressed trying to make time for everyone, including ourselves. And when it's hard to make other people hear us, we get depressed.

Today you really need a boozy lunch with your best friend. Tonight you want to snuggle up with your partner. Tomorrow you're going shopping with your mum. No one person – partner, friend or parent – is the most important in your life. This chapter is all about the numbers on your speed dial, the people you call when it all goes wrong and balancing your needs with theirs. Forget about insignificant others.

'It's all this "we" that really gets to me. I sometimes wonder where my friends have gone,' says Mary, 29.

Clea, Alan and Louise thought exactly the same thing when Rebecca started seeing her new boyfriend. 'Her phone was always engaged,' says Alan. 'And when you did get through she was always busy doing something with him – shagging probably,' says Clea. In the end, Louise insisted Rebecca ditch the boyfriend for a night out with her mates: 'I was blunt about it: we really missed her.'

'When Louise read the riot act I was a bit taken aback,' says Rebecca. 'I knew I'd been wrapped up in my boyfriend, but I didn't think they'd mind. You know what it's like when you meet someone new.' During their night out she realised how much she'd missed them. 'We had a great laugh and so much had gone on even though it had only been about a month since we'd met up.'

Rebecca is still learning to balance her friends and her partner. It's not something that comes naturally to any of us – we'd like to see everyone and do everything, but we can't. Our time, energy and emotional reserves are limited. There are only so many hours left when you eventually escape from work and, if you live in London, it takes ages to get anywhere. 'I'm usually too tired to get dolled up and go out,' says Mary.

'Keeping up with everyone is an effort,' says Rebecca. 'But it's worth it.'

Mary wishes her friends would try so hard. 'I just feel a bit lonely. I'm fed up doing everything on my own. I feel like they've forgotten me now they've got partners, and I envy their companionship. When they do crawl out of the bedroom they go out together and talk about coupley stuff.'

Living with the person or persons you have sex with is just not natural. We're one of the few animals to do so – the rest meet for as long as it takes to get pregnant then split, biological imperatives met. Not for us this speed dating *à la* Darwin. Whole pronouns, 'we' and 'our', have evolved to explain our obsessively 1-2-1 relationships. We simply can't live without one another: you + me = we. Anything else is second best: cod roe to caviar, Morgan to Gucci, Kylie to Madonna.

I try not to say we. I am one part of a we. But I am, first and foremost, me. I only say we if someone refers to my partner and me in that way. Failing that, it's me and him. Because there's nothing worse than an oppressively coupley couple. You following me?

'I feel like a freak,' says Mary. 'I am the person my friends worry about pairing off. I am the odd number. We singletons are in the minority. It seems like I'm the last girl standing.'

Well, it may *seem* that way, but Mary is not alone. In 1971 just 17 per cent of all households were composed of singletons, according to government figures. Now over a third have fridges full of meals for one. Single women now buy one in seven properties in London. That's a lot of loners – but, despite being a distinct and growing demographic, many loners still feel like losers. Mary does. And so does India, the otherwise successful 28-year-old singleton drifting round her flat in Clapham that we met in Chapter 9.

'I'd like a boyfriend, but I'm not going to rush into something just to make the numbers up at dinner parties,' says Mary. But numbers aren't the problem. It's belief. Most of us still feel we should have a partner, even if we're happier or better off on our own. A partner is a marker of success – just like the job, the house and the salary. That's wrong. I worry much more about friends in unsuitable relationships than I do about my occasionally needy single friends. However, loner will continue to mean loser until we accept it's sometimes better to be single.

Mary's equally single flatmates act as a couplefest support group. 'Summer is just one big wedding, so we take one another along as guests and everyone thinks we're lesbians, it's hilarious. When couples row, we thank our lucky stars we're free agents. But I think we're all secretly wondering who'll be the next to go.'

We're now getting married a lot later. If we do at all. For the first time ever, fewer than half of those who can walk down the aisle are doing so. The average bride is now twenty-eight and her groom is thirty-two. The combined thirtieth and engagement is no longer unusual. But despite the decreasing popularity of marriage, it's still held up as the holy grail of relationships.

'I don't care what anyone says, there's still a lot of pressure to get married and have kids,' says Mary. 'My mother is always casting up my sister's wedding. Even if I meet the right guy I might not get married because I am so sick of marquees and bridesmaids.' If she does, there's no shortage of magazines to advise her on which meringue dress to choose. 'Apart from anything else, weddings cost a fortune.'

Despite enjoying cake as much as the next man, I avoid weddings when I can. I find them oppressive and slightly embarrassing – a public display of affection gone too far. I don't understand why a couple would want me and a hundred of their closest friends to watch as they tongue one another in the presence of a priest. Love is beautiful enough without confetti. That's not to say I don't like being invited. And I have supported very close friends and beloved relatives in their public commitment.

'I never thought married life would be different,' says Elizabeth, 28, who recently got hitched under a giant sculpture of a cat skeleton in an art gallery. It wasn't an everyday wedding, but her reasons for marrying, and her response to being a wife, are commonplace enough. Elizabeth and Colin lived together for nearly ten years before becoming Mr & Mrs. All habits, foibles and issues were ironed out long ago. So what's new?

'A lot of people say married life is just the same. I'm in the camp that feels something is different, but I couldn't really describe what that something is.'

Okay . . .

'I suppose it has to be the sense of permanence that comes with the "I Do". It just feels closer, somehow, not that we weren't close before, but it's a different, deeper kind of close. Before, we were just going out – it was hard to plan for the future because there were no guarantees. Now I feel sad for people who are not married. They're really missing something.'

But *what* exactly?

Most of the married twentysomethings I spoke to talked about feeling closer – shared bank accounts, shared space and, hopefully, shared dreams. Short of being surgically conjoined, there's no way of getting closer to a person. But it's not just about emotional proximity, it's about pressure.

'I think you make more effort than when you were just going out,' says Leona, 27, who will soon celebrate her second anniversary. You do your hair extra nice? You hit the gym? What?

'You live more in the future when you're married, so it has to work. I wouldn't want it to fail after making those vows together in front of everyone I know and care about. We promised to love one another for ever. It's not just embarrassment, it's letting them down. So we make a lot of effort to sort things out and keep it together.'

'It's as much about the way other people think about you,' says Ben, 26, who got married last year. 'Friends take your relationship more seriously and that can help when you're in it for the long haul. They support you through rows rather than encouraging you to move on to the next conquest.'

And there are practical reasons for making it work.

'We are entangled in every way,' says Leona. 'We share the mortgage. The car is ours. We're the nominated beneficiaries on our pensions. I don't really own much any more – everything is shared. That's not a bad thing, it's just a thing. But it makes it harder to walk away.'

So why, when she already lived with her boyfriend, did Leona want to get married?

'My mother died two years ago and it prompted me to make my own family. I wanted my own unit.'

And Ben? Why did he put himself through the horror of wearing a kilt in front of two hundred people?

'I got married to make my life more stable. I needed to settle down. Basically, I realised I was messing around too much. I'd wake up in the morning and look at the lady lying next to me and feel a bit shit. I didn't go celibate or anything, but I started looking for a more serious relationship.' Ben met his wife-to-be at university but they didn't go out then. 'I never imagined marrying the hottie I saw around campus. The feeling I got when I discovered she fancied me too . . . it's probably one of the best in the world.' A few months later they were engaged. Nearly four years later they were married. 'We had to save up for the wedding but it was worth every penny.'

So did Leona turn her boyfriend into her husband to create a stable environment for children? 'I don't want kids,' she says, stroking her admirably flat tummy. 'That's why I got cats.'

Like many twentysomething women, Leona isn't racing to stretch-mark city, and her decision is reflected nationally. According to government figures, birth rates are at their lowest since 1924. More than 20 per cent of women with degrees now choose to remain childless (compared with 15 per cent in the general population). And less than 33 percent of households now contain children, compared with 35 per cent in 1979.

'There are so many reasons *not* to get pregnant,' says Leona. 'Luckily my husband agrees. Right now we're making a choice, but if you told me I couldn't have kids and took that choice away I'd be shattered.'

'I'd like to find a husband before I have kids,' says Mary. 'Even in these enlightened times family is inextricably linked to marriage.' So what if she stays single – will she stay childless?

'I'd like to have kids anyway, but I don't know if I could afford to on my own.' Presuming she could (and few can), how would she go about it? 'I wouldn't buy sperm or anything mad. I'd probably adopt. There are plenty of babies that need homes. I think it's selfish to make more. But I wouldn't have an abortion if I fell pregnant.'

'Our main problem will be dropping to one salary after being used to a large disposable income,' says Ben. Cash is all that's stopping him from ditching the condoms. 'We can't afford babies right now. We'd have to buy a bigger place and find a nanny.' Neither comes cheaply in London.

'It's also a bit of a lifestyle choice. If we had a baby we couldn't work as hard or party like we do now. We're currently doing some of the things we won't be able to when the rug rats arrive.' Like small white mountains of coke and long, expensive holidays. 'I reckon the wife will start swelling within the next two years. We both really want kids – that's what we're here for, right?'

Fortunately for Ben, his wife agrees. But it's not always the case that both partners agree on having, or not having, children. Some couples split because one wants kids and the other doesn't. A quarter of all families are now headed up by single parents. Mine was. And only 3 per cent of single parent families are run by fathers. It's almost always mothers, like mine, that are left holding the baby.

'I didn't plan to have children,' says Deb, 27. Yes, *children* plural. Twins, in fact. Oh, and she popped them out in the summer between her first and second year at university. 'I didn't know until I was four months pregnant.' So much for a consequence-free Fresher's Week fling.

'I decided to keep them. I felt too far gone to have an abortion.' Could she continue studying? 'I didn't plan to. I thought

I would have to drop out. But the university was great, actually.' Shame the father wasn't.

'He didn't want to know. I mean, we weren't going out or anything. He said he came to uni to get a degree and have fun not start a family. We had this huge row and I remember thinking I was going to miscarry because of the stress.'

Daddy couldn't care less, but both sets of grandparents were delighted. 'His parents were brilliant. The way they saw it, they had two grandchildren on the way. They were actually a bit disgusted at the way he reacted. But that's his choice. I'm not angry at him any more.'

With the support of both sets of parents, Deb continued studying for her exams and preparing to give birth. 'By exam time I was enormous.' She had her medicals at the university health centre and was given an extra room in halls to use as a nursery.

But it wasn't easy when she came back for her second year with twins in tow.

'Babies are noisy,' says Deb. Duh. Understandably, some of her neighbours complained. 'There was nothing I could do, so they moved out. The new people didn't bother so much.' In fact, they took turns babysitting. That year and the next the twins had a bit of a communal upbringing, with the grandparents helping out when essays were due and finals came up. 'It didn't do them any harm.'

But what about her – does she regret her decision?

'What would be the point? There were times when I didn't want to come back from the bar and change nappies or do a feed. I didn't get to go travelling or do a lot of the student things. But I got to be a mother, and now, I love it.' Amazingly, Deb graduated on time. 'And I got a 2:1.'

There aren't many twentysomething mums with twins, a degree and no partner. Female graduates such as Deb usually have their first child at twenty-eight (for women without a degree it's twenty-three). Those of us who choose to be parents are waiting longer to start trying. At the Chelsea and Westminster Hospital, first-time mothers are now thirty-five on average. And, as we've seen, we're not that into marriage any more.

So how are most twentysomethings organising their 1-2-1 relationships? We're obviously not doing what our parents did, or even what they want us to do. As with new workstyles and everything else, we're pioneering a new way of running our long-term relationships: serial monogamy. We're the S&M generation.

Rebecca moved in with her boyfriend six months after meeting him. 'I would have moved in sooner if I could've got out of my lease.' They've lived together for just over a year now. How's it going? And how is it different?

'It's a lot easier to have sex without flatmates floating about,' says Rebecca, a confirmed screamer. 'I was always worried about making noise. It got to the point where we'd wait till everyone was out and then do it really quickly before they came back.' Gags were too kinky. 'And my boyfriend lived in a shared flat.' Moving in together was the only solution.

Oddly, since they've been able to do it any time, they've had sex less. 'It's just nice having the option,' says Rebecca. 'And we've got more than one room to do it in now.'

According to government figures, cohabitees like Rebecca and her boyfriend now count for 16 per cent of households (up from 3 per cent in 1971). Why marry when you can live in sin?

'To me it's just a bit of paper. My parents got divorced, so I know how easily it can all fall apart. And I'm not religious or anything. I don't really see the point. I like the fantasy – the dress and everything – but that's a wedding, not a marriage. Maybe I'll change my mind when I get older.'

But what about all that security and future stuff mentioned by Leona, Elizabeth and Ben?

'You don't need to be married to have all those things. I'm not an insecure person – I know my boyfriend loves me. But

I'm realistic too. We've not been going out for that long. I don't want a ring on my finger right now. I don't want to feel tied down and neither does he.'

If he did ask her to tie him up, she probably wouldn't oblige, not now. But she might have done when they first got together. This is no big revelation, but I think I should warn you that your sex life changes radically in the course of a long-term relationship. 'Sex is different when you live together. We're not as adventurous as we were,' says Rebecca. 'We shagged all the time when we first moved in, but after a while you get caught up in life. We still fancy each other, but we do it less. I'm happy with our sex life.'

Married or not, you tend to have it less and do the same things more. Which is not always a bad thing – so long as you're both happy. I've gone from so-many-times-a-day-it-hurts-in-a-nice-way to a couple of times a week. This phenomenon has been given its own acronym: DINS – double income, no sex. But I think DISS is probably more accurate – double income, some sex. It's quality not quantity. I have less sex now, but I enjoy it more (honest!)

But why shag less, especially now she can make as much noise as she wants?

'Living together is about washing-up and laundry and stuff. I think we're in the nesting phase – we're making a home and it's lovely, but it's not very sexy. Plus, we're both working so we're tired a lot of the time.' We all know about that. It's hard to spend a passionate night in the bedroom after an exhausting day at the office. And not hard in a good way. We're tired, stressed and sullied by work. Life really isn't sexy most of the time. 'You have to make more of an effort,' says Leona. 'You know your husband's body and he knows yours, so there are no surprises any more. It gets very intimate and that's what you have to focus on.'

You know it's *really* bad when you can't summon up the energy for a wank. Believe me, I've been there. That's another thing that changes when you shack up with someone.

'I have to hide my porn in the one place my wife won't look,' says Ben. 'The golf bag.' The top hidey-hole for porn is the computer – that's where you'll find mine. 'My wife and I both wank,' says Ben. 'We just don't talk about it. It's something we do on our own.' Fair enough, there's no reason couples should do everything together. But isn't there a touch of shame about having a fun-fiddle in secret?

'It was hilarious telling everyone that I do it too,' says Clea, long suspected as being sexless by her friends. Why the big secret? Obviously they'd talked about masturbation before. 'I don't know, really. It's private. And girls aren't really supposed to do it. I suppose I was a bit ashamed, no, embarrassed.'

Until Rebecca walked in on him, her boyfriend had always wanked on his own. 'He was mortified, bless him. You'd think his mum had just caught him out. He started apologising but I was quite turned on, so I watched and did myself too. It was great!'

Any guy who needs to justify a bit of solo love need only look to science for justification. In possibly the most enjoyable experiment ever, Australian scientists found that men who wank every day are less likely to get prostate cancer. It didn't say anything about blisters or hairy palms. And sadly, there was no supporting evidence for ladies.

Masturbation, and porn for those that love it, are two of the most common secrets couples keep. 'We don't exactly have secrets, but there are things we don't know about one another,' says Leona, splitting pubes. 'To tell him something – no matter how small – would be to make it bigger than it is. There's no point. We already know what we need to know about one another.'

Rebecca's boyfriend doesn't know she terminated the pregnancy he was partly responsible for.

'I thought about telling him I was pregnant, but that would have made the decision harder for me. It's my body and I'd be the one left raising it if he walked away. I'm too young to be a mum. I want to sort my career and go travelling again. I can't do that with a kid.'

Deb's managing it. But she has lots of support. And anyway, motherhood isn't for everyone.

'I don't feel bad for getting rid of it, but I wish I could tell him. I think he'd be angry but he'd get over it because, when it comes down to it, I don't think he wants to be a parent right now either.'

So why did she tell her friends and not her partner? 'They're one of the reasons I decided not to keep it. I don't want to be the group mum and I don't want to change my lifestyle. They'd be cool with it, but I wouldn't. Imagine bringing a baby to the pub?! No way. Not now.'

Ben's wife doesn't know where his porn is, but she does know where he is on any given day or night. Not that he's pussy-whipped or anything. 'We have an open relationship: she shares me with my mates, the rugby and the football clubs and I share her with work, mates and shopping,' says Ben. 'We're married, but we still go out loads and do fun stuff. Neither of us owns a pair of slippers.'

Like Rebecca, Ben and his wife are working hard to balance all the people in their lives. 'I need to see my mates, she needs to see hers, we need to see ours and we need to have time on our own. That's not even thinking about family.' Complicated?

'It's scary, but we do actually have evenings when we sit down and compare diaries! We make sure that we have a mix of meeting joint friends/family, weekends away, boozing together and all that. That said, time apart is massively important. I went on a rugby tour a few weeks back for five days. She has returned fire and is currently in Spain for a week with her mates. We end up missing each other by the end of the time apart, but everyone needs space.'

Does the mouse play when the cat's away?

'I don't think so,' says Ben. 'I've often thought about it (as you do) and I bet the wife has too. But I can't handle the thought of her with someone else. I reckon open relationships are a recipe for disaster.'

In fact, Susan, Ben's wife, does have another man in her life. But as he's gay, Ben doesn't have too much to worry about – in the bedroom department anyway. 'It's very *Will & Grace*,' says Susan, referring to the gay man and straight woman bestfriend duo in the eponymous sitcom.

So far, we've focused on romantic relationships – the married, the shacked-up and the single (because solo-love is still love, oh yes). But fag and hag is one of the great 1–2–1s of the twenty-first century. It's a non-sexual relationship between a man and a woman based on a mutual appreciation of good personal hygiene, hot men and scintillating conversation. And, if we can be serious for just a second, shared oppression.

'I don't actually like the term fag hag – it implies that you're only friends with someone because of their sexuality,' says Susan. 'It's just another stereotype.' Indeed it is. But, like most stereotypes, it contains a touch of truth. The gay best friend, GBF, is now a staple Hollywood character – if Jennifer Aniston can have one, anyone can.

'Gay men and straight women both have to put up with a lot of shit from men, straight or gay. I think that's why they bond. And gay men are usually more relaxed about their feminine side. So there's no fuss about going shopping.' For the record, my idea of hell is a shopping mall on a hot summer sale day. But you get the point.

Susan's ideal man would be metrosexual: 'Culturally gay but sexually straight.'

So what does her GBF get out of it?

'A lot,' says Stephen, *Will* to Susan's *Grace*.

'Most of my friends are straight women. I have a couple of straight male friends, but not many. A lot of them go all weird when they find out I'm gay. I just don't want to deal with that. Why make an effort to be friends with someone who hates you? Straight women have less of an issue, so I'm more predisposed to them. But I don't like them all instantly or anything.'

Stephen and Susan go out every Saturday night, alternating between gay clubs and straight clubs. 'That way we both have a chance of pulling,' says Stephen. 'I don't think my husband would be too happy to hear that,' says Susan. Clearly, they respect one another. And that's why it works for them.

Non-monogamy seems to work for Mick, Chris and Paul, the happy threesome we met in Chapter 9.

'People accept that one person cannot satisfy all their social needs, which is why we all have lots of friends. I think it's the same for sex,' says Mick. 'One person can't possibly be everything to you in bed. So why not arrange it so both partners can have the sex they want? Unless you're trying to raise kids, I don't see any reason to be monogamous.' Obviously, like Marmite, it's not for everyone. Have a look at their recommended rules for non-monogamy below.

Problems only arise when life fails to meet our (usually very high) expectations. When you're forced to feel unhappy for being single, and singledom isn't swinging because you're skint and tired. When marriage doesn't make a difference, or it does and you can't cope. When your partner doesn't want kids and you do. When your friends expect too much or give too little.

Insignificant others aren't the issue – it's the people that are most important to us we must focus on finding, keeping and balancing. 'You really start to realise who's important in your twenties,' says Ben.

But when it comes down to it, as we'll see next, the most important person is you.

The small print

Five ground rules for a happy open relationship:

1. Sort sex with your partner first

'If sex between you and your partner isn't working, you have a problem,' says Mick. Having sex with other people is about building on what you have – it's not a quick fix.

2. The BT rule

Basically, this means no shagging friends or family. 'Don't shit on your own doorstep,' cautions Chris.

3. One time only

Open relationships are generally about lust – not about love or cultivating affairs. Until they met Paul, Mick and Chris limited their sex with other people to once only. 'You don't want feelings to develop because that complicates things,' says Chris.

4. Play safe

Physically – always use condoms and get regular sexual health checks. But take emotional care too. 'Don't miss your partner's birthday because you're off shagging someone else. Make sure they know how special they are to you,' says Mick.

5. Revisit the rules

Things can change. You might want a period of monogamy – because you decide to have kids or whatever. 'We talk about our relationship every six months just to make sure everything is still okay. It's sometimes awkward, but it works,' says Mick.

Five ways to juggle all your significant others:

1. Accept you can't please everyone

You're amazing – everyone wants a piece of you. Naturally, some people are going to have to be disappointed. If it's okay for other people to cancel you, why is it so hard for you to say 'No' or 'I've changed my mind'? Don't get guilted into seeing someone.

2. Prioritise your VIPs

Partner, best friend, parent – yourself, even. Make sure that the person that matters most to you knows it. Make time for each other, even if it's just to talk on the phone undisturbed. It might seem daft programming a coffee session into your diary, but if that's what it takes . . .

3. Don't be 'perma busy'

Yes, we know you're popular. But do you need to fill every second with some kind of social activity – must you talk on the phone in the toilet? Try switching your mobile off on train journeys and reading a book or just relaxing instead. Also, don't book yourself up too far ahead – else you have no time for spontaneity.

4. What are you getting out of it?

Are you seeing people that leave you feeling like shit? Okay, we all have to do the best friend hand-holding bit sometimes, but is it happening all the time? Look at what you're getting out of the people in your life and see if you don't need to take a step back.

5. It's quality – not quantity

If you're finally seeing someone you've missed for ages, focus on them – switch your mobile off and get close, even if it's just for a twenty-minute coffee. Don't invite ten people who don't know one another out so you can kill ten friends with one dinner.

15

You, You, You

That's what your twenties are all about

'I never imagined I would change so much.'
Nick, 29, DJ (formerly Nicola)

'I'm still not sure who I am.'
Anna, 28, possible permatemp

My hair is really long right now. It's so long I can chew it. And it's big – I look like a backcombed televangelist. It takes a ton of wax, and a westerly wind, to keep my bouffant under control. And I don't even like it. But I'm resisting pressure to get it cut. Why?

I just turned twenty-seven. If I cut my hair now it'll take two years to reach this length again, by which time I'll be nearly thirty. Then I'll look like some twat that's trying to get down with the kids. My hair has become a symbol of my twenties that I plan on keeping, however inappropriate and bushy.

We've no problem leaving behind acne and all the other ugly baggage of our teens. *Au revoir* to all that. But our twenties are, theoretically, our peak, physically at least. I don't want to wave goodbye to the metabolism which lets me eat anything and stay thin. Please stay, constitution which gets me over hangovers in hours not days. Don't go, relatively flat stomach. I beg you.

'I am in mourning for my twenties,' says Anna, even though she still has two years of twenties to go. 'I feel like it's the end of my youth. I have to be an adult now.' Adult – what does that mean?

'Well, I'm temping – that's not a job.' Yes it is. 'No, it's not. Everyone else has a career, and I've got no clue what I want to do. I'm still renting a room in a friend's flat and I haven't had a boyfriend for two years. I haven't had a shag for six months.'

So that's what an adult is. Someone with a lifelong career all mapped out and a loyal partner waiting for them in a home they own where regular sex takes place. By Anna's definition, most of the people I know – many of them in their forties – have yet to become fully-fledged adults.

'I just feel like my life should be better than it is,' she says, checking her mobile for messages.

And that's the essence of the quarterlife crisis. Feeling you should be having, doing or being more. Like you're missing out. There's a better party, job, flat, partner or whatever out there, and you're the only person who can't find it.

Truth is, we're all looking for it, and the reason none of us have found it is because *it doesn't exist*. What we have found is that our twenties are surprisingly expensive, occasionally ugly and intensely competitive. No wonder we feel stressed, inadequate and somehow not quite as good as our peers. Anna feels poorer, less successful and less together. She feels, even though she's only twenty-eight, that her life is in crisis.

'I don't know where to go from here. I thought I'd find some sort of direction, but I haven't. The older I get, the more settled and successful everyone is, the worse I feel. I just want it to happen for me too.'

Every twentysomething feels this way at some point. But, as we've seen, even those with all the outward trappings of success

– job, house, partner, cash – have problems; free-floating anxiety about who we are, what the future holds, who we'll end up as. The sad thing about Anna is that she's spent so much time worrying about how well everyone else is doing and her impending thirtieth birthday that she hasn't really enjoyed her twenties at all. You really don't want to be that person.

So this is it – the decade when the shit really hits the fan. You leave home then move back. You go travelling. You get a job then quit it. You get another job and quit that too. You have your first big relationship and your first big break-up. You have your first orgasm, hopefully. You catch crabs and promise to be more careful. You have kids or find you can't or get a dog instead. You buy a place, or try to. You find God, change sex, grow a fringe (then cut it off). Basically, you get a life.

Like Christina Aguilera's look and the sky above us, we are ever changing, but it's in our twenties that we alter most radically. I am not the same person now I was at twenty-one and thank God. I've had my buckteeth fixed for a start. I don't want the same things I did then.

Your sense of self impacts upon where you're going, who you're going with and how you'll get there. Your identity is at the core of your quarterlife crisis – not your job, flat or partner, complex and challenging as they can be. If they seem that way, it's because we still define ourselves too much by what and who we do, where we live and what we earn. So, if your job/partner/flat is shit and that's your life, it follows that your life seems shit. You need to work out who you are, or who you want to be, before you can truly get it together. Consider this chapter 'quality you time'.

Nick, 29, started his twenties as a woman. He'll end them as a man.

'I thought I had it all worked out,' he says. In his second year at university he came out to his parents as a lesbian and had relationships with women for the next eight years. 'I still do [women] but as a man, not a woman.'

And you thought you were confused.

'I always knew there was something different about me – even as a child. I wanted to dress and act like my brother, but it wasn't just tomboy stuff. I didn't realise until I was older, until I had the vocabulary and the framework, that I actually wanted to *be* a boy.

'I wasn't unhappy as a dyke, and my family were okay enough with it. I met a lot of wonderful, brilliant women and had a couple of good long-term relationships. But even when things were going well I felt something was wrong.'

Nick, then still Nicola, was diagnosed with depression when he was twenty-five. 'I couldn't understand why I felt so bad, so worried. And everyone around me thought it was all in my head because I had a lovely girlfriend and a good job and a nice flat and everything.'

Prozac and therapy were prescribed. It didn't take Nick long to find out why he felt so bad. 'Those feelings were really near the surface. A month into it my counsellor asked me what I'd change about my life if I could. Without thinking I said "my gender".'

Four years later and *lots* has changed.

'I had a double mastectomy and my nipples reshaped so they didn't just look like flat tits. The scarring is really minimal – you wouldn't notice if you were at the gym with me.' Testosterone has lowered his voice and given him hair in all the right places. 'It took me nearly six months to grow a beard. It's a bit wispy but I'm so proud of it.' The biggest physical change is a work in progress – his final sex reassignment.

'I want a penis but I'm not sure which procedure to go for.' Very basically, these can involve growing the clitoris into a micropenis, fashioning a penis from the vagina using what's there and a flap cut from the forearm, and – newsflash – sewing on a lab-grown penis (coming soon to a tranny near you). 'Some ops aren't available on the NHS, which would mean saving up and going abroad. I've been lucky I haven't had to do that so far.'

Changing sex is, perhaps, the least expected expense anyone could encounter in their twenties. 'My clothes were always butch, but I've bought a new wardrobe.'

Compared with the monumental physical changes, the emotional and social consequences of his sex change have been intensely difficult.

'My girlfriend at the time dumped me. She said she wanted a woman, not a man. I was really hurt, especially because I needed her support. Now, looking back, I understand her decision. But she could have been nicer. I still see her around. I can't work out if she doesn't recognise me or she's blanking me.'

Nick's parents had a mixed reaction. 'I think my mother always knew, so she's managed to accept it. But my father and my brother have a real problem thinking of me as a man. Dad cried when I had my breasts removed. He said he can't understand why I didn't just stay as a lesbian if all I wanted to do was have relationships with women. I hope he'll come round.'

A few of Nick's friends had similar problems. 'I was surprised by how many people, even in the gay community, were negative. They didn't want to know me. I am still the same person, I just have a different gender now.' And he lost his job as a civil servant. 'I hated my job anyway. They didn't sack me, but they weren't exactly accommodating. There were a lot of nasty jokes. I needed a lot of time off for treatment and it was very stressful. I thought about suing them, but I don't want to get into that sort of anger. I'd rather get on with my life.'

So Nicola is now Nick. So far, so talkshow. But to get there he's had to sacrifice his sense of self and his security – his job, the love and respect of his father and brother, and some of his friends. 'I turned my life upside down.' More like inside out. 'There are still times when I look at myself and wonder what

I'm doing. I've lost so much. But you know what? I'm happier. I'm not depressed any more. I know who I am.' And that's the base he's building his new life on.

All right, this is a bit of an extreme example, but the principle remains the same: it's in our twenties that we really start sorting out who we are. The decisions we make don't need to be popular – they just need to be right. For us. That's not to say we should be contrary or go out of our way to harm or offend other people, but *they* need to deal with that, not you. If your parents don't think you should go back to uni but you go anyway, tough. If your best friend thinks your partner's a loser, tough. And if they were right all along? Tough.

'I don't talk about my faith much,' says Lyn, 27, committed Christian and arts events manager. No wonder. Most of us stopped going to Sunday school long ago, if we ever went. I only invoke God if I'm feeling particularly grateful or especially angry, and even then I don't really mean it. The last Bible I saw was in a hotel. 'I know it's not cool to be a Christian,' says Lyn, 'but it's a fundamental part of who I am.' Fundamental, eh?

Each Sunday Lyn attends her local Church of England. She prays every day and night. The crucifix she wears is pretty and it's not just decorative. She's the genuine article – a twentysomething Christian – even if she's as quiet about it as a church mouse.

'People think my parents dragged me to church, especially because I'm black. In fact, they're suspicious of the whole thing. My mum actually came to church with me to make sure I wasn't in a cult!'

I met Lyn twice before she told me she was a Christian. When I asked how she coped with life in her twenties, she reached for her crucifix and said, blushingly, 'Jesus.'

'My faith is an anchor. Things change, but Jesus is always there. I'm not an extremist or anything – I'm not against divorcees marrying or gays or anything like that. I just believe in Christian principles and apply them to my life.'

Faith, hope and charity – I do all three. But I don't believe some omniscient beardie miraculously impregnated a woman in what is now Israel over 2,000 years ago. 'Neither do I!' says Lyn, defending her faith for the thousandth time. 'I just take the message and update it for my life now. It gives me a structure and perspective. If things are really bad at work, I think about the suffering of Christ and the fact that the world is going to continue long after I have left it.' Personally, I pour a glass of wine or phone a friend.

Lyn is about to undergo a very big, public change.

'I am being baptised in church. My family is coming and, in front of the whole congregation, I'm going to be reborn.' Is she changing her name? 'No, nothing like that. I'm just formalising my commitment.' Bit like a wedding really.

What difference will it make?

'I think I'll feel stronger. I won't let anti-Christian jokes go as much. I'll be more honest about who I am.'

Like Nick, Lyn has experienced a good deal of discrimination because of who she is. Increasingly, she chooses not to hide away. This makes her life tougher, but why should she be in the closet any more than me? Although only in their twenties, Lyn and Nick have both been reborn, cheesy as that sounds. Their new identities 'anchor' them.

Nick and Lyn have made choices, but sometimes the events that change us are unplanned and unwelcome. All we can control is our response to them. Your identity will always be partly defined by what/who you do, where you live and the people you surround yourself with. But if you rely too much on any one part of the equation – and something goes wrong – you immediately lose a sense of who you are. 'We' suddenly becomes 'I' if your relationship goes wrong, and what do you say at parties if you lose your job? Therapists talk about balancing your internal and external locus of evaluation (what you think of yourself versus how other people think of you).

Basically, it's knowing who you are and where your sense of self comes from.

'I never thought we'd end up this way,' says Jo, 29. She's just left the man she married last year after going out with him for six years. 'That's seven years, for what?'

There was no big drama – no walking in on hubby doing her best friend or anything. 'I want kids and he doesn't. It's that simple.' Well, not quite. She wants a family now, before she gets any older, and he wants to wait, till his career is more settled.

'Everything I've done since we met has been about preparing to start a family. I am not a lawyer because I love the law – I chose this career because it's lucrative and stable and I can return to it easily after having a baby. I got married when I did because I want my children to have two youngish parents and two sets of grandparents. Now I feel like my whole life from leaving university was a waste of time.'

Surely they must have talked about when they were going to have kids. Why was this such a big shock?

'He changed his mind after we got married. I think it was all too much. When I told him I wanted to start trying, he just kept putting it off. It was this and that. I gave him an ultimatum and he walked away. I still can't believe he did.'

Jo's sense of identity was bound up in being a wife and mother-to-be. Now that's been taken from her she's lost. 'I honestly don't know who I am any more. I've never really liked my job, but now I hate it. There's no need for me to earn that much now I won't have kids to support. I reckon I'll quit in the next six months.'

She has, at least, kept the house they bought together – for now. 'He's moved in with his brother while we sort out the divorce. I always earned more than him, but the property is in both our names. I'm not going to let him have it. This is my home. It's all I've got left.'

If my partner dropped a bombshell on me now – 'I'm leaving you if you don't get your ridiculously long hair cut' – I'd be distraught. Part of what defines me is my relationship with him. But – and Jo is the first to admit this – her entire identity was wrapped up in her husband. Not just part of her, all of her. That's why she's totally devastated.

'I loved him from the moment I met him. It sounds mental and old-fashioned, but I wanted him to father my babies.' What if he changes his mind again? 'I won't have him back – I can't trust him any more. What if he decides he doesn't want to be a dad the week before it's born or a year after?

'I built my life around him as my husband and the father of my children. I took this job so I could support us all. And we bought a home together. I don't know what to do now. I really don't.'

Jo put all her eggs, and somebody else's sperm, in one basket. Her whole identity has been compromised by someone else's decision. The same thing happens when you define yourself solely by what you do, and you lose your job; how much you earn, and you get a pay cut; or where you live, and you lose your home.

Eventually, Jo will rebuild a new, hopefully more holistic, sense of self. She'll get a new career, she might have to move house and there are always plenty of men around, should she start looking. But she won't depend too much on any one element. She doesn't feel it now, but she'll probably be fine. 'I suppose it's better that this happened now, but I'd rather things had gone to plan.'

Few twentysomethings plan to change their gender, like Nick, or find religion, like Lyn. I didn't plan to write this book. And Jo didn't plan to split from her husband, but his feelings about being a father changed. Fair enough – things do. We do. For most of us, switching careers, ditching partners and moving around is as challenging as it gets. And we've seen just how difficult that can be.

So, have you got it together yet? Have I? Has anyone? Well, that depends on how you define 'together'. It's not about whether your friends think you're fine, your family approves, your partner is pleased or your boss praises you. It's about feeling good about yourself whatever you're earning, wherever you live, whoever and whatever you're doing. It's an ongoing process. Never has so much been expected of a generation, yet never has it been so hard to achieve it. Things are hard for us twentysome-things – the very least we can do is be easy on ourselves (and if that means slamming some instant gratification on the credit card, so be it).

So . . . you don't know what you're doing or where you're going or whether you should buy a flat, get a pension or go travelling. Who cares? You have the rest of your life to work that shit out. The decisions we make now *are* incredibly impor-tant, but they're rarely irreversible. In the meantime, I think I'll get my hair cut. Just a little bit shorter. I can always grow it back.